Joyce's Wake and Other Full-length Plays

Michael G. Casey

With an Introduction by the Author

ISBN 978-1-9160264-5-2

First edition, 2019

Published by Azimuth Publishing
Dublin, Ireland

Photographic images used in the cover via Wikimedia.

Layout, cover design by iCulture

Please visit michaelgcasey.com

INTRODUCTION

In 2013 a number of playwrights and directors attended workshops run by Conall Morrison (Director with the Abbey Theatre, Dublin, and with the Lyric Theatre, Belfast). These inspiring sessions resulted in the formation of the Pavilion Playwrights and later, the Umbrella Theatre Company (UTC).

Four playwright / directors ran this company: Gerard Dalton, Celia de Fréine, Michael O'Meara and myself. It was an honour to work with these talented and dedicated people, and indeed with all of the superb actors who made themselves available to UTC. I learnt early on to value the feedback of actors. Whenever an actor had difficulty with a part it was usually the writer's, or possibly the director's, fault. A good production is the result of an interactive process where everyone contributes; it cannot be otherwise. This, at any rate, was the guiding collaborative philosophy of UTC.

During the following four years UTC was prolific, producing seven full-length plays and three rehearsed readings, using the following Dublin-based theatres: The Pavilion, Mill, Lexicon, Trinity College Players and the Teachers' Club. In addition, an astounding forty short (ten-minute) plays were produced, mainly for the National Gallery of Ireland, where each short piece was based loosely on paintings on display in the gallery, e.g., those of Vermeer, Caravaggio, Osborne, Burton et al. During each play the painting in question was projected on to a screen behind the stage. These shows were extremely popular and full houses were the norm.

Two of the plays in the present volume were brought to full production by UTC, 'Joyce's Wake' and 'The High Priest of Hackballscross'. A few comments should be made about both plays:

The title of the first does not imply the wake of James Joyce; it is in fact the wake of his children, especially Lucia who suffered incredibly because of her father's lifestyle and obsession with writing his two great books, 'Ulysses' and 'Finnegans Wake'. Was their sacrifice worth it? (In another play, 'Joyce at Last', to be published in Volume Two, James Joyce himself ruminates on this question when Lucia is in an asylum in the UK and he is coming close to the end of his life. This play was also produced by UTC and put on in Dublin, and, by invitation, in the Henrik Ibsen Museum, Oslo – a perfect location, given Joyce's unbridled admiration for Ibsen.)

The second play, 'The High Priest of Hackballscross', is a light-hearted treatment of a Passion Play being put on by the local drama group in a small town. A play within a play, it highlights the parallels between the occupation of the Holy Land and the occupation of Ireland, and it deals with the often-hidden relationships between local people which are laid bare under the pressure of performing. Tension, and the bonding that is part of the acting experience, reveal some surprising truths about the characters.

The play 'Wherewithal' is a contemporary one,

set in a small town in Ireland. 'Wait Now' was performed as a rehearsed reading. This play is dedicated to Samuel Beckett and is more modernist in tone, though not, I hope postmodernist. 'Get Up' is futuristic and largely political. I hope readers and theatre folk will enjoy them.

In addition to thanking my colleagues in UTC and the hundred or so actors who kept up an association with us, I must also thank the 'hidden' people, lighting and costume experts, stage managers, front of house staff and theatre managers, without whose help few if any productions would have been possible. Gratitude is also due to the local authority of Dún Laoghaire for modest but indispensable grants.

I must also thank my wife and family for putting up with my absences, though it is conceivable that they were not unduly bothered by these.

"The beauty of play scripts – when done well, as here – is that they plunge us into the action. Our imagination engages from the start. The great range of these plays, from Joyce's troubled daughter through careening passion play to the absurd at play in multiple dystopian futures, is in the end a stream of questions around who we are, what we want, and what awaits us all."
—Peter FitzGerald

BOOKS PREVIOUSLY PUBLISHED
BY MICHAEL G. CASEY

Come Home, Robbie, a novel, published by The O'Brien Press, 1990

> "...page-turning urgency ... spine-tingling compulsion ... the sheer quality of the writing lends the story some of the stature of heroic tragedy."
> —The Education Times

Treadmill, an award-winning Chapbook of short stories, published by Tipperary Arts Centre and Start Magazine, 2008

> "...Casey brings to life vivid characters who captivate, amuse and engage ... (He) has a wry observation and quick wit."
> —Mike McCormack

Ireland's Malaise: The Troubled Personality of the Irish Economy, published by The Liffey Press, 2010

> "...(Casey) shows the same Confucian wisdom as his hero, T.K. Whitaker in his brilliant new book."
> —Eoghan Harris, The Sunday Independent

The Visit, a novel, published by The Anaphora Press, 2011

> "...a small Irish town deals with a major event ... an interesting addition to the genre ... clear-eyed ... vivid description..."
> —Denis Fahey, Historian

> "...a lovely clear prose style ... some great characters and beautifully crafted vignettes."
> —Stella Kane, Quartet Books Ltd

Broken Circle, a collection of poetry, due to be published by Salmon Press in Spring 2020

> "...very powerful, intelligent poems made their presence known immediately ... (Casey) uses casuistry and persuasiveness to rival Robert Browning's dramatic Monologues..."
> —Derek Selen

Michael G. Casey's most recent novels, *Smudged Mascara*, *Maura's Dance with Uncle Sam*, *The Killing of Ros Grenham*, *Proving Ground* and *Divers Kinds*, from Azimuth Publishing, are available in Kindle and print versions through Amazon.

DEDICATION

For my father

TABLE OF CONTENTS

JOYCE'S WAKE

A Play in Two Acts

CHARACTERS AND ACTORS

LUCIA JOYCE — Tara Maguire
Charlotte Hamel

GIORGIO JOYCE — James Daniel Murphy

JAMES JOYCE — Martin Brennan
Michael Heavey

NORA JOYCE — Brid Turner

SAMUEL
BECKETT — Colin Carpenter
Conor Marron

HELEN KASTOR
FLEISCHMAN — Sarah Lawlor

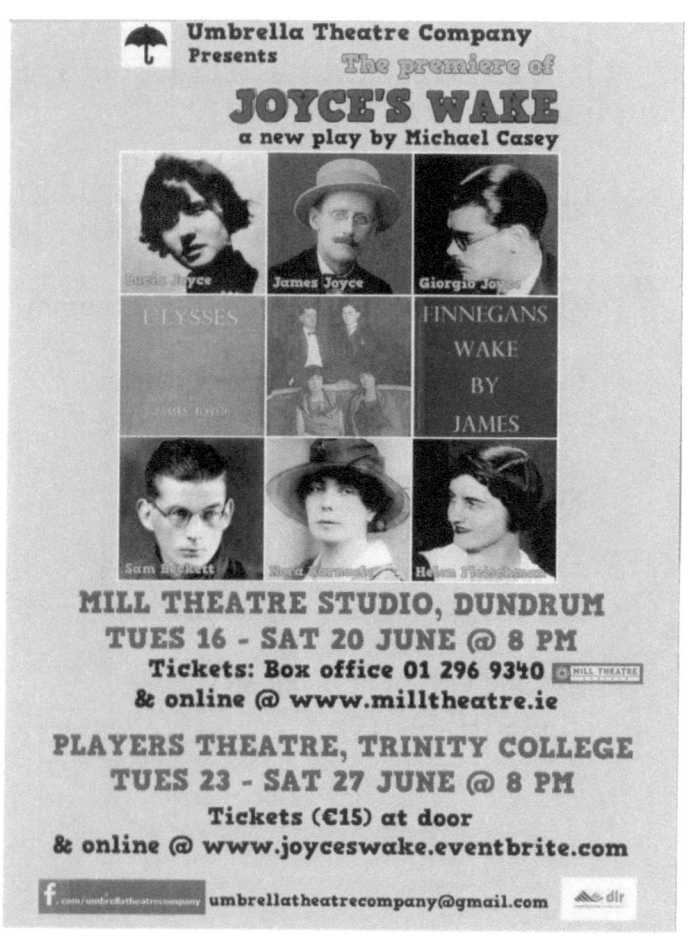

Flyer for the première of *Joyce's Wake*, 2015
front (original in colour)

JOYCE'S WAKE

A Two- Act Play by Michael Casey

MILL THEATRE, MAUREEN O'HARA STUDIO, DUNDRUM

Tuesday 16th (Bloomsday) – Saturday 20th June 2015 @ 8pm

And

PLAYERS THEATRE, TRINITY COLLEGE, DUBLIN

Tuesday 23rd - Saturday 27th June 2015 @ 8pm

Umbrella Theatre Company presents the premiere of **JOYCE'S WAKE** by **Michael Casey**, in the **Maureen O'Hara Studio, Mill Theatre, Dundrum** from **Tuesday 16th June 2015 (Bloomsday) until Saturday 20th June**. This new two-act play will then transfer to the **Players Theatre, Trinity College, Dublin**, from **Tuesday 23rd to Saturday 27th June**.

JOYCE'S WAKE traces the Joyce family's period in Paris, from 1922 to 1940. James Joyce is, at last, a celebrated writer and has begun Finnegans Wake, which will be his final masterpiece. His work and lifestyle have created havoc for his two children, Lucia and Giorgio. Neither has the self-confidence to develop fully. When Samuel Beckett enters Lucia's life he is attracted to her. However, he gradually realises that she may be mentally disturbed. Worse lies in store for Lucia and Giorgio.

Did Joyce have any conception of the suffering of his children and is great literature worth this kind of sacrifice?

CAST (In order of appearance)
Lucia Joyce - Charlotte Hamel
Samuel Beckett - Conor Marren
Giorgio Joyce - James Daniel Murphy
Nora Barnacle (Joyce) - Brid Turner
James Joyce - Martin Brennan
Helen Fleischman - Sarah Lalor

Creative and Technical Management
Playwright: Michael Casey
Director & Set Design: Gerard Dalton
Production & Stage Management: Michael O'Meara, Mark Aylward
Lighting: Pat O'Grady
Costume Co-ordination: Celia de Fréine.

There will be an interval between Act I and Act II

Umbrella Theatre Company was formed in 2013 by theatre-makers and playwrights, Gerard Dalton, Michael O'Meara, Celia de Fréine and Michael Casey with the objective of creating and presenting new writing and innovative drama within a community of theatre artists in Dublin and Dun Laoghaire -Rathdown Council area. Umbrella has received an Arts grant from Dun Laoghaire - Rathdown County Council in 2014 and 2015.

Sample of audience comments after recent performances by Umbrella Theatre Company
'I thoroughly enjoyed Umbrella's Theatre performances in the National Gallery and thought it was the most fantastic afternoon's entertainment. The actors were incredible.'
'It was the most amazing event I have been to for some time!'
'Well done guys. We recommend it to everyone.'
It was a memorable experience.'

Contact: umbrellatheatrecompany@gmail.com

Flyer for the première of *Joyce's Wake*, 2015
back (original in colour)

ACT ONE

PROLOGUE

Autumn. Afternoon. 1954. A projection shows a large institutional building, bearing a plaque – Northampton Mental Hospital. LUCIA, a woman in her late forties in a dishevelled white robe, sits in a corner of a small cell-like room. She is sedated and has a haunted look on her face.

LUCIA: (*To herself*) Who am I again...? Yes, Issy, the daughter of Earwicker. But why did he make me two people? Two ... He knew I went from one to the other. To escape ... Sometimes I was Kitty O'Shea when he was Parnell ... I had no choice. Issy the temptress...
(*She reads from 'Finnegans Wake'.*)
"She climbed over the bannistars; she gave a childy cloudy cry. Nuee! Nuee! A lightdress fluttered ... She was gone and into the river ... there fell a tear, a singult tear ... a leaptear.

11

But the river tripped on by her ... lapping
though her heart was brook: ... Weh! O Weh!
I'se so silly to be flowing but I canna stay..."
(*She looks up.*)
He said he wrote the book for me. Babbo said
it. A dreamworld for me. (*Pause*) Maybe it
was for him. But I forgive him anyway. I
never "flispered to Finnegan, to sin again..."
(*A timid knock is heard on the door which
opens slowly. SAMUEL BECKETT is
admitted. He is also in his late forties. He is
carrying a parcel.*)

BECKETT: (*Nervously*) Hello, Lucia ... I brought
you a few books...

LUCIA: I have plenty to read here.

BECKETT: Oh, 'The Wake'. Yes, there's plenty
there.

LUCIA: How do you know?

BECKETT: I helped your father with parts of it ...
Don't you...?

LUCIA: Were you a 'Pappa Pal?' Did you dance
with him?

BECKETT: (*Uncertainly*) I'm Sam Beckett, Lucia.
Do you not...? Don't you ... remember me?
We once...

LUCIA: You're old.

BECKETT: I know. The years have flown by.

LUCIA: Do you know I'm in this book?

BECKETT: Yes.

LUCIA: As two people. Not just one.

BECKETT: (*Sadly*) Yes.

LUCIA: Why did Babbo do that?

BECKETT: I don't know, Lucia.

LUCIA: Did he think I wouldn't understand it?

BECKETT: No, No. He wrote it for you...

LUCIA: (*Quoting*) "...sad and weary I go back to you, my cold father ... my cold mad feary father..."

BECKETT: (*Upset*) There is resurrection too, Lucia ... In the book ... Recovery...

LUCIA: Not for everyone ... Not for "Nuvoluccia in her lightdress." He was too "Dadda for me to dance." (*Pause*) Though I did dance once...

BECKETT: You danced superbly...

LUCIA: But not well enough ... Not ballet ... No ... (*Beat*) ... Babbo is dead now...

BECKETT: Yes ... He died in Zurich ... Thirteen years ago.

LUCIA: When they went to Zurich they left me in Paris ... with the Nazis...

BECKETT: It was a ... an impossible time...

LUCIA: And Giorgio's marriage collapsed.

BECKETT: Yes...

LUCIA: It was bound to ... And Mama? How is she?

BECKETT: Nora is ... fine...

LUCIA: She never visits me...

BECKETT: (*Shocked*) What ... never?

LUCIA: Miss Weaver sometimes and Giorgio ... but Mama never...

BECKETT: (*Surprised*) Not once?

LUCIA: Not once ... Why would she...? Why would she visit me?

(BECKETT *rests his head in his hands. A spotlight stays on* LUCIA *'s face for a moment and then picks out the book.*)

Lights down.

SCENE ONE

Joyces' apartment. Spring. The early twenties. Projections show scenes of Paris. Some dust sheets cover items of furniture.

GIORGIO: (*Off*) Don't stop, Lucia … Oh a graceful move … Brava…!
(LUCIA *dances from the wings onto the stage in the style of Isadora Duncan.* GIORGIO *follows her clapping to the rhythm.*)

GIORGIO: Good, Lucia … right on the beat … very good … Excellent…!

LUCIA: (*Breathlessly*) … I am so thirsty…

GIORGIO: Just another ten minutes. You can do it, Lucia. You'll feel the better of it…

LUCIA: You're a slave-driver … Giorgio … This was only meant to be … a warm up.
(*There is a sudden loud knocking sound from Joyce's study.* GIORGIO *and* LUCIA *stop immediately and look guiltily at each other.*)

LUCIA: We're upsetting Babbo. We have to stop.

GIORGIO: *He* doesn't need much silence when he barges in drunk every second night. Remember Trieste?

LUCIA: Oh, I do … I have dreams about it … But still, his writing is what counts. Everyone says how great it is.

GIORGIO: But how are we supposed to improve if

we can't practice? I thought that once we moved here to Paris we'd have plenty of opportunity. Anyway, your dancing is really coming on, Lucia. I wish I could say the same about my singing. Jesus, there I go again. Why do we feel that we have to measure up?

LUCIA: We have to do it for Babbo. He works so hard. He says we all have talents and we must express them ... Though sometimes I don't know what to express. He used to talk to me about a secret wood with a river running through it. Everything was all right in that wood...

GIORGIO: Fantasy stuff, Lucia. We can't even speak French well ... Still, we can understand each other. That's the main thing.

(NORA, *fashionably dressed, enters. She tousles* GIORGIO'*s hair.*)

NORA: Are you finished practising already?

GIORGIO: Dada banged on the wall.

NORA: He did, did he. Well, we'll see about that...
(*She walks determinedly towards the study door.*)

LUCIA: No, don't, Mama! He doesn't like being interrupted...

NORA: (*Stops in her tracks*) And he didn't even unpack all his damn books...
(*As* NORA *removes some books she finds the family portrait.*)

NORA: Ah, here's the family portrait ... Let me hang that up ... em ... where? Over here I think ... Yes...

(NORA *hangs it up and looks at it admiringly.*)

NORA: There! All present and correct.

LUCIA: It's not a good likeness of me.

NORA: Your father says that if he ever finds a woman who's happy with her own picture he'll send flowers to the Pope … It's fine … Now I'll go and sort him out…

GIORGIO: Don't bother Mama. We were more or less finished anyway.

NORA: Just remember, you have as much right as he has around here … Lucia, that modern dancing looks a bit … cheap … Would you not change to ballet?

LUCIA: It's not cheap. It's expressive. Anyway, you have to start ballet when you're four or five…

NORA: Well, you know my views … You'd better go and get dressed.

(LUCIA *exits.*)

GIORGIO: I suppose we can't eat until he deigns to come out?

NORA: He's working on some difficult part. God knows what. That last book nearly blinded him and now he's off scribbling again. 'Work in progress', he calls it. We'd better leave him be for the moment.

GIORGIO: 'Work in progress' … not very original is it?

NORA: Well, he has another title but I'm under oath not to reveal it.

GIORGIO: It's a matter of supreme indifference to

me.

NORA: (*Laughing*) I can't say it's keeping me awake at night. (*She places a hand on his shoulder.*) I can't believe you're twenty-four, Giorgio. Twenty-four! Where in the world did all the time go? (*Pause*) Incidentally, that young man, Beckett, is due shortly. He's about the same age. You could make friends with him. He could tell you more about Dublin –

GIORGIO: He's replacing Tom McGreevy in the École. He's a lecturer. I wouldn't be talking the same language as him.

NORA: (*Sighing*) I know that feeling. But, Giorgio, a person shouldn't be judged by how good they are with words. That's just wrong. Anyway, I don't think Sam takes himself too seriously –

GIORGIO: (*Defensively*) It's not an issue for me – whatever about Lucia.

NORA: She feels left out or something … I'm not sure what it is exactly. But you're good to her, Giorgio, and she appreciates it. Maybe I could do more, but I don't know what she needs. I'm at a loss –

(*A bell sounds.*)

NORA: That must be Sam Beckett. Will you tell your father he's here?

(GIORGIO *knocks timidly on the study door and goes in.* NORA *goes to the main door to admit* BECKETT. GIORGIO *re-emerges.*)

GIORGIO: He says he'll be out in a minute.

NORA: He wants to make an entrance … Come in,
Sam. It's good to see you again.
(BECKETT *is tall and thin. His hair is
plastered down – unlike the style of later years.
He is wearing a new suit that seems too small
for him.*)

BECKETT: (*Shyly*) I hope I'm not intruding …
These are for you, Mrs. Joyce.
(*He hands her a simple bouquet of flowers.*)

NORA: Thank you, Sam. These are lovely. And it's
Nora by the way. (*Pointedly*) I'm not *Mrs.*
anything. You met Giorgio briefly the last
time?
(*She puts the flowers in a vase on a sideboard.*)

BECKETT: Yes. Nice to meet you again, Giorgio.
(*Both men shake hands and, at* NORA'*s
promptings, sit down.*)

GIORGIO: I thought Tom McGreevy might be with
you.

BECKETT: He's not feeling well.

NORA: Probably hungover more like. Just because
it's Paris doesn't mean you young men can
drink like fish and lose the run of yourselves.

BECKETT: (*Laughing*) I didn't drink at all in
Dublin.

GIORGIO: There's that name again. Can you tell
me, Sam, what on earth is so fascinating about
that city?

NORA: It's a good question. I never liked the place
much or the people. A penny looking down on
a farthing.

BECKETT: I think most of it is in your father's

imagination, Giorgio.

NORA: Speak of the devil.

(*The study door opens and* JOYCE *walks slowly and with upright gait into the living room. He is wearing a suit with a waistcoat, and an eye-patch.*)

JOYCE: Ah, Mr. Beckett. It's good to see you again.

BECKETT: It's very good of you to invite me back, Mr. Joyce.

NORA: (*Grinning, in an aside to* GIORGIO) Mr. This. ... Mr. That ... Mrs. Fiddle-de-dee ... Look at the lovely flowers Sam brought.

JOYCE: (*Peering, raises eye-patch*) Caltha Palustris, and ... Glebionis Coronaria, if I'm not mistaken.

NORA: Daisies and Marigolds ... (*Pointedly*) Do you know how to grow them?

JOYCE: I certainly do not ... So, Mr. Beckett, how long will you stay at the École?

BECKETT: I'm not sure ... Maybe the same length as Tom ... Mr. McGreevy ... I've no real plans.

GIORGIO: We have that in common...

JOYCE: Not to plan is often planning by default. We just don't know we're doing it. (*Pause*) So, does your new job pay well?

NORA: Jim! You can't ask such personal questions.

JOYCE: Rephrase. Are you on the same incremental scale as Mr. McGreevy?

BECKETT: I would imagine so. It's much the same job, I gather.

NORA: That's none of your business, Jim.

JOYCE: Well, writing then. You'll have plenty of time to write. McGreevy only had to give two lectures a week. He became a Boulevardier of sorts, though a good poet. But I imagine you will want to engage the Muse more seriously.

BECKETT: I'm not really a writer … just an academic … a critic.

JOYCE: You need to be a thinker for that.

BECKETT: And for your … more creative work as well.

(With a bored expression GIORGIO *leafs through music books.* NORA *and* BECKETT *take notice but* JOYCE *does not.)*

JOYCE: No. There's not much thinking involved. I just borrow a classical structure and pile on the details. I'm not the architect or even the builder. Just the hod-carrier –

NORA: *(With a mischievous grin)* Just like what's-'is-name…? What is that name again? Yes, yes … it's coming back to me … The hod-carrier…

JOYCE: *(Alarmed)* No! Don't say it. It's 'work in progress' –

NORA: Calm down. I'm joking. God, it's only a name…! Don't worry, Sam. All will be revealed in time…

JOYCE: *(Recovering composure)* Well, whatever you do, Mr. Beckett, make sure it is different, original. Anyone could have written 'Dubliners' but not too many could have done 'Ulysses'. And I think I can say with some certainty that nobody could write one sentence of ... ahem ... 'work in progress'.

NORA: Who would want to? It's all ráiméis...

(LUCIA *enters from the right. She is striking in a simple dress and with her jet-black hair freshly done. She immediately catches* BECKETT*'s attention.*)

LUCIA: Excusez-moi. Je vais à mes leçons de danse...

NORA: Lucia, this is Mr. Beckett from Dublin.

LUCIA: (*Taking his extended hand*) Enchantée. J'espère que vous avez trouvé Paris...

NORA: The King's English please.

BECKETT (*Confused.*) But I understand ... Oh, sorry, of course ... Ballet-dancing, Miss Joyce?

LUCIA: Modern expressionist dancing, Mr. Beckett. Just like the painters – except with movement. (*She does a seductive twirl.*) They say I'll be the next Isadora Duncan.

JOYCE: (*Proudly*) Better, if you ask me. Soul rather than technique. And the spirit of Issy ... Lucia, Mr. Beckett is taking over from Mr. McGreevy at the École. He'll be on the same pay scale.

LUCIA: (*Huskily*) I hope you won't resemble Mr. McGreevy in other ways –

NORA: Please, Lucia. There's no need for that sort of talk...!

LUCIA: Well, this is gay Paree. We're very liberated here. (*More darkly*) Some people are very unconventional. They don't even bother to get married. It's like a secret wood. Normal rules don't apply.

BECKETT: I see, yes … I am delighted … to meet you at last, Miss Joyce.

LUCIA: I suppose Babbo has been pestering you for information about Dublin, wherever that is. Tom McGreevy is from Kerry, so that's no good. No, it has to be Dublin for Babbo.

JOYCE: (*Fondly*) Are you suggesting, Miss Mignon, that your father is obsessed by a city?

LUCIA: Yes, I am. When you're not obsessed by me –

NORA: You'd want to get a move on. That dance teacher is a stickler for punctuality.

LUCIA: Don't fuss, Mama … I hope to see you again, Mr. Beckett.
(*She trails a scarf across his shoulders as she walks towards the door.*)

BECKETT: I-I look forward … to that … very much.

GIORGIO: Hold on, Lucia. I'll be with you.

JOYCE: Take taxis. There and back.

NORA: Listen to that … No expense spared. You'd think we were born to luxury.
(LUCIA *and* GIORGIO *exit.*)

JOYCE: They're such talented children. You must hear Giorgio sing some time.

BECKETT: I would love to … May I ask if there is any literary talent … in evidence?

NORA: (*Not fully in jest*) Oh, I diluted that inheritance. The mad woman from Galway.

JOYCE: (*Groaning*) Not again.

BECKETT: (*Guiltily*) I'm … sorry if … I only –

NORA: It's nothing, Sam. Just normal sparring.

(NORA *begins to read the Daily Mail.*)

JOYCE: You told us the last time that you come from Foxrock. Of course that's not Dublin at all. It's a Protestant part of Wicklow.

NORA: Oh Lord, he's off again!

BECKETT: Em … not exactly … Anyway, I studied at Trinity College…

JOYCE: So, you got into Dublin once in a while. Right, so let me ask you this. The two statues in front of Trinity…

BECKETT: Edmund Burke and Oliver Goldsmith…

JOYCE: Yes, but which is closer to the main gate?

BECKETT: Equidistant … I always assumed so…

JOYCE: But not true, however. Goldsmith is closer by two and a half feet.

BECKETT: That is extraordinary!

NORA: Look at him. He's happy now. Just look at him.

JOYCE: We all need our small triumphs. I met an American writer last Wednesday … Herring … something … no, Heming – way. He told me that language should be used sparingly. Simplicity, he said, was the ultimate goal.

NORA: And you told him, no doubt! Of course, you did.

JOYCE: I merely suggested that simple language was appealing to simple souls. He was quite upset. Not a great victory perhaps, but it got me through the day … You'll find, Mr. Beckett, that one of the great advantages of Paris is not the people you meet or even the toleration of the more bizarre tastes, but rather its distance from Ireland and especially its distance from the Celtic Twilight and the contrived effusions of Mr. Yeats and his fellow sprites.

BECKETT: I like Yeats's poetry but, I agree, his Movement seems a little 'manufactured' for my liking. Forging the conscience of the nation has to be more organic … as you have pointed out.

JOYCE: Yes, 'Movements' as you call them, should be confined to the water closet.

BECKETT: I am hoping … if you agree … to do a piece comparing Dante and yourself –

NORA: (*Laughing*) There's no comparison!

JOYCE: Most commendable. I would help if I could but I'm really snowed under by my present project … 'Work in…'

BECKETT: Is there anything … I could do … to help – ?

JOYCE: (*Opportunistically*) That is most kind. Yes, there is so much work. I would appreciate another hand on deck.

NORA: Slave labour, you mean.? He's got four or five other helpers, not counting Paul Léon. (BECKETT *stoops and picks something from the floor.*)

BECKETT: Lucia … Miss Joyce seems to have dropped a slide from her hair.

JOYCE: (*Pondering*) Slide … Odd word. For a curlpin. Not a glissade. Actually the opposite, a fastener of sorts. And a bijou de femme. Remarkable.

NORA: Why don't you keep it for her, Sam?
BECKETT: (*Enthusiastically*) I will. I'll keep it safe
 for her...
 (*He puts it in his inside pocket.*)

Lights down.

SCENE TWO

Spring. Early afternoon. The apartment. Offstage,
GIORGIO *is singing 'Non Più Andrai', from*
'Figaro', to his own piano accompaniment.

(LUCIA *enters, dancing and clapping.*)

LUCIA: Wonderful, Giorgio. Bravo. Bravo. You'll
bring the houses down on all our heads –

NORA: It was very moving. You really should go to
University to study music –

LUCIA: (*Petulantly*) What about me?

NORA: Both of you. The Sorbonne is only down the
road from here.

GIORGIO: We wouldn't get in. Do you know what
the entrance exams are like? I've looked into it.
We're not even fluent in French.

NORA: Maybe it's not as hard to get in as you
think.

GIORGIO: It is. It's a nice thought but it won't
work. How many different schools did we go
to in Trieste? Twelve? Thirteen? We wouldn't
get through the front gate of the Sorbonne.

NORA: Well, you'll find your feet, I'm sure.

GIORGIO: I don't know if … my voice is good
enough. And I…

NORA: What?

GIORGIO: (*Embarrassed*) Well, I find it difficult …
to stand up in front of people.

NORA: That's just a matter of practice and

experience. (*She tousles his hair.*)

LUCIA: What about me? I'm not French. I'm not Irish or Italian, Austrian or Hungarian, or Swiss ... I used to dream that I wasn't anyone. Just a kind of space...

NORA: They were just nightmares, Lucia. We all had those. (*Pause*) Incidentally, Sam found a slide of yours. He's coming over today to go for a walk with your father.

LUCIA: Good. Nice Sam. But Babbo's already gone out.

NORA: (*Nods*) To *listen* to the river, would you believe that? When Sam calls I'll send him there. ... You know, he's much more knowledgeable about Ireland than your father. He agreed with me that Michael Collins was a much more heroic man than De Valera. He'd have reunited Ireland if he'd lived.

GIORGIO: How did he die ... this Collins?

NORA: Shot through the head in a cowardly ambush. All the good men died. The crowd in charge now are hypocrites and chancers.

GIORGIO: I don't know much about it.

LUCIA: I don't know anything about it and I don't want to know. Babbo only cares about Dublin, writing, and white wine. Oh wait ... someone called him the literary Parnell. He liked that.

(*A bell sounds and* NORA *goes to the door.*)

NORA: That must be Sam now ... Come in, Sam. You're welcome...

BECKETT: Thank you, Mrs. Joyce. ... Nora ... Oh

hello, Miss Joyce. I ... I found your slide last week.

(*He hands it to her; she lets her fingertips linger on his palm.*)

LUCIA: Thank you so much, Sam. You should call me Lucia.

BECKETT: I will ... I will. Thank you ... And I'm Sam ... Well, you know that ... I mean, *call* me Sam ... Oh hello, Giorgio, forgive me...

LUCIA: So you're going down to the Seine to meet Babbo?

BECKETT: Is he gone already?

NORA: Sometimes there's no holding him.

BECKETT: Am I late...? Oh Lord!

NORA: No. It's his fault. He'll be well through the first bottle when you arrive.

BECKETT: (*Anxiously*) I'd better go now.

NORA: Don't let him get you started on the drink, Sam ... Maybe you could, you know, keep an eye on him –

GIORGIO: Mama! You can't ask Sam to be his keeper. It isn't fair.

NORA: (*A little crestfallen*) Maybe you're right, Giorgio.

LUCIA: (*To* BECKETT) Give my regards to Babbo.

BECKETT: (*Surprised*) What...? Oh, I will...

LUCIA: And give him this from me. (*She kisses* BECKETT *on the cheek.*)

BECKETT: I will ... How...? I'll try ... Yes.

(BECKETT *exits left.*)

NORA: What's going on, Miss?

LUCIA: That's for me to know.

(She looks at the slide in her hand and smiles.)

Lights down.

SCENE THREE

Summer. Late night. LUCIA *is in the living room. She is swinging one leg and studying her fingernails.*

LUCIA: (*Loudly*) Where's Giorgio?

NORA: (*Offstage*) He's gone out to meet his
    friends.

LUCIA: Friends ... friends. Who'd be friends with
    any of us? The no-country Joyces of nowhere-
    land.
    (NORA *comes out from the study carrying a
    few sheets of paper.*)

NORA: Jesus, I don't know what he's at in there
    day after day. Here, listen to this. (*She reads
    haltingly.*) "... Woman with curlpins ...
    haggish expression, peaky nose, trekant mouth,
    fithery wight, ... Welshrabbit teint, Nubian
    shine, nasal fossette, turfy tuft, undersized, free
    kirk, no age..." What in God's name is all that
    about? I haven't a clue. No one could figure
    out that gibberish. Harriet Weaver is right.
    He's losing his wits. And if she cuts off the
    spondulicks, we'll all be in queer street...

LUCIA: (*Reflectively*) It's not so hard to follow.

NORA: (*Shocked*) What? You can understand that
    ... the rubbish I just read out?

LUCIA: Sort of. I think he's talking about a middle-aged woman. She used to be a beauty. Like Cinderella. And she's now flowing along like a river, approaching the 'change' and old age. I think death comes into it too.

NORA: Good God! I've heard everything now...
(*She stares at her daughter as if seeing her for the first time.*)
I don't believe it. (*Pauses*) Or maybe I do. (*Pauses*) Did you finish the wash-up?

LUCIA: Yes. And broke a cup ... They're out every second night. Where are they tonight?

NORA: Oh, his usual haunt down by the river, drinking and *listening to water*. Jesus, Mary and Joseph, I don't know who's worse. I was hoping Sam would be a good influence. But I think he's overawed by your man. Men are all the same anyway ... Why didn't you go to the theatre with Giorgio instead of moping around here all evening?

LUCIA: He's probably with that Helen Fleischman. She's a bit of a salope if you ask me ...
Divorced too ... She'll lead him astray.

NORA: Easy on, Lucia. I hear Helen is from a respectable American family.

LUCIA: A rich family –

NORA: So?

LUCIA: And she's ten years older. And, if you want my opinion, I think it was Babbo she set her cap at first...

NORA: Stop it!

LUCIA: The truth must come out...

NORA: I told you to stop! I don't want any of that kind of talk in this house.

LUCIA: Anyway Helen's too old for Giorgio ... Am I allowed say that much?

NORA: That's enough guff out of you! ... You tell *me* something, now Miss. What's the real reason you stayed in tonight?

LUCIA: I don't know what you mean.

NORA: Well, he is attractive. And gangly like your...

LUCIA: Who?

NORA: Who? Who? Sam of course.

LUCIA: Yes, he is sort of like Babbo.

NORA: (*With restraint*) A pity about the boils though.

LUCIA: What boils ... I didn't notice any boils...

NORA: On his neck ... He's very athletic. Boxing and cricket.

LUCIA: Cricket? What's cricket?

NORA: It's an English game, played with a bat and ball –
(*Sounds of incoherent singing precede the entrance of* JOYCE *and* BECKETT, *who are inebriated.*)

LUCIA: (*Jumps up*) They're here.

NORA: (*Grimly*) And not in very good condition by the sound of it.

JOYCE and BECKETT: (*Singing*) I gave it to Nellie / to stick in her belly / ... the leg of the duck / Oh, what a time ... we had to...
(*They flop on the sofa.*)

NORA: Stop it! I won't have such carry-on in this

house. In front of Lucia, too.

(BECKETT *straightens up on seeing* LUCIA, *though she's laughing.*)

BECKETT: Oh, most sorry … Miss Joyce … Dreadfully sorry…

JOYCE: How about … this one … Sam…? How's … it start again…? I've lost the key … ta … tumm … ta … to the door…

NORA: Lucia, don't take any notice of this pair. Go and get some coffee. Go on! And you two. Sit quiet!

(LUCIA *flounces out with a poor grace.*)

JOYCE: Ah, Nora. (*Sings*) C'mon Sam … Of the good stuff let's have more / 'Cause I've lost the key to the Door / … And come next Lent I will unbare / my penitent buttocks to the air…

NORA: I warned you about him, Sam. I warned you. Look at the state of him! The neighbours are laughing at him … at us.

JOYCE: Fetch me my guitar, woman.

NORA: I most certainly will not.

JOYCE: (*Singing*) First he tickled her / Then he patted her / Then he passed the female catheter / For he was a jolly old medical, jolly old medical / pox doctor of mine … Always remember. To copulate is fine / to masturbate divine –

NORA: I warned you!

JOYCE: This one's all right. (*Sings*) Whack fol de dah / Dance to your partner / Welt the flure / Your trotters shake / Wasn't it the truth I told ya / Lots of fun at … Oh, No … (*He stops abruptly, realising the danger.*)

NORA: (*Triumphantly*) I know why you stopped. I'll say it unless you sit quiet. I'll say it!

JOYCE: (*Chastened*) You wouldn't. No ... no, don't...

NORA: Oh, wouldn't I?

JOYCE: All right, Molly. I'll be quiet.

NORA: (*Sharply*) Don't call me that. I have my own name. Do you hear me now? I have my own name.

JOYCE: Sorry ... Where's Lucia, my inspiratrice...? Ah, the good girl. An cailín maith ... Issy ... Isis. My deepseep daughter ... bourne out of medsdreams unclouthed when I was pillowing in my brime...

(LUCIA, *laughing off, enters, dancing. She glances at* BECKETT*'s unruly hair and smiles.*)

JOYCE: My deepseep daughter ... before becoming Anna Livia Plurabella or Kate ... but never a seahag –

NORA: Be quiet! Cut out that codology!

BECKETT: How is ... the ... how is the dancing ... Miss Joyce ... Lucia?

LUCIA: Excellent. Would you like to dance with me, Sam?

BECKETT: (*Awkwardly*) Oh, yes ... I would ... but I've two left feet ... I'm afraid...

LUCIA: I can teach you, if you like ... We can teach each other...

NORA: Not now. It's late, Lucia, and you have that choreography class in the morning.

LUCIA: It's all right for Giorgio to be out late with
    his gigolo but I have to go to bed.

NORA: You'll thank me for it later. Go on now!

LUCIA: Another time, Sam. (*To* JOYCE) Don't
    worry Babbo, if I ever take a fancy to anyone,
    you won't lose out.
    (*With a meaningful glance towards*
    BECKETT, LUCIA *exits, doing a few graceful*
    dance steps)

JOYCE: (*Half mumbling*) I don't mind being … a
    vieux beau. Her suitors … are mere striplings
    … Whereas we can dream … rêverons …
    Conceived on St. Lucy's Day, the Feast of
    Light that combats blindness – (*Touches his*
    eye-patch.)

NORA: Don't mind him, Sam. With any luck he'll
    fall asleep.

JOYCE: (*Alert*) Did you know, Giorgio's girlfriend,
    Helen, is a Jewish heiress…?

NORA: Shut up about her…!

JOYCE: Her people are the cutlery kings of New
    York … Truckloads of cash … Yes, the old
    ship is coming in at last … if I may mix
    metaphors…

NORA: So you don't care about Giorgio's
    happiness…? (*Annoyed, canny, she makes a*
    knocking sound on the table.) Who could that
    be at this hour of the night? (*She goes to the*
    window.) I think it's Ms. Weaver – God
    Almighty…

JOYCE: (*Suddenly alert*) Jaysus, Miss Moneybags
    … what does she want…?

NORA: A return on her investment, I'd say. She *is*
    your patron…

JOYCE: (*Quickly on his feet*) She mustn't see us
    like this…! Sam, you go in that room. Hurry
    … Hurry!
    (BECKETT *exits right and* JOYCE *goes into
    his study.* NORA *goes to the door, opens and
    closes it, pretending she has admitted
    someone.*)

NORA: (*Loudly*) Hello Ms Weaver … How nice to
    see you … Come in … Come in … Yes, Jim is
    in the study … Jim! Harriet Weaver is here to
    see you!

JOYCE: (*Off, controlling slurs*) A second please …
    if you would be so kind … I'm just finishing
    an important paragraph…
    (JOYCE *emerges. His hair is freshly combed,
    his bearing steady, careful and upright.*)

JOYCE: Ah, Miss Weaver … My dear Harriet …
    It's so good to see you again … (*He looks
    around.*) What the hell…? What…? Ah Nora,
    that's not fair … Ah, God, it's not funny …
    You nearly put the heart sideways in me…

NORA: An important paragraph! That's sobered
    you up!! Maybe you'll behave now … As a
    matter of fact Harriet Weaver *did* call earlier
    and left this envelope for you.

JOYCE: Let's see…
    (JOYCE *opens the envelope.*)

NORA: I don't see why she doesn't put my name on
    it sometimes … How is it that you don't need
    your glasses when you're counting money…?

JOYCE: A goodly bonus if my poor eyes don't deceive me. I can get that fur coat for Lucia now. I promised her –

NORA: Over my dead body ... Give it here. (*Sounds of knocking go unnoticed.*)

JOYCE: New clothes for you too. Who ever said I was frugal? I'm generous to a fault. When I have it.

NORA: Give it to me ... If you don't, I'll have the children baptised.

JOYCE: They're too old. That threat doesn't wash anymore. (*He peels off several notes and hands them to her. Knocking is heard again.*) Christ, who's that?

NORA: (*Laughs*) It's poor Sam. He's still hiding. (*Loudly*) It's all right, Sam, you can come out now.

(BECKETT *enters diffidently.*)

BECKETT: Has Miss Weaver left already? Is everything ... all right?

NORA: Not too bad at all. Let me remind you again, Sam, never to lend money to that man. He'd bleed a nation dry. Poor Ezra Pound ran off to Italy to get out of his clutches.

JOYCE: Ah, you're all too serious. Just like the French critics. Can't see the fun in anything.

NORA: Oh it suits you to say that now, tumbling over from drink. And with a full wallet. Go on now. Up to bed.

BECKETT: I'll be off too. Sorry about ... Say goodnight to Lucia for me.

JOYCE: Take a taxi. A taxi there and back.

(NORA *sees* BECKETT *to the door. JOYCE
takes some money out of his wallet and looks
fondly at it.*)

NORA: Come on, you. Bed.

JOYCE: Just because I have money!

NORA: Sleep is all you're good for since you
started that damn 'Ulysses' eighteen years ago.
Sleep and snoring.
(*He leans on her as they exit to the right.*)

Lights down.

SCENE FOUR

Autumn. Evening. The apartment. JOYCE *is seated behind a desk, poring over a manuscript.* BECKETT *is standing with several sheets of paper in his hands.*

JOYCE: Have you checked the fourth section?
BECKETT: Yes. And I've done the corrections.
JOYCE: Amendments or emendations?
BECKETT: Happily, only the latter.
JOYCE: Good man. (*Picks up a letter, lifts up the eye-patch, and uses a magnifying glass.*) I have a letter here from the Shakespeare Company, from Miss Beach herself. Apparently, there's a copyright problem with 'Ulysses'. Mmmn. I think the Sapphic Beach is up to her old tricks. She's trying to pull the wool over my one good eye. But she won't finagle me.
BECKETT: Is there anything I can do?
JOYCE: No. Padraic Colum is the man for the job. He'll put the kibosh on her little scheme. (*Pause*) Incidentally, have you figured it out yet?
BECKETT: What? Figured out what?
JOYCE: You know … the … the title…
BECKETT: Of this? (*Holds up manuscript.*) I'm not sure … but I think it's 'Finnegans Wake'. Am I

right?

JOYCE: (*Grins*) But don't tell anyone yet ... apart
from Nora. She knows ... Why don't you write
a review of it later? I'd help you get it
published and that would help my sales. One
hand washes the other.

BECKETT: I'd love to. It's a fascinating,
compendious, work. Dream-like, even
Freudian –

JOYCE: Dream-like, yes. But Freudian, never.
Shakespeare said it all, long before that
Viennese chancer.

BECKETT: I love the passage where Anna Livia
thinks about the conception of her daughter ...
"what wouldn't you give to have a girl? Your
wish was mewill.. And lo, out of a sky..." The
reference is to Lucia I think –

JOYCE: (*Defensively*) Well, a text can mean
different things.

BECKETT: The female characters are really strong,
Anna Livia in particular. And her different
personalities.

JOYCE: I know they're strong. They sometimes
scare the bejasus out of me ... Of course
Harriet Weaver thinks I'm gone mad. But you
have to keep forging ahead.

(NORA *and* LUCIA *enter.*)

NORA: (*To JOYCE*) You had three bottles of white
wine last night and were calling for another.
Sam doesn't drink half as much and he's
twenty years younger than you are.

JOYCE: He doesn't *need* it yet ... Anyway, you

should see him when he gets together with
Tom McGreevy.

NORA: That's not the point. You'll have to cut
down. Your health is poor. When will you get
sense?

(LUCIA *notices the boil on* BECKETT*'s
neck.*)

LUCIA: That boil must be painful. Sam.

BECKETT: Oh, I suppose I'm used to them now.
They let the badness out.

LUCIA: There's no badness in you, Sam ... Let me
... (*She goes to squeeze it.*)

JOYCE: (*Squirming in horror*) Aaaagh. Aaaaagh.
(*He puts a hand over his good eye.*)

NORA: Don't, Lucia. Go and get some lint.
(LUCIA *goes out to the living room and
rummages in a drawer.*)

NORA: (*To* JOYCE) Don't be so squeamish. (*To*
BECKETT) You might be run-down, Sam.
You should take cabbage water. I could make
you some –

(LUCIA *returns and carefully places the lint
on* BECKETT*'s neck.*)

LUCIA: Or I could make a poultice for you.

BECKETT: Thank you. But I couldn't impose ...
That's a lot better. No, I'm not run down. I've
always had these damn boils...

LUCIA: Poor Sam. Suffering in silence. Silently
suffering Sam.

JOYCE: What about *my* arthritis and failing sight
and bad stomach?

NORA: Exercise and temperance are what you need.

JOYCE: You're a hard Galway woman, Nora
    Barnacle.

LUCIA: Poor badly bullied Babbo.

    (GIORGIO *and* HELEN *enter, laughing.*)

GIORGIO: I think you've met everyone, Helen.

HELEN: Yes, I guess so … I'm delighted to meet
    you all again.

LUCIA: Hello Mrs. Kastor-Fleischman. How is
    your son?

HELEN: (*Smoothly*) He's fine, Lucia. Thank you for
    asking. By the way I have a nice Schiaperelli
    dress that would suit you. I'll bring it round the
    next time.

GIORGIO: We came in Helen's car this time. It's a
    Roll Royce.

JOYCE: Do you drive, Helen?

HELEN: Oh no. Too technical for me, I'm afraid.
    We have a chauffeur.

NORA: A chauffeur?

HELEN: Yes, I'd be lost without him.: (*Looking at
    papers lying around*) This place seems to be a
    hive of creative activity.

JOYCE: But will there be any honey to show for it
    at the end of the season?

HELEN: Oh, I think there will be. Pots and pots of
    honey.

LUCIA: And how would you know?

HELEN: (*Ignores* LUCIA) Sweet, sweet honey. Oh,
    by the way, Sam, Peggy Guggenheim sends
    her regards…

BECKETT: (*Embarrassed in front of* LUCIA)
    Who…? Oh, yes, I met her very briefly …

after a seminar…

HELEN: She's buying up paintings at a rate of knots … They love to see her at art auctions.

JOYCE: She must be very wealthy…?

HELEN: Yes. She's even going to buy a gallery to house the paintings…

JOYCE: A gallery…? As in a whole building…? I know something about painting. Maybe I could advise her?

HELEN: I'd be delighted to introduce her to you … And I'm absolutely certain she would benefit greatly from *your* advice…

NORA: Oh God above … give me strength…

GIORGIO: We only dropped by to pick up those theatre tickets.

JOYCE: Oh yes, for the 'Master Builder'. Here they are. I got them from Paul Léon.

HELEN: Maybe you'd like to use them yourselves. I know you're a fan of Ibsen.

JOYCE: Oh, I've seen that play so many times…

HELEN: Why not come with us? We could pick up more tickets … Or we could get a box … The Théâtre du Palais Royal does have boxes I think … That would be fine and dandy…

NORA: It's completely booked out, I'm afraid … Isn't that right, Jim?

JOYCE: What…? Booked out…? Oh, yes. I believe so. Go on you two young things and enjoy yourselves. Take a taxi … Oh, no … you don't need to.

HELEN: Well, thank you very much, Jim. We must all have dinner together soon … On me … (*To*

GIORGIO) We'd better skedaddle, Sweetheart.
(HELEN *throws kisses as she and* GIORGIO
exit.)

LUCIA: She thinks she can bribe me with a dress ...
She has Giorgio on a string...

JOYCE: Oh, now, she's sunny and gay ... good for
what ails ye...

LUCIA: There's another side to her, if you ask me.

NORA: She called you 'Jim'. A wonder it wasn't
'Shem' ... Who does she think she is?

JOYCE: I thought you didn't like formality.

NORA: Giorgio will have his work cut out with that
one. Mark my words. I'm telling you now.

JOYCE: But the money, Nora. Buckets of the stuff.
Houses in New York and in the Pyrenees...

NORA: She wants Giorgio's name to hide her
Jewishness...

JOYCE: Why would anyone want to do that...?
They make a handsome couple ... Look on the
bright side ... Giorgio could be set up for life.
Maybe money can't buy happiness but it can
get you a better class of misery.

LUCIA: There is no bright side. Giorgio is caught in
a trap ... What do you say, Sam...?.

BECKETT: Oh, it's not my place to ... comment
...: (*Consults watch.*) I have to run too ...
papers to mark.

JOYCE: What about the cross-checking with Paul
Léon? It's a crucial passage. And my eyesight
is not up to it.

BECKETT: (*Guiltily*) Will tomorrow be all right?

JOYCE: (*Reluctantly*) Early.

BECKETT: (*Nods*) Before the cock crows once.
NORA: (*To* JOYCE) He's doing you a favour. It's
    not as if you're paying him.
    (BECKETT *and* LUCIA *kiss passionately in
    the vestibule.* NORA *watches from the study
    door. She is thoughtful rather than displeased.*)

Lights down.

SCENE FIVE

Autumn. Night. Living room of the apartment.

JOYCE: (*Handing a letter to* NORA) I can't read
  this scrawl. Could you read it for me? Those
  eye operations aren't doing any good.

NORA: It's from Malbois, the singing coach. He
  says that … Giorgio's voice is not quite … a
  true bass. It is an in-between register with an
  … indifferent timbre. It does not float on the
  breath … nor come from the abdomen as it
  should…

JOYCE: Oh Lord … What else…?

NORA: Then he says … that Giorgio lacks stage
  presence … and is of nervous disposition …
  There is not the self-assurance needed for –

JOYCE: That bloody man, Malbois…! He has
  exceeded his brief … Who does he think he is?
  Freud?

NORA: What have you done now?
  (LUCIA *and* GIORGIO *and* BECKETT *enter.*)

LUCIA: Who is Monsieur Malbois?

JOYCE: A pianist, a very good one. He
  accompanied Giorgio last Wednesday evening,
  remember?

GIORGIO: (*Darkly suspicious*) I think he's more
  than that. I may not be a genius, but I'm not an
  idiot either…

JOYCE: What do you mean?

GIORGIO: He's a voice instructor, isn't he? Well, what's the verdict? Let's have it.

JOYCE: You have a wonderful voice –

BECKETT: I agree with that … absolutely…

GIORGIO: That's your opinion, Dada. What is his? What did Monsieur Malbois say? In that letter…

JOYCE: He's only one –

GIORGIO: Christ, as bad as that…? (*To* NORA) Were you in on this?

LUCIA: Mama's not in on anything.

GIORGIO: Oh, what's the point … (*He walks quickly towards the door.*)

NORA: Giorgio … please!

(GIORGIO *exits right and slams the door behind him.*)

JOYCE: (*Sadly*) The best laid plans … I meant well…

NORA: (*Loudly*) You should have told me what you had planned. Giorgio is very sensitive about these things. It wasn't fair to spring that on him.

JOYCE: I have a headache now. Lucia, Could you fetch my other glasses?

LUCIA: Fetch this. Fetch that. Oh, all right. Babbo can be very demanding.

(*She exits right with a flounce.*)

JOYCE: My 'Mignon's' in good form anyway. For this relief, much thanks.

NORA: (*Noncommittal*) Mmmmm.

BECKETT: (*Looking at watch*) Are you sure … it's

all right ... for me...

NORA: To stay the night? Of course, Sam. That was the arrangement. It's much too late for you to leave now. You wouldn't even get a taxi at this hour.

> (LUCIA *returns with the glasses which she places on* JOYCE'S *nose.*)

JOYCE: Sancta Lucia, bringer of light –

> (LUCIA *dances for a while.*)

LUCIA: I'm off to bed for my beauty sleep. Goodnight everyone.

ALL: Goodnight.

> (NORA *peers at her curiously. Just before exiting* LUCIA *turns and gives* BECKETT *a knowing look.*)

JOYCE: Is there any more wine?

NORA: No. The cupboard is bare.

JOYCE: Well, maybe it's time for us all to turn in. Let us dream. Rêverons ... But not of Lucifer...

NORA: You'll be all right on the couch, Sam. I've left you some blankets.

BECKETT: I'll be fine. You go on. And ... thanks.

> (*After* NORA *and* JOYCE *exit,* BECKETT *wrestles with the couch. He removes watch, glasses, pullover and shoes and arranges them carefully on the floor. He wriggles awkwardly into the bed. The lights go down. After ten seconds or so the lights come up slightly to reveal* LUCIA *standing in the doorway in her robe. She sits on the edge of the couch. She takes his head in her hands and kisses him.*

After a while BECKETT *pulls away.*)

LUCIA: What's wrong?

BECKETT: (*Awkwardly*) Nothing … I mean here
… in your parents' house…

LUCIA: I know.

(*They both laugh nervously, trying to keep the
sound down.*)

BECKETT Christ, if he came in now…

LUCIA: Babbo would understand. He's a man of
the world. Several worlds…

BECKETT: Several worlds? Yes, I know what you
mean. You're very close. You even talk like
him sometimes … Like he writes.

LUCIA: (*Surprised*) I do?

BECKETT: Yes, the same rhythm. It's amazing.

LUCIA: That's a wonderful compliment. You're a
very nice man, Sam. And you help Babbo.
Which is good because he's nearly blind, even
though I bring him light.

BECKETT: (*Wryly*) Less about him. What about us?

LUCIA: You can't leave him out. He gets in
everywhere. He tried to get me to go with Tom
McGreevy. But he's a homosexual. Most of
our friends are.

BECKETT: I know Sylvia Beach is –

LUCIA: (*Laughing*) Oh Sam. She's a Lesbian.

BECKETT: That's what I mean. (*He moves to kiss
her.*)

LUCIA: Everyone should say what they mean. No
more and no less. Not like him. I can sort of
follow it, but a lot of people can't.

BECKETT: I know. I find it difficult –

LUCIA: Do you like my eyes, Sam…? Do you think I should get my hair bobbed again?

BECKETT: Yes to eyes. No to hair. I like it just the way it is.

LUCIA: I love Giorgio's voice, whatever that man said. But he deserves better than Helen Fleischman.

BECKETT: Everything will work out all right, Lucia. Don't worry.

LUCIA: Are you sure, Sam?

BECKETT: Yes … Yes.

LUCIA: I used to have … terrible nightmares. I'm always afraid they'll come back.

BECKETT: I won't let them.

LUCIA: That's good, Sam … because they were awful … Even though I knew they weren't real.

BECKETT: I know that feeling.

LUCIA: You do?

BECKETT: Oh yes. I have demons of my own.

LUCIA: We're alike, you and me.

BECKETT: Yes, we are.

LUCIA: (*With sad intensity*) I like it when you hold me, Sam.

(*She embraces him tightly; they lie slowly back on the couch.*)

Lights down. Music of 'The Lass of Aughrim'.

End of ACT ONE

ACT TWO

SCENE ONE

Autumn. Night. A restaurant. Sounds of chatter.
BECKETT *and* GIORGIO *walk to a table in a restaurant, carrying their drinks.*

GIORGIO: (*Slurring slightly*) Sometimes he tries
    too hard.
BECKETT: I suppose every father tries. He told me
    that family was the most important thing to
    him.
    (*They sit.*)
GIORGIO: That's a good one! And I suppose
    writing comes second? Oh, I can't blame him.
    That's the problem. No one to blame. He was
    dragged around Dublin by his own father by all
    accounts. Do you know how many times we
    had to change apartments in Trieste? Twenty-
    six times…
BECKETT: Good God!
GIORGIO: Twelve different schools. (*Pause*) He

humiliates me without meaning to. I sometimes wish he was just a simple bastard I could hate.

BECKETT: Relationships are so ... damn complicated.

GIORGIO: You sound like Professor Jung ... I find it difficult to talk. Who's going to listen to me? He's everywhere. I'm in the shadow.

BECKETT: You'll find your own way. We all have to once we're pulled out of the womb. It's not easy for you, the son of an expatriate, a famous man of letters. But when you marry and settle down it will all be very different ... Listen to me! What the hell do I know...?

GIORGIO: Who wants a failed singer who can't stand in front of an audience?

BECKETT: Helen Fleischman seems very fond of you.

GIORGIO: (*Laughing*) Lucia calls her a 'gigolo'. I think she means me.

BECKETT: Why not take a leaf out of Lucia's book. She's always very ... lighthearted.

GIORGIO: (*With a querulous look*) Light...? Lighthearted...?

BECKETT: Maybe that's not it exactly...

GIORGIO: Where is Lucia by the way? I thought you were meeting her here this evening?

BECKETT: I am. But I have to meet Tom McGreevy first. I'll be back in plenty of time.

GIORGIO: Well, take a taxi there and back.

(*Both laugh.*)

(*Reflectively*) In a way, we're both orphans. We're also bastards, technically speaking. That bothers Lucia more than me ... We spent our lives in one room or another with our father locked in his study. At night he went out drinking and came back roaring and singing and telling us how great he was.

BECKETT: (*Heatedly*) He has the greatest admiration for you and your talents –

GIORGIO: (*Maudlin*) Talents? Singing and dancing! Don't you see? He tried to mould us, fashion us. He is the great artificer, Daedalus. If he is, then who am I? (*Pause*) Icarus, that's right, and we all know what happened to him ... He tried to fashion Mama, too, but she was too strong for him. Lucia is another matter ... Don't you see ... we're not his children. We're his characters – raw material for making his characters...

BECKETT: Oh, now ... He ... (*Awkwardly*) ... he loves you both...

GIORGIO: (*Shrugs*) All I know for sure is that I've spent years going to the 'Studio de la Voix', trying to prove myself, knowing all the time that it is impossible to measure up ... Lucia will be tested soon at the Bal Bullier, a big dance contest. Why do we have to perform all the time? Anyway, Lucia had it worse than me...

BECKETT: I don't follow.

GIORGIO: A genius can do anything ... get away with anything ... create fantasy worlds where everything is all right...

BECKETT: What're you getting at?

GIORGIO: We all wear different faces, Sam ... Anyway, forget all that ... Blood under the bridge. (*Pause, more upbeat*) I've been thinking about proposing to Helen. She's older ... but we get on so well together ... She's coming here later...

BECKETT: Well, you must make your own decisions. Good luck to you, whatever you decide.

GIORGIO: If she accepts, it would probably mean leaving Lucia on her own with ... them. Unless Helen agreed to ... We'll see ... We'll see ... (*Looks blearily at him*) I think there's going to be another war sooner or later. It will change everything.

BECKETT: I wonder.

GIORGIO: Hell is on its way ... but maybe it has some advantages over limbo.

BECKETT: Not too many I think ... Of course, neither exists.

GIORGIO: You may be wrong there ... (*Pause*) ... Look around ... Where do you think this is ... Are we really alive ... I mean really...?

BECKETT: Maybe you should ... ease up on that brandy, Giorgio. It's strong stuff.

GIORGIO: Don't patronise me, Sam.

BECKETT: Sorry, I didn't mean to...
(*He leaves a couple of bills on the table.*)

GIORGIO: I see ... you're wearing one ... of his old neck-ties...

BECKETT: (*Pleased*) Yes. He gave me a gift of this one.

GIORGIO: Generous to a fault … Be careful it
    doesn't become … a yoke around your neck…
    (HELEN *enters smiling.*)

HELEN: Hi Honey, I see you've started without me.
    Good for you.

BECKETT: Sit here, Helen. I'm going.

HELEN: Not on my account, I hope.

BECKETT: No. I have to meet McGreevy. But I'll
    be back. Leave you, love you.
    (BECKETT *exits.*)

HELEN: I see you've had a few already.

GIORGIO: I like the way you said that. No censure
    … no veiled criticism.

HELEN: You should know by now I'm not like that.
    Live and let live is my motto.

GIORGIO: I'm sure your son appreciates that
    approach.

HELEN: He's a good kid. If it ain't broke … you
    know. Besides, we have a great Nanny … It's
    not a problem for you, is it, George … the fact
    that I have a son…?

GIORGIO: No, not at all. I'm very fond of David …
    He reminds me a little of myself at that age…

HELEN: I'm so glad you feel like that, Honey,
    because we just get on so well. So very well.
    My first husband … oh … it doesn't matter…

GIORGIO: No. Go on. You can tell me anything,
    Helen.

HELEN: Nothing much to tell, really. I was young
    and made a mistake. I thought he was Mr.
    Right. But he had issues … He wasn't as
    relaxed and tolerant as you … But then few

people are … By the way, do you know
Gertrude Stein?

GIORGIO: No. Though I think I've heard the
name…

HELEN: She runs a big literary salon. I'm sure your
Dad would know her.

GIORGIO: I'm sure he would…

HELEN: I wonder if he might get me an
introduction … I have some short stories I'd
like to have published. Would you ask him for
me?

GIORGIO: Certainly…

(*She kisses him.*)

HELEN: You're a darling … Have you heard the
joke about Gertrude Stein?

GIORGIO: No, I don't think so.

HELEN: Here goes: She's the Mama of Dada.
Pretty good … isn't it?

GIORGIO: I'm sure … it is…

HELEN: George, there's one other thing I want to
ask you … Sometimes in your home, I don't
know exactly what's being said. I know a little
Italian but not enough. I often feel excluded …
Sometimes I even imagine that Lucia is
cussing me out…

GIORGIO: No, she's not … Don't worry about that.
But I'll have a word, anyway…

HELEN: Good. That would be great…

GIORGIO: You know I'd do anything for you,
Helen…

HELEN: I'm beginning to believe it, George.
You're an ace, a real friend…

GIORGIO: I was hoping ... we'd gone beyond friendship...

HELEN: I think we have, George.

GIORGIO: In fact I've been working up to something...

HELEN: What might that be, Darling?

GIORGIO: Well ... it's about you and me ... us...

HELEN: Yes, You and me make us.

GIORGIO: We love each other...

HELEN: We do. I can't deny it.

GIORGIO: Then why wait? Let's get married. I haven't got a ring yet ... But ... later. What do you say?

HELEN: Give a girl a chance to gather her wits!

GIORGIO: (*Deflated*) Oh ... OK ... How long will you need?

HELEN: Not too long ... I've already thought about it ... the answer is Yes!

(*Both stand and hug.*)

GIORGIO: Great answer, Helen ... Superb...

HELEN: How could I refuse you, Darling? Waiter! A bottle of your best champagne ... Krug Vintage...

GIORGIO: And two large brandies ... We can make cocktails ... to celebrate ... We can have a party when Lucia and Sam get here...

HELEN: Lucia is coming here...?

GIORGIO: Yes.

HELEN: You know, Darling, this is so personal ... so between *us* ... I think we should go somewhere else to celebrate ... on our own. How about *La Coupole*? We'll have plenty of opportunities to invite others later on … But just you and me on this very special night? OK?

GIORGIO: Whatever you want, Helen.

HELEN: That's great, Honey. Waiter! Cancel the order.

(GIORGIO *and* HELEN *exit.*)

Lights dimmed briefly.

SCENE TWO

Later that night. The same restaurant. As LUCIA *enters she sees* HELEN *and* GIORGIO *leave. She looks out after them. She sits, fidgets, looks at the menu, consults her watch.*

(BECKETT *enters in a rush.*)

LUCIA: (*Relieved*) Sam, about time. I was beginning to wonder.

BECKETT: Sorry I'm late. I had to wait almost thirty minutes for a tram when I left McGreevy. There's a strike, I think. Always some strike or other. Liberty, equality, but no fraternity...

LUCIA: Well, you're here now ... I saw Giorgio and Helen leave here arm-in-arm. She was looking very content...

BECKETT: He probably proposed to her...

LUCIA: Proposed...?

BECKETT: He was talking about plucking up the courage...

LUCIA: He's walked right into her trap...!

BECKETT: Give it time, Lucia ... Everything will work out, you'll see.

LUCIA: You believe in miracles...

BECKETT: Maybe I do ... *You're* here for a start...

LUCIA: (*Brightening*) That's a nice thing to say,

Sam … Let's look at the menu. I'm thinking of
having asparagus soup and the salad.

BECKETT: That's fine for me too. Good choice.

LUCIA: It should help clear up your boils. Purify
the blood, as Mama would say.

BECKETT: (*Laughs*) The old remedies are the best
remedies.

LUCIA: The waiters haven't come near me. They
fawn over Helen … But they seem to dislike
me for some reason.

BECKETT: Oh, now. I would doubt that.

LUCIA: (*Cranes forward intimately*) I often think of
that first night on the couch in the apartment…

BECKETT: I know. Right there in the living room.
It was amazing.

LUCIA: Right under Babbo's nose. (*Pause,
tenderly*) It was your first time, Sam?

BECKETT: Em … did it show?

LUCIA: (*Puts her hand on his*) It was wonderful …
And real.

BECKETT: I'm glad … relieved too…

LUCIA: We should sleep together more often, Sam.

BECKETT: That would be great … but I'm still
afraid of your father. And your mother. I don't
know what they think about … us.

LUCIA: They're bohemians. Anything goes.
(*Pause*) Anyway, they like you … Babbo
appreciates your help … And Mama thinks
you're a good friend for Giorgio…

BECKETT: I'm glad to hear that…
(*He notices that she has gone into a sort of
trance.*)

61

BECKETT: I'm glad because … Lucia, are you …
all right…?

LUCIA: This service is appalling! (*She looks
angrily around.*) Hey, you stuck-up Frogs, how
about some service…?

BECKETT: Easy on, Lucia…!

LUCIA: If you think I don't exist, you're wrong …
dead wrong…! I'm not going to disappear …
I'm not…!

BECKETT: (*Alarmed*) Lucia, for Goodness Sake…!
(*She tries to set fire to the menu.*)

BECKETT: My God, what are you doing…?

LUCIA: I'm the light-bringer, didn't you know? But
they still hate me…
(*Alarmed, and shocked,* BECKETT *takes her
by the elbow and accompanies her out of the
restaurant.*)

Lights down.

SCENE THREE

Autumn. Early afternoon. The apartment. LUCIA *and* GIORGIO *are in the living room.* LUCIA *is looking untidy. Sounds of a river flowing swell to a crescendo and then fade away.*

GIORGIO: You have your dance competition
  coming up soon.
LUCIA: Oh, that. Should be a cake-walk ... How's
  Mrs Helen Kastor Fleischman?
GIORGIO: Fine. She's fine. Thanks for asking.
LUCIA: She's not right for you – you shouldn't
  have got engaged.
GIORGIO: I know it's hard for you, Lucia. –
LUCIA: Hard? No it's not hard. I'm just trying to
  warn you. She has money; her family has
  money. She just wants to be part of Babbo's
  more famous family. She has no name ...
  She'll take your name, and more...
GIORGIO: Lucia, I don't like to hear that sort of
  talk ... What about you and Sam?
LUCIA: Oh, Sam. He's a virgin ... or was ... (*She
  examines her face in a hand-mirror.*) I never
  much cared for my eyes ... Sometimes I have
  no face, just a blank space ... No face, imagine
  that.
GIORGIO: I mean is it going anywhere? You and
  Sam.

LUCIA: Everything goes somewhere ... maybe back to the beginning ... I am ... Lucia Joyce ... Stupid name. He gave me nothing ... Remember those nightmares?

GIORGIO: Yes.

LUCIA: I hope Lucia never has them again ... And the teachers who hated us because Babbo was often drunk...? And because we're bastards?

GIORGIO: I remember.

LUCIA: I might become engaged to Sam, I don't know yet. Assuming he doesn't mind bastards ... or soiled goods. Maybe he does ... maybe he doesn't ... Expressionist dancing, not ballet. Have you heard anything like that? Expressionist singing...? (*Beat*) I need better clothes ... But not Fleischman's cast-offs... (*She suddenly flings the hand-mirror on the floor.*)

GIORGIO: (*Unsurprised*) Did you take your Veronal today?

(*He cleans up the mess.*)

LUCIA: That's none of your business!

GIORGIO: It is my business, Lucia. I'm your brother ... How are you getting on with Professor Jung?

LUCIA: Oh, him? Babbo calls him the Tweedledum of Zurich. How can he be any good then? He's worse than the Tweedledee of Vienna ... I'm fed up with them all. (*Pause*) I'm tired, Giorgio ... so tired...

GIORGIO: (*Sadly*) I know ... I know ... But you really should try to take better care of yourself

... You're a good person, Lucia...

LUCIA: I heard Padraic Colum saying that Mama
wasn't good enough for Babbo ... But then
who is...? I am his inspiratrice or little Issy ...
Mama is jealous of me. Imagine that...? I'm
not good enough for him ... or for anybody ...
(*Loudly*) I don't belong here!
(*She tries to light paper doilies on a plate.*
GIORGIO *gently takes the lighter from her*
hand.)

GIORGIO: You are part of this family, Lucia.
(*He shows her the family photo.*)

GIORGIO: There you are ... There...

LUCIA: Is that me...? No ... No ... That's a
different person ... I don't belong anywhere.

GIORGIO: Calm down, Lucia ... Shush.
(*He puts his arm around her shoulder and*
strokes her hair.)

GIORGIO: Shush. I'll take care of you ...
Somehow.

Lights down slowly.

SCENE FOUR

Spring. Night. The living room is empty. The door bursts open and LUCIA *rushes in. She throws off her cape to reveal a silver dance costume. She is very distressed.* JOYCE, NORA *and* BECKETT *follow her into the room.*

NORA: Calm down, Lucia. It's not the end of the world.

LUCIA: (*Shouts*) It's the end of me. I lost. I lost. I should have won.

BECKETT: You were the best by far.

JOYCE: Everyone knew that except the judges. The audience were shouting, 'Nous reclamons l'irlandaise.' By popular acclaim, you won.

LUCIA: That's no good to me. All my so-called friends were there … Laughing … I've been beaten down. Again. Why did you put me through that, Mama…?

NORA: Me? I didn't arrange it … I had no idea…

JOYCE: Expressionist dancing is still too avant garde. They prefer older forms, including the African style that won this evening…
(*He gestures to* BECKETT *to go to her. He hesitates, then takes her hand and pats it diffidently.* LUCIA *pulls her hand away.*)

NORA: Where's Giorgio?

BECKETT: He was … upset. I think he went to see

Helen. Her driver called for him...

LUCIA: (*Agitated*) Giorgio can't sing. I can't dance. I can't hold on to Sam. Because we're bastards. That's why. It's as simple as that!

NORA: Lucia, please stop.

LUCIA: (*Shouts*) Why should I stop? You made me a bastard. All my school friends knew it. Bastard! Bastard! You made me one. I couldn't make myself a bastard, could I? No, you made me one ... you made me a bastard...!

NORA: How dare you!

JOYCE: (*Anxiously*) Lucia, not ... to your mother ... please...

LUCIA: (*Confronts* NORA) You tricked him. But you couldn't get him up the aisle. You never helped me when he –

NORA: Shut up! (*Slaps her*) ... I'm sorry ... Oh, God, I'm sorry –

(LUCIA *pushes* NORA *and runs ou*t.)

JOYCE: Christ Almighty....

BECKETT: I'd better...

JOYCE: (*Shakily*) Stay ... Stay ... The worst is over ... She'll calm down ... That dance contest was so unfair...

NORA: You're a bigger fool than I thought ... if you believe that.

JOYCE: I don't know what you mean ... She'll settle down when the disappointment passes...

BECKETT: I think ... in the circumstances ... I should...

JOYCE: (*Shrewdly*) Sit down, Sam ... What did she mean about not holding on to you? I thought you two were getting on well.

BECKETT: Well, it … it … didn't … you know …
develop … I'm probably not … suitable … for
her…

JOYCE: That's too bad. May I ask what happened?

BECKETT: Em … differences … arose. … I
mean…

NORA: What are you trying to say?

BECKETT: Just … that … there appeared to be
some … incompatibilities … What I thought
was … liveliness … well, you know…

JOYCE: No, I don't know!

NORA: (*Combatively*) Do you think she's …
unwell?

BECKETT: I … I … don't –

JOYCE: Is that it? I never thought you were so daft.
Your first instinct was correct. Liveliness.
That's Lucia's rare gift. Liveliness … But you
shouldn't have led her on, Sam. That was
unfair.

BECKETT: Lead her on…? I didn't … think … I
did … Oh, Lord…

JOYCE: But you brought her to lunch so often.

BECKETT: (*Blurts*) At *her* invitation … Sorry … I
shouldn't have said that.

NORA: Why didn't you refuse? You're a free agent.

BECKETT: Lately … I would bring … Tom
McGreevy … or Jack Yeats … or
Ponisovsky…

NORA: (*Loudly*) Chaperones! Oh, God, that must
have killed her.

BECKETT: (*Distraught*) I never thought … I'm so

sorry ... Oh, Lord what can I say...?

NORA: (*Grimly*) I think you'd better go...

JOYCE: Wait...

NORA: I mean it.

BECKETT: (*Rising*) I'm so sorry ... (*Begins to weep*) I would never ... never do anything ... to hurt ... Lucia ... You must believe that... (*He looks back once and exits left.*)

NORA: (*Half to herself*) I'm sorry too.

JOYCE: (*Wistfully*) I thought there was potential there. They got on so well together ... (*Pause*) He was the best amanuensis I ever had.

NORA: She's not well, Jim.

JOYCE: You too? She's just at an awkward age. And that, combined with her liveliness or giddiness ... You know, I think Paul Léon's nephew is interested in her.

NORA: You can't interfere.

JOYCE: There's nothing wrong with giving Nature a nudge along.

NORA: (*Loudly*) Don't meddle. You don't know anything about real life. It's all just words with you, all just bloody words ... Children! I should have had my womb taken out years earlier. You never gave me any help with them. How could you? Your books are your children. You're a child yourself.

JOYCE: (*Stoutly*) I love them both dearly.

NORA: You never showed it. They had to perform for you, to earn your praise. They're not actors. They're real people. Well, you've done it now. Lucia isn't well. You might as well know ...

I've been sending her to see Professor Jung.

JOYCE: (*Shocked*) You what? I can't believe you did that ... He's a charlatan ... worse than Freud any day....

NORA: Do you know what he said? He told her she was drowning. Drowning!

JOYCE: Don't mind that old guff. She's not drowning ... she's not ... she's not...

NORA: Say it! Mental illness. The words terrify you. Face up to it. You used to worry about your own mind, didn't you? You used to wet the bed, thinking about all those lunatics who lost their minds to syphilis. Face up to it now. Your daughter is mentally disturbed. Hebephrenia is what Professor –

JOYCE: (*Alarmed*) No ... no ... Lucia is just prey to sudden impulses ... And I know it hasn't been easy for her ... But she'll be fine when she gets over this disappointment and when she gets some rest. The holiday in Ireland and the visit to Harriet Weaver in London will do her the world of good. You'll see.

NORA: (*With resignation*) You're as daft as she is ... Oh, go to bed. But, you haven't heard the last of this.

JOYCE: Are you coming? (*He moves towards the door.*)

NORA: In a while. I've some things to do ... Oh, and by the way, Helen won't marry Giorgio unless he's made legitimate ... Her parents insist on that. They're very strait-laced.

JOYCE: So?

NORA: *We* have to get married.

JOYCE: Us? You and me?

NORA: Yes. Who else?

JOYCE: Fine. Whatever. I'll ask Paul Léon to do the paperwork.

(JOYCE *exits.* NORA *looks after him, then shakes her head in disbelief.*)

Lights down.

SCENE FIVE

Early summer. Early evening. GIORGIO *and* HELEN *are in the apartment having drinks.*

HELEN: It's eerily quiet … Of course Lucia is still in England with Harriet Weaver. I wonder how she's getting on.

GIORGIO: Not too well … There were some incidents…

HELEN: You don't have to worry about her, Sweetie. She'll find her own way, never fear. We all have our ups and downs. Why, I have moods myself sometimes…

GIORGIO: I'm not so sure … We may have to look after her…

HELEN: You worry far too much, Honey … Anyway we'll probably be spending half our time in New York. Remember you'll have a stepson … (*Enthusiastically*) And I imagine we'll be starting our own family soon.

GIORGIO: We can talk about it again … How did your meeting with Gertrude Stein go? (HELEN *looks out window.*)

HELEN: The damned chauffeur is always late … Gertrude Stein? She's a strange creature. I got the impression that she is ashamed not only of her sex but also of her Jewishness. She thought that Jim was condescending towards Jews in

'Ulysses'.

GIORGIO: Jim…? I don't think that can be right.
He identifies with Jews more than with any
other people … Anyway, did she like your
short stories?

HELEN: It's hard to say. I don't think she liked *me*.
She kept looking at my clothes. Maybe I
should have dressed in rags … like some of the
painters who were there … One guy, Picasso,
looked like a tramp … I'm not kidding …
Maybe if your Dad looked at my fiction…? If
he gave it the thumbs-up, I'd be well on my
way.

GIORGIO: I'll ask him if you like … or you can.

HELEN: Maybe I could pluck up the courage … By
the way, I brought you a little gift, a bottle of
20-year-old Armagnac.
(*She puts it on the table.*)

GIORGIO: That's most generous of you, Helen.
We'll have some later … Now what's the latest
on the wedding.

HELEN: Well, we've agreed on a civil ceremony …
probably the *mairie* in the Sixth
Arrondissement. But Daddy is insisting on a
big party afterwards in New York. The
numbers already stand at over 300 but will
creep up I think. Does that bother you,
Darling?

GIORGIO: No. It's your big day, Helen. Whatever
you want is fine with me … Will I have to
crush a glass underfoot?

HELEN: No. I think we can do without all that

schmaltz and old-fashioned symbolism ...
Have you decided on the best man yet ... Sam
Beckett or Tom McCreevy?

GIORGIO: Sam is travelling a lot lately. It'll
probably be Tom...

HELEN: You don't have any French friends?

GIORGIO: Not really...

(JOYCE *enters.*)

JOYCE: I hope I'm not interrupting.

HELEN: Not at all ... I was wondering if ... No, I
shouldn't ask...

JOYCE: Go ahead, Helen. You can ask me
anything.

(JOYCE *sits.*)

HELEN: Well, it's about some short fiction I've
written ... I was wondering if you might ...
look it over for me...

JOYCE: Well, of course, Helen, I'd be delighted. I
wonder if my eyes would be up to it though.
Better if you dropped by some time and read
the material to me. How about Wednesday at 3
p.m.?

HELEN: That would be fantastic. I'm most grateful,
Jim.

JOYCE: A couple of bottles of good Chablis would
make the work go swimmingly.

HELEN: No problemo ... in fact a super idea...

GIORGIO: I thought we were supposed to go
shopping for wedding clothes...

HELEN: That can wait, Sweetie. Anyway, I can
have someone do most of it in New York.

GIORGIO: Well, we'd better make tracks for Les

Deux Magots before the potage gets cold.

JOYCE: Try the onion soup. It's a meal in itself. And the oysters aren't bad either ... Enjoy the evening. A chauffeur there and back...

(HELEN *kisses him on the cheek as she and* GIORGIO *exit.*)

JOYCE:(*Loudly*) Nora! Where did you get to?

(NORA *enters*)

NORA: I waited until that woman left.

JOYCE: Ah now, Nora, your future daughter-in-law...

NORA: More's the pity. She's seduced Giorgio and now she's bombarding him with expensive gifts. She's on the make...

JOYCE: I know you and Giorgio are very close...

NORA: It's nothing to do with that. He's being led up and down the garden path. We ... never had the money to buy him expensive things...

JOYCE: He wouldn't be impressed by that...

NORA: He mustn't be your son then ... And you're going to help her with her writing ... You're flirting with her, you stupid old goat ... When will you get sense? Never. Never. Never ... Do you think for one moment that I'm going to let you alone with her on Wednesday when she brings over her scribblings and two bottles of wine. Think again ... Have you no regard for me or your son?

JOYCE: It was a totally innocent arrangement...

NORA: Was it now...? Do you take me for a fool...? You're not God's gift to women, you know. Some of us can actually manage to survive without you…

JOYCE: Oh merciful hour … Nora, all right, you have a point. I'll change the arrangement … Now, did you get a chance to look at that letter I'm going to send to Harriet Weaver.

(NORA *produces a letter from her pocket.*)

NORA: This thing? Have you not even a titter of sense? *We* asked *her* to look after Lucia in England. It was unfair and we shouldn't have done it.

JOYCE: She put Lucia in an asylum. She had no right to do that. No right. It was high-handed and unacceptable – as I say there in the second paragraph…

NORA: Lucia tried to set Harriet Weaver's house on fire. What was the woman supposed to do?

JOYCE: She may be a patron of the arts but that does not give her the right … to diagnose … to put my … our … daughter into an asylum…!

NORA: You still can't say it … No, you'll deny it to the end.

JOYCE: Give me the letter. I'll re-write it…

NORA: No, I won't … Good Christ, writing and re-writing won't change anything … It never does.

(*She crumples the letter.*)

Lights down.

SCENE SIX

Autumn. Evening. HELEN *is sitting on her own in the Joyce apartment.*

HELEN: (*Loudly*) Any luck?

GIORGIO: (*Off*) Yes, I've found it.
(*He enters carrying a passport.*)

HELEN: A passport is an important document, George. You should be careful where you leave it…

GIORGIO: Thanks for that advice!
(*He takes a swig from a hip flask.*)

HELEN: Don't snap at me. You know I have to go back and forth to New York … And, by the way, you could try a little harder to develop your singing career over there.

GIORGIO: I'm not one of your projects, Helen … And did it ever occur to you that I have no interest in being famous…?

HELEN: Oh for Chrissakes, you have to do something … something other than drink! You're pissing your life away…

GIORGIO: Drink brings me peace of mind…

HELEN: And I don't?

GIORGIO: No, you do not. You're always carping and criticising … And I never know what kind of mood you're going to be in…

HELEN: I never knew you could be so cruel … You

know I'm carrying your child...

GIORGIO: (*Chastened*) I'm sorry, Helen ... I went too far...

HELEN: I'm not feeling well ... I think maybe I should go to the New York Clinic for a rest...

GIORGIO: Again...? The last time you went in was because the critics didn't like your short stories ... I mean ... don't take this the wrong way, but is it really necessary...?

HELEN: Disappointment goes deep in me. You probably wouldn't understand ... Daddy does...

GIORGIO: And Daddy knows best...

HELEN: What does that mean?

GIORGIO: You listen to him ... When have you ever taken my advice ... or even asked for it?

HELEN: You know I'm highly-strung, but I don't think you fully realise what that means. My father does.

GIORGIO: Well, if Daddy's girl wants to go for another rest cure who am I to stand in her way? (*He takes another swig from the flask.*)

HELEN: (*Tearfully*) That cruel streak again...

GIORGIO: You seem to have a knack of bringing it out in me...

HELEN: It's always my fault, isn't it? You can be a sonovabitch at times ... d'you know that? But I know what's eating at you...

GIORGIO: What?

HELEN: You know damn well...

GIORGIO: What on earth are you talking about...?

HELEN: You've never forgiven me for not allowing

Lucia come live with us … That's it, isn't it?
GIORGIO: We should have done more for her…
HELEN: Two is enough in a marriage…
GIORGIO: What the hell does that mean?
HELEN: You figure it out.
GIORGIO: Christ … I can't believe this.
(*He holds his head in his hands.*)

Lights down.

SCENE SEVEN

Winter. Night. Ten years later. The furniture in the apartment is being packed up; the suitcase is visible. All of the characters are about ten years older. BECKETT has grown in confidence. JOYCE is grey and frail, and given to stomach pain. NORA is placing fresh flowers in a vase.

NORA: Ahhh ... daisies and marigolds ... You remembered.

BECKETT: Caltha Palustris and Glebionis Coronaria, if I'm not mistaken.

(They both laugh. NORA puts the family photo and toy kitten in the suitcase.)

NORA: God Almighty, will that man ever settle in one place? We're on the move again. I've become world champion at packing ... It's very good of you to drop by, Sam.

BECKETT: I couldn't let you all go without saying 'au revoir'.

(NORA sits. GIORGIO enters, followed by JOYCE.)

GIORGIO: Stephen went to sleep the moment his head touched the pillow.

NORA: The apple doesn't fall far from the tree. I can hardly believe we have a grandson.

JOYCE: Wonderful new life...

BECKETT: A fine lad. Stephen ... after Dedalus.

Am I right? Everything is the same ... and yet different ... By the way, congratulations on your weddings. Plural.

NORA: Thanks, Sam.

GIORGIO: (*Not fully in jest*) Better late than never ... for them.

BECKETT: (*Nervously*) How has ... Lucia been...?

GIORGIO: Not so well, Sam. She'll be here soon. (*Pause*)

NORA: The war will change everything.

JOYCE: Hitler hates Jews apparently ... He's a good Catholic of course ... Did you hear that my brother, Stan, was threatened with expulsion from Italy because he spoke out against the fascists? What kind of world is Stephen going to grow up in...? We're going to Switzerland. What are your plans, Sam?

BECKETT: I've volunteered for ambulance duty here in France.

JOYCE: You must be mad. Never volunteer for anything. France won't hold out a week. She's far too civilised to fight.

NORA: Are you fit enough? What about your ... illness?

BECKETT: My nervous breakdown? I saw a head-doctor in England. I'm not too mad now, I hope.

JOYCE: (*Carefully*) You're not ... embarrassed about mentioning that...?

BECKETT: Not in the least. It's almost a fashion statement. You're nobody unless you've had a breakdown.

NORA: (*Looks pointedly at* JOYCE, *to* BECKETT)
And then you had the misfortune of being
stabbed.

BECKETT: Yes, by a pimp.

JOYCE: I hope you weren't interfering with his
trade.

BECKETT: (*Laughs*) I was waiting for a bus. He
just came over, excused himself, and stabbed
me. A freak event. In retrospect it was quite
funny.

JOYCE: You were stabbed by a pimp. Imagine what
Hitler will do to you! Ireland will be neutral,
despite the fascist proclivities of Yeats and his
crowd. Go back there, Sam. You're not a
fighter. And it's not your war.

GIORGIO: (*Drinking*) He'll do what's right. He's a
man of principle.

BECKETT: I wouldn't go that far. But I don't really
have many commitments. Speaking of which,
how is Helen, Giorgio? I was so sorry I
couldn't make the wedding.

GIORGIO: Actually we're going through a difficult
patch right now. Helen is not very well …
She's spending some time in a clinic in New
York.

BECKETT: I'm sorry to hear that. I hope things will
improve.

NORA: Well, life goes on. We all have to go on, for
Stephen's sake, if not our own.
(LUCIA *enters left and throws her coat over
the back of a chair. Her hair is longer than
before and her clothing dishevelled.*)

BECKETT: (*Gets nervously to his feet*) How … are you … Lucia…?
(*He goes to kiss her on the cheek but she turns aside.*)

LUCIA: Who are you? Sam? God, you're so scrawny.

NORA: Why don't you go and have a nice lie down.

LUCIA: (*Shouts*) Huh! C'est moi qui est l'artiste. Moi! Moi! (*She stabs a finger against her breast several times.*)

JOYCE: Of course, Lucia. No one doubts that.

GIORGIO: Don't patronise her.
(LUCIA *picks a daisy from the vase, removes the petals one by one and lets them drift to the floor.*)

LUCIA: I never liked this game. It does not appeal to me.
(*She crushes the flower and lets it fall, keeping only a single white petal – perhaps representing her love for* Beckett.)

LUCIA: Just a tiny petal, that's all … Of no significance … And broken. We're all broken … Even Helen. The name she wanted wasn't enough … what is…? Nothing … It's all space … emptiness…
(*She exits right, clutching the petal in her hand.*)

JOYCE: She'll calm down … This war has us all on edge.

NORA: (*To* JOYCE) Still … After all this time … After the nightmare she caused Miss Weaver…

JOYCE: Don't mention that woman to me.

NORA: Don't take it out on her. I never thought you were a bully until I read that letter you were going to send her.

JOYCE: (*Loudly*) She put my daughter in an asylum! How did you expect me to react?

GIORGIO: Face up to it. She needs help, professional help.

JOYCE: Not you as well ... I told you, she'll be fine. Can't people be absent-minded nowadays? I know I am.

GIORGIO: And I suppose you think my marriage is fine.

JOYCE: It can be rehabilitated ... with help from all sides. *We* got married to satisfy Helen's people. Why don't they rally round now?

GIORGIO: Because there's nothing to save. I rushed into it ... to get away ... I got it wrong again, didn't I? You can't escape when ... when ... it's inside...

(*He points to his heart.*)

JOYCE: What about Stephen?

GIORGIO: (*Wells up*) It breaks my heart ... (*He turns away.*)

NORA: I'm sorry, Sam. We're washing our linen in front of you.

BECKETT: Don't apologise ... I feel part of ... I'm sorry. ... (*Beat, awkward silence*) May I ask about 'Finnegans Wake'? How was it received?

JOYCE: Ah, generally all right. Except for the po-faced French critics. (*Shrugs*) But what have I left now? That book drained me. What have I left?

NORA: (*Sharply*) What you always had and never appreciated. Your family.

JOYCE: That was always a priority.

GIORGIO: A priority? Good God, I've heard everything now. This is priceless...

JOYCE: It may surprise you to know ... (*He winces in pain and holds his stomach.*)

NORA: What's the matter?

JOYCE: That damn colitis is acting up ... It's not so bad now. It comes and goes.

NORA: I told you to have it seen to. It could be an ulcer.

BECKETT: You should go to the doctor.

JOYCE: I will ... It's easing off now ... By the way, I've read some of your stuff, Sam. 'Murphy' is a clever book. There's something there. A seed that will grow.

BECKETT: Ah, but could anyone have written it?

JOYCE: No, they could not. So, you pass that test with flying colours.

BECKETT: I don't think I've found my voice yet...

JOYCE: Writers have several voices. Tone is what you mean. Oh, you'll find that all right ... (*Muses*) Some kind of stark, pared prose with a dash of Schopenhauer maybe ... a bleak view of things, at any rate.

NORA: Whatever you do, Sam, come out of that man's shadow.

GIORGIO: (*To* NORA) You tell *him* that! That's good ... damn good. (*To* BECKETT) Limbo is your space, Sam. We both have that in common.

BECKETT: I think you may be right.

JOYCE: Leave Hell to Dante.

GIORGIO: (*To* JOYCE) So, what about you? Heaven?

JOYCE: I don't think so. Here. (*He points to the ground.*) And some kind of inner space.

GIORGIO: What the hell is so wrong about just living your life? From one day to the next? (*Pause*) No answer...? Why am I not surprised? (*Pause*)

JOYCE: This war, though, will finish everything. I should know. Ireland is the original battlefield.

BECKETT: Bludefilth?

JOYCE: (*Nods*) Primal betrayal. All myths and religions are about betrayal. The child is betrayed from the moment of birth.

GIORGIO: (*Sarcastically*) Tell me more. This is rich ... I thought writers had a sense of irony... (LUCIA *enters right. Her clothes are in worse disarray. She sits.*)

NORA: Are you all right, Lucia?

GIORGIO: She's in a trance.

JOYCE: She's dreaming.

GIORGIO: (*Sharply*) Christ, she's not dreaming! It's a catatonic trance. She's had several in the last few weeks, in case you didn't know.

NORA: It's best to leave her alone when she gets like this.

(NORA *covers* LUCIA *with a shawl. She and* GIORGIO *return to the table.*)

BECKETT: (*Concerned*) Is there anything I can ...

is there anything she needs?

JOYCE: Actually, I have a gift for Lucia … When she took up illuminated lettering she turned out to be brilliant at it. As good as the monks who worked on the Book of Kells. She does all of those wondrous animals and eternal whorls. It's almost as if Anna Livia has come to life … Well, Voilà!

(*He turns and produces a book from a drawer in the sideboard.*)

JOYCE: I hold in my hand Lucia's first published book, 'Chaucer's Alphabet'. It is a wonderful edition. I hope it will be the first of many. Congratulations, Lucia!

NORA: (*Holding her head*) I don't believe this…

(*He goes to present the book to* LUCIA *who pays it little or no attention. He lays it on her lap.*)

JOYCE: Well done, Lucia. I wish *I'd* found a publisher as easily.

GIORGIO: (*Sarcastically*) She's as talented as I am. Jesus mercy!

JOYCE: Wh-a-at?

GIORGIO: We've tried singing, dancing, sketching, calligraphy. What else would you like us to excel at? And then you go and sponsor that singer, Sullivan. How the hell do you think that made me feel? I was written off by Malbois and then you go and find yourself another protégé. I should be jealous of Sam, for God's sake. (*Loudly*) Do you really think an illustrated book is going to help Lucia? Even in

your wildest dreams do you really think
that…? Another damn book…

JOYCE: (*Stunned*) That whiskey is no good for you.

GIORGIO: You almost sound like Helen. Anyway,
you're hardly a model of temperance.

NORA: Please! Enough wrangling…! Sam is here.

GIORGIO: I rest my case. No offence, Sam. Maybe
Herr Hitler was robbed too, as a young man. I
hear he had unusual parents.

NORA: (*Upset*) That's not fair, Giorgio. I did … we
did our best…

GIORGIO: Lucia should be in a hospital. I'm going
to put her to bed now.

(GIORGIO *gently leads* LUCIA *out. She is
docile and takes his arm.*)

JOYCE: It's sad to see her so withdrawn.

NORA: You'd prefer arson. You'd like to see her
throw another chair at me, or break windows…

BECKETT: (*Delicately*) I hope I didn't …
contribute to…

NORA: No, Sam. We were wrong to blame you. I
apologise for that.

BECKETT: There's absolutely no need. (*Pause*) I
wish … I wish things could have been …
different … (*Pause*) I have to … go…

NORA: Not on our account?

BECKETT: No. Suzanne is expecting me.

NORA: Ah, yes, Suzanne. How is she?

BECKETT: Very well, thank you. She's a
wonderful woman. Practical, down to earth –

NORA: Like me.

BECKETT: Maybe, maybe. You could be right.

JOYCE: We need to be kept on the right road by
women good and true.
(BECKETT *kisses* NORA *and embraces*
JOYCE. *His face begins to crumple.*)

BECKETT: Goodbye…

NORA: Not goodbye, Sam.

BECKETT: I hope not … You were … are … like a
family to me.

NORA: You picked a great one.

BECKETT: (*Takes her literally*) I did … I want to
say … how much your friendship … meant to
me. You welcomed me when I arrived …
(*Emotionally*) You had no one to welcome you
when you went to Trieste … It makes a
difference, believe me…

JOYCE: No speeches, Sam. Limbo, remember.
Stark, spare.

NORA: We'll see you after the war, Sam. Take care
of yourself. And no heroics.

BECKETT: Don't worry … Say goodbye to Lucia
and Giorgio for me … I'll write as often as I
can.
(BECKETT *weeps as he walks towards the
door. His murmur of 'au revoir' is barely
audible.*)

NORA: A good friend, a good man.

JOYCE: Yes. He'll find the right tone sooner than
he thinks.

NORA: (*Surprised and annoyed*) You're very
aggravating! Writing isn't everything. Why
does everyone have to be a talented artist?
Why can't you admire people for just … being

alive?

JOYCE: You blame me, don't you?

(NORA *shrugs and turns away from him.*)

JOYCE: I wanted what was best for them – if you forgive the cliché.

NORA: (*Loudly*) I don't give a good Goddamn if it's a cliché or not! Anyway, you're wrong. You wanted what was best for you. Not for them. For your image. We were all supposed to be some kind of mirrors reflecting your light. The world has to revolve around you, and if it doesn't, you make up a world that does. All your characters are born in your image and likeness, to give you praise. Finnegans Wake is your mad world. I hope you feel at home there.

JOYCE: (*Quietly*) It's not my world.

NORA: (*Disbelieving*) Oh no? Then whose?

JOYCE: Don't you know?

NORA: (*Shrill*) How on earth would I know? How would the Galway woman know anything?

JOYCE: I made that world for –

NORA: Go on. Why? Just so you could play word games and show how smart you are – ?

JOYCE: (*Hotly*) No! No! I made it for Lucia ... For Lucia ... She'd be fine in Finnegan's world. Dreams, impulses, the flow of water ... That's how she thinks...

NORA: (*Quietly*) Is there a secret wood with a river? A place without any rules?

JOYCE: (*Surprised*) Yes, a fantasy world.

NORA: And is there a river like an old woman?

JOYCE: Yes, when the river Liffey enters the sea.

NORA: (*Almost to herself*) She *did* follow it … My God … (*To* JOYCE) So, you do realise that she's –

JOYCE: Different. Yes. Giorgio is different too. It's not their fault that the ordinary world doesn't give them a place.

NORA: (*With quiet intensity*) So you do them out of a normal life, and then you make a fantasy world for them? I want to tell you something. (*Loudly*) You're not God!

JOYCE: Don't you see, Nora. It's atonement. It's the only thing I could do. What else … could I do…? There was … nothing else…

NORA: (*Sharply*) Atonement for what? For what? (*Pause*) Don't tell me. I don't want to hear…

JOYCE: (*Chastened*) For not being a … good father. For being driven to other things, to sacrifice and redemption … I never meant to … harm her. You must believe that … Jesus, you should have known my own family. We were all tormented in the cradle. For years I was Oedipus … terrified of blindness and punishment … If my work was acceptable the dues would be paid. They would be safe … (*Pounds his chest.*) What can we do? I'd change everything to see Lucia and Giorgio happy. But I can't … (*Weeps*) I can't. (*He takes out a handkerchief and dries his eyes.*)

NORA: They paid for your work … What's done is done. Lucia was precocious too. Maybe she couldn't help that. (*She puts her head in her hands and then looks directly at him.*) It can't be undone.

JOYCE: (*Weeping*) I hoped it could ... but it's too late ... (*Pause*)

(NORA *points to the book.*)

NORA: You paid to have that book published, didn't you?

(JOYCE *nods his head which is already bowed.*)

NORA: (*Not unkindly*) Another bloody book ... You fool ... You never had much common sense ... Well, I suppose your books were sort of children to you ... But imagine Lucia and Georgia having to compete with books ... with made-up stories...

JOYCE: (*Kneading hands*) Terrible ... terrible ... (*With great effort of will*) But ... I don't think ... I could have done ... anything differently ... I had to write ... *had* to ... Am I damned?

NORA: No plenary indulgences ... maybe a fool's pardon.

JOYCE: That'll do me...

(*Pause*)

JOYCE: You were going to leave me once. Remember?

NORA: Once? Several times ... I don't know why I'm still here.

JOYCE: (*With an effort*) I never strayed...

NORA: Tell me something I don't know. (*Pause*) And I never betrayed you...

JOYCE: I know.

NORA: Remember how you used to worry about

Giorgio not being your son? Do you still have doubts?

JOYCE: No. I was so uncertain back then ... I suppose you never lose it completely.

NORA: The real you was bad enough ... but not as bad as you thought. And I'm not saying that just because you wrote a few good books ... Did you think we'd end up here like this thirty-six years ago when we took the boat and ran away from home?

JOYCE: No. But I'd do the same again.

NORA: Finnegan, begin again...?

JOYCE: Yes. Like a shot.

NORA: Well, you achieved everything.

JOYCE: I achieved nothing. I should've paid ... more attention to the children. (*Pause*) ... Listen to the rain. The rivers will be in flood soon.

NORA: You and your rivers – flowing on and on...

JOYCE: But not forever ... It's nearly full time.

NORA: What?

JOYCE: I don't think I've much time left.

NORA: (*Upset but trying to disguise it*) You'll go on for years.

JOYCE: This war will see me out ... We can't always go around in circles. I see the end of the line –

NORA: Stop it!

JOYCE: (*Leans closer to her, urgent tone.*) Listen ... I don't want to be buried in Ireland –

NORA: I don't want to hear that kind of talk.

JOYCE: (*With the same urgency*) Promise me you

won't let them –

NORA: (*Crossly though on the verge of tears*) I'll have you cremated ... that'll solve everything –

JOYCE: Promise me –

NORA: (*Loudly*) All right! All right! Whenever a decision has to be made.

JOYCE: Thank you ... I think you still care deep down...

NORA: (*Cross and weeping*) Why do you think ... I stuck with you all this time?

JOYCE: Barnacle glue ... I'm glad you did.

NORA: Well, I did.

JOYCE: I know.

> (*He has difficulty rising from his seat. She helps him up.*)

NORA: (*She blows her nose.*) Come on ... Any regrets?

JOYCE: None ... with you ... Only the children...

> (*He leans on her as they exit together.*)

Lights are dimmed. Projection of a storm. Lights brought up again quickly.

SCENE EIGHT

LUCIA *enters the living room in her night-dress. She wanders around in a trance. She touches familiar objects, looks at the book 'Chaucer's Alphabet'. She takes an old soft toy out of the suitcase, holds it, and puts it back. She picks up an unframed family photograph and holds on to it.* GIORGIO *enters from the right in a dressing gown.*

GIORGIO: Lucia, what are you doing up? It's almost four o'clock.

LUCIA: (*Dazed*) I ... can't sleep...

GIORGIO: Not those dreams again? I'm sorry...

LUCIA: For what?

GIORGIO: For everything. I should have looked after you better ... When we were growing up...

LUCIA: You did...

GIORGIO: I didn't really understand what you were going through...

LUCIA: You were a child too.

GIORGIO: Then I got married and travelled ... Dada was caught up in his writing. Nothing else mattered to him.

LUCIA: And the fantasy world ... I know. I don't blame him.

GIORGIO: You're very forgiving...

LUCIA: I'm ... not ... I'm not well, Giorgio...

GIORGIO: (*Sadly*) I know ... it's so unfair ... after everything you've been through...

LUCIA: I'll have to go back to hospital...?

GIORGIO: (*Weeping*) I know. God help you.

LUCIA: Will I ever get out...? I don't think so ... Helen will ... But not me...

(GIORGIO *bows his head.*)

I've been saying goodbye to ... some of these things...

(LUCIA *indicates the suitcases. Then she begins to tear her image out of the family portrait.*)

GIORGIO: Don't ... Please don't...

LUCIA: I have to ... I was never really part of... (*She crumples up the picture of herself and throws it on the floor.* GIORGIO *picks it up and keeps it.*)

Will you visit me sometimes in the asylum?

GIORGIO: Yes, as often as possible. And Dada and Sam too. And your nephew, Stephen ... And Harriet Weaver.

LUCIA: I don't think Mama will visit me.

GIORGIO: She will.

LUCIA: No, I don't think so. She won't. She blames me...

GIORGIO: I thought Sam might understand. I thought he might make a difference ... But he turned out to be a writer too.

LUCIA: It's important ... books are important...

GIORGIO: I know ... But so are you ... So are you. (*He places his arm around her shoulder.*)

GIORGIO: Come, Lucia, try to get some sleep.

LUCIA: I'm afraid ... I won't wake from those
    dreams ... I don't want to close my eyes.
GIORGIO: Don't worry, Lucia ... You will wake...
LUCIA: (*Shakes her head*) No, I won't ... (*She
    turns back for one last look at the apartment.*)
    No ... no...

As they walk towards the exit, GIORGIO *picks up
the illuminated book, as if to give it to* LUCIA. *Then
he lets it fall back on the table. A spotlight follows
them both out the door then comes to rest on the
torn family portrait. All lights come down.
Darkness. The music of 'The Lass of Aughrim' is
heard.*

    *An EPILOGUE details, on screen, later events
in the lives of the main characters, including a
photograph of Lucia in her Bal Bullier dance
costume. The final slide shows the headstone of
LUCIA ANNA JOYCE. She is buried on her own in
Northampton – far from the family grave in Zurich.*

END

THE HIGH PRIEST OF HACKBALLSCROSS

A Play in Two Acts

CHARACTERS AND ACTORS

VICTOR HENNIGAN　　　Ian Condron
School teacher and Director of
play; early thirties.

LIZ　　　　　　　　Denise O'Connor
A young district nurse in love
with VICTOR; plays the part
of the Virgin Mary; late
twenties.

MRS B　　　　　　　Ann Kennedy
Doctor's wife; plays the part of
Magdalene.

SARAH　　　　　　　Aoife Fagan
MRS B's daughter; plays the
part of Salome; she falls for
MARK.

PADDY MALONE　　　　John Clarke
　　　　　　　　　　　　Pat O'Grady

A victualler and pipe major;
cast as Pontius Pilate.

STEPHEN FARRELL　　Martin Brennan
Town Clerk; plays the part of

Caiphus, the High Priest.

FATHER DUNPHY   Michael O'Meara
Priest and manager of Victor's
school; self-appointed adviser
to VICTOR.

MARK TAYLOR   Evan Darcy
                               Alan Grant

Bank official; auditions for the
part of Christ.

DR LYNCH   Imelda McDonagh
Expert theatre critic and
adjudicator.

MULLINS   Nathanael O'Leary
VICTOR'S student; helps
backstage and plays the part of
Roman centurion; he fancies
SARAH.

ACT ONE

SCENE ONE

Set in a small town in the fifties a couple of weeks before Christmas. A slightly raised stage upon the actual stage. Desert backdrop. Palm trees. Mountains in the distance.

    (MULLINS *enters, picks up a script and reads melodramatically.*)

MULLINS: I find no fault in this man. The Curator of Judea speaks … Free Barabbus! Free Barabbus!
(He wobbles a sheet of aluminium.)
And the earth shook and the rocks were split asunder…
(VICTOR *enters left and stands for a second on the dais. He is carrying scripts and a newspaper.*)

VICTOR: Cut it out, Mullins, and go on about your business

MULLINS: (*Sarcastically*) Yes, Sir. Right away, Sir!

VICTOR: (*Crossing to centre stage*) And Mullins...

MULLINS: What is it now?

VICTOR: It's the *Procurator* of Judea, not Curator. As Captain of the Guard you should know that. By the way, tell the sixth-years I need four more spear-carriers here on Wednesday night. Now (*Claps hands*) haven't you some sets to work on?

(VICTOR *looks at the newspaper.*)

Seismic eruptions, Mullins. Forces loosed upon the earth. (*Nodding towards newspaper*) They've exploded a new type of Atom bomb in the Pacific. Where will it all end? (*He sits at the desk and busies himself with the scripts.*)

MULLINS: Sure, we're bunched.

VICTOR: (*Absent-mindedly*) Hmnmmm? Could be, Mullins. Could be. ... Nice shirt.

MULLINS: The brother in America sent it.

VICTOR: Ah, emigrants' remittances ... Where would we be without hand-outs? What is the future, Mullins? Who's got any ... and who gives a damn? (*Pause*) Strindberg, I thought would be nice. Even Ibsen ... O'Casey maybe ... But no ... a Passion Play. How can we have a 'happening' with a passion play? (*More seriously*) We'll have to do it ... Somehow ... And not just because we're opening the theatre ... Mullins, what do you think of this place anyway? The restoration ... Did they do a good job?

MULLINS: I wouldn't know, would I?

VICTOR: I remember when it was a church. My

grandmother was baptised here. (*To himself*)
She was happy to live and die in the town. We
have wider horizons now in the fifties ... At
least I have...

MULLINS: I didn't hear that last bit, Sir...

VICTOR: Not for your ears ... There must be a way
... to get this dog's dinner of a play to work ...
Hey, what're you doing to that palm tree?

MULLINS: It's kind of obvious. I'm painting it.

VICTOR: Oh God, not green and brown ... And
what are those? (*Points*) Those round things?

MULLINS: Coconuts.

VICTOR: Coconuts...? No. No. I don't want real
trees. More a suggestion of trees ... stylised,
you know. Naturalism won't work, and we
can't afford it. (*Sighs*) I'll show you later. Go
back to your sawing ... Coconuts, I ask you.
(*Enter left* LIZ, *an attractive and forceful
young woman*)

LIZ: Ah, my public awaits. Soon you shall feast at
our glittering banquet. Don't all applaud at
once. (*To* VICTOR:) So, how's it going, Herr
Direktor?

VICTOR: Ah ... I've been working on the Caiphus
angle. But I don't think I have it yet ... In fact
the whole thing could be a complete mess, Liz.
And there's only three weeks to go.

LIZ: Don't worry. That's plenty of time ... for pros
like us.

VICTOR: (*Ruefully*) Then, of course, there's Mrs
B...

LIZ: (*Smiling*) There's always Mrs B.

VICTOR: She could be disastrous as Mary Magdalene…

LIZ: Oh, I don't know. She's well cast as an old tart.

VICTOR: (*Unamused*) And, needless to say, I don't have a Christ yet.

LIZ: Now that could be a problem. Hamlet without the prince. And I don't think our beloved Pastor is going to give in.

VICTOR: What the hell is Father Dunphy's problem with that? Christ was a man, wasn't he? Why can't he be represented on the stage?

LIZ: It's just fear if you ask me? Father Dunphy is afraid that no one in the town would be good enough to play Christ. What if he got his lines wrong and was laughed at…? Look, don't worry about it. It's not Oberammergau.
(*She leans towards him and touches his cheek.*)

VICTOR: Mullins, you can go for your break now. The cast will be here any minute. The cast, God help us
(*Exit MULLINS, marching. VICTOR and LIZ embrace and kiss. She sprawls wantonly on the desk to embarrass him.*)

VICTOR: Em … Get up, Liz. They'll be here soon…

LIZ: (*Banteringly*) But, Dollink, you've got me all hot and bothered now. Give a girl a chance … Come on, cheer up. No one expects a major production.

VICTOR: I'm surprised at you, Liz. Standards are important. Besides, I just heard this morning that Dr Lynch is going to adjudicate … She scouts for the Abbey, you know.

LIZ: Aha! And I thought this was art for art's sake...

VICTOR: It is ... It is. That too. Of course. But come on, a good word from her would make all the difference. Don't you see ... It could be my way out...

LIZ: *Your* way out. What about good old us?

VICTOR: Our way out. You know what I mean. We have to do a good production, something really fine. Avant garde maybe, like Beckett's recent play. Just because it's a traditional Passion Play doesn't mean we can't innovate...

LIZ: Maybe not ... But we know how it ends ... Anyway, don't go overboard with the arty-farty stuff. Here in Hack we like meat and potatoes. And we like villains with mustachios. The gospel story is a bit of a melodrama anyway, if you think about it.

VICTOR: No, no ... no. For a smart woman you sometimes frighten me, Liz. I want a ... a scorching production. Something that puts the old Passionsspiel in a new light, rocks people on their heels...

LIZ: (*Smiling*) And Mrs B. and the rest of us are going to help you do this? Victor, my dear man, I don't think you have the ingredients. Have you ever tried to make an omelette without eggs? Anyway, what's all this about leaving your job?

VICTOR: (*Pauses reflectively*) Maybe I liked teaching once ... but not anymore. And I think it's beginning to show...

LIZ: You mean Father Dunphy's noticed it?

VICTOR: (*Defensively*) Well, yes ... if you must know. Anyway, this town is killing me by inches...

LIZ: (*Pensively*) Ah-ha, I'm beginning to see why this play means so much.

VICTOR: Well, let's keep that to ourselves. It's our secret.

LIZ: I'm getting used to keeping secrets.

VICTOR: (*Holds her*) That's my point. In Dublin we'll be free as the air...

LIZ: I wonder...

VTCTOR: Yes. We can get a flat, somewhere near the canal ... Pembroke Road maybe. Move in together ... properly. You'll see. No more skulking in side streets, following each other home. No more getting out of bed at three in the morning. It's not just a dream ... we can make it happen...

LIZ: There is another alternative, you know ... Or is marriage too dull for a free spirit like you?

VICTOR: It's a matter of timing, Liz. We'll drift into that later.

LIZ: Drift...? Drift...? Don't sweep me off my feet, whatever you do, you wild romantic.

VICTOR: You know I can only concentrate on one thing at a time. For now the play's the thing. It's absorbing all my energies...

LIZ: (*Smiling*) Yes, I've been noticing that.

VICTOR: Yeah, well, first things first. Let's knock the socks off the adjudicator and then we're

home free ... Now, how is your part coming
along?

LIZ: I don't know. Maybe I'm not immaculate
enough for the part. Suppose Father Dunphy
finds out that a fallen woman – ME – is
playing Mary?

VICTOR: God, don't say that! I've enough worries.
(*Cups hand to ear*) Speaking of which ...
Ssssh...
(*Enter left,* MRS B., *a gushing middle-aged
woman in a flowing scarf, followed by her
clinging daughter,* SARAH.)

MRS B.: (*In an affected accent*) Coooeee...!
Blessings to all. Are we late, Darrlings? Come
on, Sarah, don't dawdle. Our esteemed
Director awaits. Oh, hello, Liz. Didn't see you
there. Having a little special coaching from
Victor or can anyone join in?

LIZ: (*Archly*) I was on time.

MRS B.: Punctuality is not a virtue in a woman,
Darrling. Keep 'em waiting and pent-up is my
motto. Lean and keen ... Don't sigh, Sarah.
God, what a day! The Hunt Ball went on till
the wee hours and then I had to deal with
hordes of shawlies in Bob's surgery all
afternoon ... I was in more need of medication
than any of them, I can tell you. The punch
Lady Babs served was very strong ... It
reminded me of the stirrup cup on Coronation
day...

LIZ: We're here to rehearse.

MRS B.: You know, I noticed something odd about

Caroline Hartford. And Bob tells me she's had
bouts of morning sickness...

SARAH: Mammy!

MRS B.: What? It's Mummy – or Mum!

SARAH: Mammy!

VICTOR: (*Hurriedly*) How about the costumes, Mrs
B.? How're they coming along?

MRS B.: I got the material, wholesale of course.
And even as we speak, St. Callista's orphans
are hard at work on them. Our maid, Peggy, is
supervising them. The soldiers' helmets are a
bit of a problem though...

SARAH: Maybe we could borrow some from the
fire brigade and stick plumes on them.

MRS B.: No, Sarah. That wouldn't do at all.

LIZ: It might work, if we used tin-foil...

(*Enter* PADDY, *a burly, extrovert man in his
fifties.*)

PADDY: (*Breathing heavily*) God bless all here. I
came in the front to avoid his nibs, Caiphus. I
saw him in Carroll's Lane on his way here.
Gave him a wide berth, the little pen-pusher...

VICTOR: Paddy, we're supposed to work as a team.
An ensemble. Stephen is playing an important
part as Caiphus.

PADDY: Oh, we'll bury our differences on the
night. But you know what he did on the Town
Council yesterday? Turned down the proposal
for a proper covered-in-dust cart. Again! Said
the tractor and trailer were good enough. I'm a
rate-payer. I can't have the bin men parking
outside my shop ... with dust and God knows

what else flying all over the meat. Foreign bodies in the chops...

MRS B.: I do sympathise with you, Paddy. The Council doesn't understand the first thing about hygiene. Bob says the open trailer is a definite health hazard. And he should know. You're absolutely right, Paddy, the town is not well served by the Council.
(*She begins to do ballet exercises.*)

VICTOR: Em..em ... What are you doing, Mrs B.?

PADDY: Her dancing press-ups. Ah, the bloom is still on you, Mrs B. You never lost it.

MRS B.: Have to ... get in shape ... for the Salome part ... It's been a while, mind you ... But it's coming back ... It's like riding a bicycle...

VICTOR: (*Diffidently*) Salome...? Emmm ... em ... We haven't actually decided on ... the dance scene yet, Mrs B. I think you should concentrate on Mary Magdalene ... for the time being. It is ... eh ... possible that Sarah would be quite good as Salome...

SARAH: Yeah, I could do the dance of the seven veils ... Easy ... I'm a good jiver.

PADDY: Oh, I don't know. If you ask me, Mrs B. still has it. 'Course Mary Magdalene was a fine lump of a girl too, with her flaming red hair...
(*He joins* MRS B. *at the 'bar'.*)

MRS B.: (*Laughing*) Oh, Paddy, you're a terror. Remember those Pioneer Socials years ago? You still have a good leg under you...

SARAH: (*With relief*) Stephen Farrelly is here ... Hello, Stephen.

(STEPHEN *enters right. He is a slightly-built, fussy man in his late thirties, with a pencil moustache.*)

PADDY: Caiphus in the flesh.

VICTOR: Ah, Stephen, better late than never.

STEPHEN: Well, are we dancing or are we going to rehearse? I have to leave at nine-thirty sharp.

MRS B.: A tryst I trust. We have to keep an eye on the quiet ones, eh, Paddy?

PADDY: Who'd have him? Not Sarah anyway...

SARAH: (*Joking*) Oh I don't know about that ... There's not a huge choice in Hack...

STEPHEN: As a matter of fact, there's an urgent meeting of the Council.

PADDY: (*Alarmed*) Jays, you're not striking a new rate ... ? We're taxed up to the hilt as it is!

STEPHEN: Council business is strictly confidential, as you well know. I can't divulge...

PADDY: Well, we know how you voted on the dust cart. It's a disgrace. The whole town is an eyesore.

STEPHEN: You can talk! I've seen that abattoir of yours ... It's a disgusting hell-hole. It should be closed down.

PADDY: (*Becoming heated*) At least I don't collect money for a handball alley for the town and then blow half of it on a dinner for the football team...

STEPHEN: That was a unanimous decision by the Council ... Not that it's any of your business...

MRS B.: Gentlemen ... Gentlemen!

LIZ: Come on, you two ... Bury the hatchet.

PADDY: Unanimous my eye ... It's all free trips
    and free lunches with you lot on the Council. I
    hope Mr. McEntee settles your hash.

STEPHEN: You're the hurler on the ditch. If you
    know so much about it, why don't you stand
    for election?

MRS B.: You should, Paddy. You'd have my vote...
    We need a sound man on the Council to get
    things done.

SARAH: (*Vamping towards* STEPHEN) Can I take
    your hat, Stephen?

STEPHEN: Yes, thanks, Sarah.

VICTOR: Right, everyone. We're going to have a
    read through the first Caiphus and Pilate scene.
    You're doubling as Claudia, Mrs B.

SARAH: Who's Claudia when she's at home?

MRS B.: Oh Sarah, Sarah. She was the wife of
    Pontius Pilate. A woman of noble birth...

PADDY: Good bit of casting there, Mrs B.

VICTOR: The rest of you know your parts, I take it.

STEPHEN: (*Looking up from his script*) You've
    changed it a lot. I've much more lines than
    before.

SARAH: But that's a good thing isn't it, Stephen?
    More lines.

STEPHEN: (*Grumbling*) Not so sure about that...

VICTOR: Caiphus is central. At least from a
    theatrical point of view.

STEPHEN: He hardly gets a mention in the bible.
    The Douay version anyway.

VICTOR: But think about what he did. He had
    Christ followed everywhere, he bribed Judas,

rigged the trial ... Caiphus was some operator.
It would be like one of our lot conning the
British Government.

PADDY: (*Showing keen interest*) Why did he do all
that ... vengeance or what?

VICTOR: As High Priest, Caiphus had complete
power over people's lives. He couldn't tolerate
this agitator, Christ, who was winning over the
people ... And doing better magic ... miracles,
I mean.

LIZ: Maybe you're reading too much into it.
Caiphus was just a bit player.

MRS B.: No. I think Victor has a good point. It
makes sense to me, Darrling.

VICTOR: Look at it this way. Judea was occupied
by the Romans. The people had no confidence
in themselves. The only identity they had,
came from their religion. Caiphus kept that
alive. Without that they were nobody, without
a future ... without hope.

LIZ: They looked forward to the coming of the
Messiah.

VICTOR: But wasn't that a sort of wishful thinking
... ? (*Pensively*) And then a nobody from
Nazareth, from the back of beyond, challenged
their faith, even sided with the Romans on
occasion. Caiphus couldn't accept that; he had
to get rid of him...

SARAH: Yeah, we did that at school. The Jews
were expecting a posh king to come in glory.
They couldn't accept Christ because he was a
poor man with no power...

VICTOR: I suppose you could put it like that …
Think of it in our own terms…

PADDY: How do you mean?

VICTOR: Well, De Valera could never get the
better of Lloyd George. But Caiphus most
certainly got the better of Pontius Pilate…

PADDY: Got ya … He was one cute boy, that
Caiphus. (*Glances at* STEPHEN.)

VICTOR: O.K., places everyone. Now, Liz, for the
moment, you stand in for Caiphus's wife,
Esdra. She was the daughter of Annas, the
previous High Priest.

PADDY: So Caiphus married well too?

VICTOR: Absolutely. Married the boss's daughter.
He didn't miss a trick. Sarah, you're the
serving girl … O.K., Stephen, from the top.

STEPHEN / CAIPHUS: (*Stilted and quite nervous*)
Ah, Procurator, thank you for seeing me at this
late hour.

PADDY / PILATE: (*Plodding and script-bound*)
Have you something to report, Caiphus?

MRS B. / CLAUDIA: (*Hamming*) Shall I ask the
servant to bring wine? We got a shipment from
Rome … a rather fine Beaujolais…

VICTOR: No ad-libbing, Mrs B. There's no
Beaujolais in the script … Paddy, go on.
(*Enter* MULLINS *and his imaginary troops.*
He marches about.)

MULLINS: Left … Right, Left … Right…! Arms at
the ready…!
(MULLINS *moves in* SARAH*'s direction and*
brushes against her. She steps back.)

VICTOR: (*Wearily*) Mullins, not now.

MULLINS: You said we had to practice...

VICTOR: Dismiss your troops ... and finish those flats.

MULLINS: Troops, Fall out...

(MULLINS *goes to back of stage and picks up a hammer.*)

VICTOR: Paddy, go on.

PADDY / PILATE: Oh, very well. Bring some wine. Now, Caiphus, what is it you wish to tell me?

VICTOR: Mullins, stop hammering for the moment...

MULLINS: I thought I had to finish these flats...

VICTOR: Could you hammer more softly...?

(MULLINS *looks up to heaven.*)

MRS B.: Also, Paddy, if you could tone down that Leeside lilt ... just a tad...

PADDY: This is worse than school ... All right, I have you. (*Clears throat*)

PADDY / PILATE: Now, Caiphus, what is it you wish to tell me?

STEPHEN / CAIPHUS: It's this Nazarene. My servants follow him daily, as you know. He continues to stir up the people with talk of sedition.

LIZ / ESDRA: He has condoned prostitution and accused my husband's Scribes of dishonesty. He has thrown out the Temple-traders...

PADDY / PILATE: I told you before, there is nothing I can do. These acts do not offend against Roman law. Besides, my soldiers tell me he's a harmless yokel.

STEPHEN / CAIPHUS: Harmless? Oh, my dear
Pilate, you have been badly misinformed. This
man blasphemes…

LIZ / ESDRA: My husband speaks the truth.

PADDY / PILATE: Blasphemy is not a crime. We
Romans have many gods. Too many, but the
people like them…

MRS B.: (*Stage whisper*) Sarah, Sarah … Serve the
wine…

SARAH: (*Stage whisper*) All right … all right! I'm
coming.

(SARAH *serves imaginary wine.*)

LIZ / ESDRA: We have but one God.

STEPHEN / CAIPHUS: Recall what happened
when your legions paraded their gods on their
standards. Thousands of us were ready to die –

VICTOR: (*Interrupting*) Not so confrontational,
Stephen. Remember, Caiphus is shrewd. He
knows he can't browbeat Pilate. He's taking
his measure to see how he can manipulate him
when the time comes … Are you all right,
Stephen?

STEPHEN: (*Abruptly*) Yes … Yes … Why
wouldn't I be…? Thousands of us were ready
to die.

PADDY / PILATE: Including you? For your God …
your *one* God?

STEPHEN / CAIPHUS: Of course. For us
blasphemy is worse than treason. It is treason
of the heart. Oh, I know Rome takes a more
practical view, thinks in structures. Your

viaducts and feats of engineering are a marvel to behold. But for us Jews it starts and ends here in the heart.

MRS B. / CLAUDIA: And this Christ is influencing the hearts of men. Is not that the real issue?

STEPHEN / CAIPHUS: I have to represent the people. As they are. Maybe we are provincial, even primitive. We have no power, no wealth. The only fulfillment of an occupied people is the law of God. Without that there can only be anarchy and rebellion.

PADDY / PILATE: But this Christ is not a Zeal … sorry, Zealot or freedom fighter, like Barabbus –

VICTOR: (*Interrupting*):More impatience here, Paddy. Pilate senses a threat but it's so veiled he can't quite deal with it. Sarah, re-fill the goblets. All right, carry on.

SARAH: (*Aside*) They're drinking fierce fast.

STEPHEN / CAIPHUS: Don't be so sure. He associates with the Zealots, especially Judas Iscariot.

PADDY / PILATE: I thought Judas was in your employ.

STEPHEN / CAIPHUS: For now. But he's playing a double game, a dangerous one. This matter is doom-laden, Pilate. It strikes at the order which you and I, in our separate ways, have to preserve.

PADDY / PILATE: I have taken note of your representations, Caiphus. We will talk again no doubt.

STEPHEN / CAIPHUS: Very well, Procurator.
Thank you for receiving us.
(*He pretends to exit.*)

MRS B. / CLAUDIA: Be wary of him, Pilate. He
has amassed a fortune from Temple tithes.
With these monies he has made friends in
Rome. He is not without influence.

PADDY / PILATE: You think he could outsmart
me?

MRS B. / CLAUDIA: Not in logic. But … he is a
trickster … a cute hoor…

VICTOR: Stick to the script, Mrs B…

MRS B / CLAUDIA: But he is a trickster.

PADDY / PILATE: I hate this country … These
people with their superstitions and false hopes.
They've got nothing, yet they believe they
were chosen by God, by their *one* true God.
It's beyond lunacy … I long for Rome.

MRS.B / CLAUDIA: Why not give that little man
what he wants? What difference would it
make? These people are all barbarians who, as
you say, believe in one god … *One* …
Imagine…!

PADDY / PILATE: You're right … But somehow I
don't think it will be so simple. It is strange
how complex this backward country is. My
longing for Rome is matched only by my
desire to leave Judea behind for good…

VICTOR: (*With somewhat forced enthusiasm*) All
right … You're getting into it. We need to
work on the timing and we need more
movement.

MRS B.: The accents were a bit off.

VICTOR: Yes. Maybe you could tone down...

MRS B.: Not mine ... I meant Paddy's...

VICTOR: We'll work on that later. I just want to get the broad shape of it for now. (*Shouts*) Mullins, We're ready for tea now.

MULLINS: As if I haven't enough to do. (*He exits.*)

STEPHEN: (*Ill-at-ease*) Caiphus ... I ... have an awful lot to say.

VICTOR: He is very important to the plot, Stephen. Try to see him as the anti-hero.

LIZ: (*Intrigued*) Most actors would kill for more lines. Is there something bothering you, Stephen?

STEPHEN: (*Defensively*) No-oo. What do you mean? No, not at all...

(MULLINS *enters with a large tray. They all help themselves.*)

MULLINS: Don't leave any for me ... whatever you do...

(MULLINS *joins* SARAH *who is on her own at the side of the stage.*)

Em ... eh ... You're a ... fine bit of stuff ... well put together, like...

SARAH: And you're a cheeky young brat.

MULLINS: How about ... you know ... a bit ... of a coort?

SARAH: With you...? Get lost.

MULLINS: Ah, go on ... I know how to French kiss...

SARAH: Feck off with your imaginary soldiers, you twerp...

MULLINS: You don't know what you're missing. All right. Troops left wheel!
(MULLINS *exits, marching.*)

VICTOR: (*Consulting clipboard*) Now we still have to cast Martha. Most of you were here when we auditioned for the part. I quite liked Brigid Nolan.

MRS B.: The Nolan's of Kilboher? Oh, Victor, I don't think so. I realise you know the family but…

VICTOR: (*Sharply*) I'm not being influenced by that. I know every family in this … town.

MRS B.: (*Grimacing delicately*) It's a question of … nature. I'm not blaming Brigid Nolan. But the family is … I don't know…

LIZ: (*Aggressively*) Poor?

MRS B.: (*Bridling*) Undependable. Let's face it, they're always in trouble. They haven't paid rates in years … The sheriff has a path beaten to their door. Stephen will vouch for that…

STEPHEN: That would be a confidential matter, I'm afraid. I'm bound by the Official Secrets Act…

MRS B.: Well, everyone knows it.

SARAH: I like her. We were in Senior Infants together…

MRS B.: Sarah, that was years ago. She went off the rails after that … Paddy?

PADDY: Mrs B. has a point. Old man Nolan sold me cattle with the staggers more than once … I don't deal with him now at all.

LIZ: What's that got to do with anything? Could we try to be objective about this. The girl is talented. She should be given a chance.

MRS B.: I don't think we could depend on her, that's all. She's a wild thing. Besides, we have a good team here. Let's keep it like that … Sarah could play Martha anyway…

VICTOR: Not if she's doing Salome.

MRS B.: (*Passing a hand over her brow*) Well, I don't think Brigid Nolan would fit in. I certainly couldn't give of my best … if she…

VICTOR: Look, let's leave it for now. It's a small part and we can decide later. I may even write it out altogether … I've bigger fish to fry.

STEPHEN: Meaning Christ?

(PADDY *makes a quick sign of the cross.*)

VICTOR: Yes. I'm still working on Father Dunphy. He's against the idea of anyone playing the part … The main part … Imagine … Righto. Thanks everyone. Let's call it a day. Tomorrow evening, … same time. We'll start using costumes as soon as possible; it'll help build atmosphere.

PADDY: Good night, Victor.

LIZ: (*With a meaningful look*) See you later … tomorrow, I mean … tomorrow…
(*Most exit.* MRS B. *stays behind while* VICTOR *gathers up his papers.*)

MRS B.: Oh Victor, could I have a private word…?

VICTOR: (*Warily*) What can I do … for you, Mrs B.?

MRS B.: A thought occurred to me at the Hunt Ball. Wouldn't it be marvellous if we could get the Church of Ireland folk in to see the play…

VICTOR: (*Puzzled*) Of course ... They can buy tickets just like anyone else.

MRS B.: But I think we should make a gesture ... Oh, I know there's a bit of tension right now. But the Royals did visit Londonderry recently ... And we should all do our bit for Northern Ireland...

VICTOR: (*Impatiently*) *London*derry ... What are you driving at, Mrs B.?

MRS B.: (*Demurely*) Well, I think a little compromise is called for ... regarding Mary. Now, I believe in the Immaculate Conception, of course ... But it might be no harm at all to ... on this occasion ... You could delete some of the references to the ... Virgin Birth...?

VICTOR: Cut some of Liz's scenes?

MRS B.: As a gesture of friendship to the Church of Ireland people ... Diplomacy ... that sort of thing ... It's got nothing to do with Liz's lines.

VICTOR: (*Putting on overcoat*) Mrs B., remind me never to underestimate you.

MRS B.: You'll think about it then? Ah, good. (*Puts on her coat.*) While I have you here, Victor, there is one other thing.

VICTOR: Oh, yes?

MRS B.: You've always said we should work as a team ... to give of our best.

VICTOR: (*A watchful look in his eyes*) Mmmnn...

MRS B.: Well ... it's not easy to give of your best when you ... sense a certain hostility...

VICTOR: From someone in the cast? Who, Stephen?

MRS B.: (*Conspiratorially*) Liz, actually. I don't think she likes me.

VICTOR: Of course she does.

MRS B.: No, I don't think so. And when there's friction it blocks the creative juices, don't you agree? Has Liz said anything to you ... about me?

VICTOR: No. (*Warily*) Why do you think she'd confide in me? Why would you think that?

MRS B.: Oh, call it intuition. Bob says I have a sixth sense ... (*More quietly*) He used to say it...

VICTOR: Well, he's the doctor ... and a dedicated one by all accounts.

MRS B.: (*Studying her fingernails*) Yes, dedicated. To his profession...

VICTOR: (*Consults watch*) We'd better get out of here.

MRS B.: Why do we do it ... Victor? Why, oh why? Oh why?

VICTOR: Do what?

MRS B.: Acting ... Donning other personalities...

VICTOR: (*Shrugs*) I'm not sure ... To test our mettle?

MRS B.: (*Moodily*) Mmmmm ... Or to hide?

VICTOR: Hiding in plain sight? Maybe that too.
(*They exit together.*)

Lights down.

SCENE TWO

The stage for the Passion Play is taking shape. The backdrop is more defined and the stylised palm trees are in place. The Hill of Calvary can be seen with three crosses at the top.

(STEPHEN *and* SARAH *are at centre stage.*)

SARAH: Your costume isn't bad ... How is the fit? (*Tries to suppress a giggle.*)

STEPHEN: O.K. A bit roomy. (*Looks at her with embarrassment*) Why don't you put something on?

SARAH: (*Flirtatiously*) I have something on. My seven veils...
(*She wafts a veil in his direction.*)

STEPHEN: Leave them on for God's sake...! You must be perishing cold ... We could be raided if you appear like that.

SARAH: Oh, now, Stephen. This is 1954. (*Moves closer to him.*) You're going to have to shave off the moustache or cover it with a fuller beard ... I think your robe is a bit loose.
(*She makes some adjustments to it in a slightly provocative way.*)

STEPHEN: It's all right, I tell you. Leave me be.

SARAH: Now, now, we can't have the High Priest looking like a laundry basket. I'll put a few stitches in it if you take it off.

STEPHEN: I'll do no such thing: What's got into you? I thought you were a quiet class of a girl.

SARAH: And I thought a bachelor like you ... had some lead in his pencil.

STEPHEN: (*Recoiling*) Behave yourself, Miss. You're your mother's daughter all right. I'll say that for you.

SARAH: (*Crossly*) Oh, leave her out of it. She always cramps my style ... Even when she's not here.

STEPHEN: You shouldn't speak like that about your mother. I happen to live with my mother...

SARAH: I might have guessed.

STEPHEN: What do you mean by that, young lady?

SARAH: Oh, nothing ... nothing at all ... (*Stands up*) Well, I'm going to listen to Juke Box Jury until the others arrive.
(*She flounces out left.* STEPHEN *begins pacing back and forth, reading the script. He notices* MULLINS *looking at him through the archway.*)

STEPHEN: Have you nothing to do?

MULLINS: Oh, I have plenty to do ... More than a lot of people I could name.
(*Enter left* FATHER DUNPHY, *a pink-faced man around sixty, wearing wire glasses.*)

FATHER DUNPHY: Good evening, Stephen ... or should I say, Caiphus? I must say you look the part in that get up. I hope you're not after my job. 'Course I'm not a High Priest ... merely an ageing Curate.

STEPHEN: No contest, Father. I'll stick to my own last. (*Forces a smile.*)

FATHER DUNPHY: How are things on the Council? The Town Council, not the Sanhedrin … Ha … Ha…

STEPHEN: Not too bad, thanks. Although there may be problems financing the public works scheme this Christmas.

FATHER DUNPHY: I can imagine. There's just not enough cash to go round these days. The dues are way down too … By the way, there's no one to do the collection at first mass on Sunday. Any chance … ?

STEPHEN: (*Resigned*) I'll do it. My mother likes to go to first mass anyway. She's done the Nine First Fridays about twenty times by now…

FATHER DUNPHY: Good man. That's the spirit. And we'll be organising the Ladies' Confraternity in a few weeks. Maybe your mother could get the altar ladies together … ? We need fresh flowers and altar linens.

STEPHEN: I'll mention it to her.

FATHER DUNPHY: Great. There's nothing like communal effort, Stephen. If we had a bit more of it we might get the country back on its feet. By the way, is Victor here? I dropped in to see him.

STEPHEN: I think he's backstage. I'll get him for you.

(STEPHEN *exits right.* FATHER DUNPHY *removes his gloves and flicks through the scripts. He notices* MULLINS.)

FATHER DUNPHY: Ah, young Mullins, hard at work I see.

MULLINS: Yes, Father. I'm glad someone noticed.

FATHER DUNPHY: Drop up to the Presbytery on Saturday. The greyhounds need walking. There'll be a couple of bob in it for you … Mmmmmm … the Hill of Calvary. You should make the cross in the middle a little bigger. And what are those spiky things?

MULLINS: Palm trees…

FATHER DUNPHY: They don't look like palm trees to me. I think you need coconuts on them. Yeah, coconuts up at the top…

MULLINS: But Mr Hennigan said no coconuts…

FATHER DUNPHY: Don't mind what Victor said … He spends a lot of time up in the clouds … You have to have coconuts … I'll get the art teacher to do a sketch for you.
(VICTOR *enters.*)

VICTOR: Mullins, you can go and sort out the shields and spears for your soldiers.

MULLINS: (*Sarcastically*) Right away, General.
(MULLINS *marches out.*)

FATHER DUNPHY: No wonder the Roman Empire declined. (*Pause*) But, you know, Victor there is an unruly element in your class. I don't think a little more discipline would go amiss. We've spoken about this before.

VICTOR: Kids have to learn from their own mistakes. They'll turn out all right.

FATHER DUNPHY: I wonder … ? More commitment, perhaps, is called for … Anyway, how are the rehearsals going?

VICTOR: All right. But I wouldn't put it any stronger than that.

FATHER DUNPHY: The Bishop will be attending, maybe even Cardinal D'Alton. I hope we can give a good account of ourselves. As you know, it will be the official opening of the theatre as well.

VICTOR: (*Looks out at the auditorium*) It took twenty whist drives, seven raffles and God knows how many jumble sales to refurbish this place. I'm hoping for a really original production ... one that will be remembered.

FATHER DUNPHY: A word of advice if I may. It might be better not to attempt anything too sophisticated.

VICTOR: (*Aside*) Where've I heard that before?

FATHER DUNPHY: We're a small community, Victor. People don't ask for much; it's hard enough to get by. The Korean War didn't help. I wonder if we have a future here on the edge of Europe at all. We seem to lack the confidence to lift ourselves up by our own efforts.

VICTOR: I suppose it's not all that long since Independence. We were used to taking orders from the British for hundreds of years...

FATHER DUNPHY: And from the Church ... I don't mind admitting that ... Yes, it's difficult for people to decide things for themselves.

VICTOR: Maybe in a small way, theatre can help confidence ... Sometimes it's necessary to

experiment to find out who you are ... Well ...
As you know, Father, my main worry about
this production is ... casting the main part...

FATHER DUNPHY: That's what I wanted to talk to
you about. I had a word with the Bishop and
he's pretty much opposed to the idea. Passion
Plays have been done for years without Christ
being represented.

VICTOR: But ... but ... I mean...

FATHER DUNPHY: You know, in some religions,
you can't even have a statue of God ... Islam,
for example ... You know, a voice offstage, or
some such device, has worked quite well in
other productions...

VICTOR: (*Carefully*) It won't work in this case.
Besides, we're going to have a most
experienced adjudicator from Dublin ... Dr
Lynch...

FATHER DUNPHY: That's hardly relevant. Aren't
we getting just a little ambitious, Victor? We
can't all forge the uncreated conscience of the
race, etcetera, etcetera.

VICTOR: In Oberammergau they have an actor
playing Christ...

FATHER DUNPHY: This is Hack, Victor. Hack ...
Besides, in Oberammergau the actor is very
carefully chosen. The process of selection by
the Church takes years...

VICTOR: (*Fighting for restraint*) You don't think
anyone in this town is suitable to play the part?

FATHER DUNPHY: Victor, my dear man, how
could anyone be suitable to play the part of the

Son of God? No audience could suspend disbelief to that extent...

VICTOR: They could if the play is properly acted and directed...

FATHER DUNPHY: I know it's becoming fashionable nowadays to question authority, but you know, authority is often right, Victor. You should try to submit. It's good for the soul.

VICTOR: An American actor played the part in a movie recently...

FATHER DUNPHY: Victor, Victor ... When you have to mention Hollywood, you've lost the argument. As well as all the false glitz and glamour, that place is run by Jews...

VICTOR: You can't say that...!

FATHER DUNPHY: I've just said it ... Relax, Victor. Just use the resources you have at your disposal. Don't try to get above yourself...

VICTOR: (*Sarcastically*) Heaven forbid!

FATHER DUNPHY: (*Points to a pedestal*) I have a bust in the presbytery that would go well there. It's one of Yeats. But no one would notice the difference ... Must go now ... The Monsignor wants his Sweet Afton ... I'll be back later. (*Just after* FATHER DUNPHY *exits left,* LIZ *enters right. She is dressed in a blue robe.*)

LIZ: I've been hiding in the arras.

VICTOR: You heard him then. (*Clenches fists*). He drives me mad, the pompous ass. Don't get above yourself, Know your place, Accept authority, Mortify the fucking flesh...!

LIZ: He means well enough. You can hardly expect the shepherd to treat his flock as equals. Remember that last Curate? He tried to stop women going to hurling matches. Said they only wanted to see the men's muscles ... The eejit...

VICTOR: Christ, we have to get out of here, Liz. We have to ... There's no future here ... no freedom.

LIZ: (*Smiling*) Don't take it so seriously. It's just a question of playing the game ... At least, Father Dunphy thinks I'm virtuous. He has no problem with my playing the Holy Mother ... That's something.

VICTOR: That's only because the church doesn't care about women...

(MRS B. *enters left and hides behind a pillar.*)

LIZ: True enough.

VICTOR: But what if ... he found out about *us*?

LIZ: So what? We're both single...

VICTOR: But we're living in sin ... He runs my school...

LIZ: Anyway, how could he find out? You're worrying about nothing.

VICTOR: Maybe we'd better stop seeing each other ... until this is over. Just in case...

LIZ: My God, I've heard everything now.

VICTOR: (*Earnestly*) This is our chance, Liz ... maybe the only one we'll ever have. Let's not do anything to jeopardise it.

LIZ: (*Drily*) Reserve all passion for the play...

(MRS B. *emerges from behind the pillar and*

moves to centre stage.)

MRS B.: Don't tell me I'm early, Darrlings.

LIZ: (*Startled*) Oh, hello ... Have you been there long?

MRS B.: No. Just got here, this second.

VICTOR: Excuse me for a few minutes. I want to go backstage to check the lighting.

LIZ: Can't you do that later?

VICTOR: I'd better do it now. Before the others arrive. I won't be long.

(VICTOR *exits.*)

MRS B.: Victor is so talented, don't you agree?

LIZ: (*Feigning indifference*) I suppose so. I hadn't really thought about it.

MRS B.: Isn't it amazing how talent will flower even on poor soil? I mean his father was no great shakes as a provider. Hardly did a decent day's work in his life. The malt stores carried him for as long as they could. And he died roarin', as they say. Cirrhosis of the liver.

LIZ: That's not a very nice thing to say.

MRS B.: But it's the truth. And poor Victor was dragged up. Hardly had a seat to his trousers...

LIZ: (*Losing composure*) That's enough, Mrs B.!

MRS B. (*Cannily*) Oh, I'm sorry, my dear. I didn't realise you ... and he ... ? Forget I said anything ... Just forget it.

LIZ: What are you really trying to say?

MRS B.: Nothing. I'm just surprised at your reaction ... I wasn't to know you'd take it amiss...

LIZ: (*With controlled anger*) If you've something to say just spit it out...

MRS B. (*Looking around as if for support*) I'm at a loss. I really don't know how to reply to you...

LIZ: (*Very deliberately*) Mrs B., maybe there is something I should tell you ... To clear the air, as it were.

MRS B.: Oh? What might that be?

LIZ: Well, as you know, my job involves regular visits to the fever hospital...

MRS B.: You're a District Nurse ... So ... ?

LIZ: I often meet your husband, Bob, on his rounds in the hospital...

MRS B.: I would imagine so ... And ... ?

LIZ: Well, I've learnt a lot from him. A word here ... a word there...

MRS B.: Like what?

LIZ: (*Pauses*) Oh, this and that ... some surprising things...

(*Takes a compact from her handbag on a nearby chair and applies lipstick. MRS B. adjusts her wig.*)

MRS B.: About medicine and patients ... I suppose?

LIZ: Not necessarily ... Some matters closer to home...

MRS B.: Like what? What're you trying to say...?

LIZ: I understand that certain items ... go missing from the pharmacy...

(*Enter left SARAH with a plate of sandwiches, and PADDY who is dressed in a saffron kilt and piper's tam.*)

SARAH: Grub's up. Ham sandwiches. Only the last few left.

LIZ: (*Gaily*) Paddy, I think you're in the wrong

costume.

PADDY: I've just come from a pipe band meeting. Didn't have time to change. (*Takes a sandwich*) Might as well have one of these while we're waiting. Mmmm, very good.

MRS B. (*Rallying*) You look good in a kilt, Paddy ... You have the hips for it ... Our maid makes a reasonable sandwich. But that's about it I'm afraid. Her casseroles are dire.

SARAH: Stews...

MRS B.: Casseroles!

SARAH: Stews!

PADDY: (*Opening the sandwich*) I hope this is our ham now.

MRS B.: Of course. Is there a better butcher in Hack?

PADDY: No. There is not. Still, it pays to advertise ... Why do you think I'm going through this torture of acting? You'd be surprised how many people come into the shop after the play. To meet the star!

STEPHEN: I thought your meat sold itself.

PADDY: Goodwill is important for retailers. You civil servants wouldn't understand that.

STEPHEN: Well, I wouldn't buy a pig's trotter from you ever since I saw that abattoir ... Oh God, the state of it...

MRS B. (*Forcing a laugh*) Now, gentlemen, artistic differences are one thing ... but let's not fall out over meat. We're all hams, aren't we?

PADDY: (*Puts an arm around her shoulders*) Mrs B. always keeping the peace. You're a great girl. Give us a squeeze.

MRS B. (*Simpering*) Don't start, you amorous
butcher –

SARAH: (*Interrupting*) Mother, did you bring the
mustard?

MRS B.: Try the wicker basket!

STEPHEN: (*Tersely*) Where is Victor? He shouldn't
keep us waiting.
(*Looks away quickly from* SARAH *who
rehearses the dance of the seven veils.*)

LIZ: He'll be here shortly.

STEPHEN: I suppose my part will have expanded
again. (*Looks offended as the others giggle.*)

LIZ: You're lucky. My part's been cut. I don't know
why ... Or do I ... ?
(*She looks towards* MRS B.)

MRS B.: Victor knows what he's doing.

PADDY: He does. I've learnt a lot from him about
the bible.

STEPHEN: Like what?

PADDY: Well, Nazareth was a one horse town just
like Hack. Nothing good ever came out of it...

STEPHEN: Except beef ... and tripe.

MRS B.: Go on, Paddy.

PADDY: And the Jews had to be cute-hawks to
survive under the Romans. The Holy Land was
occupied just like we were. He makes it real ...
the politics of it. I wish they'd taught us like
that at school. I might've passed the Intercert.

STEPHEN: Not a chance of that ... But I wonder ...
I suppose the Jews and the Irish do have a lot
in common.

SARAH: Like what?

STEPHEN: Emigration for a start. They had the
Holocaust; we had the Famine … Similar
populations, political influence in America,
emigrants' remittances to the old country….

SARAH: It makes sense to me.

PADDY: (*Grudgingly*) Well, you might have a point
there.

LIZ: (*To* MULLINS) By the way, did you manage
to get the carpentry tools for St. Joseph?

MULLINS: I moved heaven and earth to get them.

LIZ: Be a good lad and put them in the prop room.
(MULLINS *picks up a canvas satchel of tools,
salutes and exits.*)

MRS B.: You were very good, Paddy, to give him a
part-time job in the abattoir.

SARAH: Mammy! Cut it out!

LIZ: I don't think you should patronise him.

PADDY: You don't have to worry about him. With
that brass neck, he'll go far.
(VICTOR *enters right.*)

VICTOR: Nice costumes, Mrs B … With the
exception of Rob Roy here. I want to tell you
all there's a surprise lined up for later.

MRS B.: What is it? Do tell, Darrling…

VICTOR: It wouldn't be a surprise then.
(MULLINS *enters, drilling his imaginary
soldiers.*)

MULLINS: Legion halt! Troops fall out. Take up
your positions!

PADDY: You'll never make the F.C.A., lad. Or
even the pipe-band…

MULLINS: Who'd want to? I'll leave that to the old windbags...

PADDY: Watch it, Son...! See what I said about a brass neck?

SARAH: You'll have to excuse him, Paddy. He's wet behind the ears.

LIZ: Easy. Easy. Don't let our artistic temperaments get the better of us.

VICTOR: Right, let's get on. The scene we're going to do is Caiphus's last appeal to Pilate. Stephen, you have to make this credible. Let the costumes help you ... grow into them. Liz and Mrs B., pretend you're part of Pilate's household. I'll stand in for Christ...

MRS B.: Does this mean we're not going to have a Christ after all?

VICTOR: Wait and see. I've organised something for Father Dunphy later.

MULLINS: (*Whispering*); Hi Sarah. I'll give you another chance, if you want. We could go for a bag of chips after...

SARAH: Get away from me, you little scut...

PADDY: I'm still not clear about Pilate's character. I mean is he a weakling or what?

VICTOR: He was a military man early on in his career. Then he became a politician. Does that answer your question?

PADDY: (*With a knowing nod*) Say no more. A weakling, and a gobshite as well.

LIZ: But he was interested in truth.

VICTOR: Yes, but he didn't have the guts to live by it. All right, places everyone.

(The cast mount the raised stage. PADDY *and* STEPHEN *stand.* VICTOR *nods to* PADDY.)

PADDY / PILATE: *(Haltingly but a little more fluent than before)* Caiphus, do you understand what it is you demand? Crucifixion doesn't just kill; it destroys, slowly and with great cruelty.

STEPHEN / CAIPHUS: *(Breathing heavily)* I know it. I have seen many crucifixions.

PADDY / PILATE: Bring in the prisoner.
(MULLINS *pushes* VICTOR *forward rather aggressively.*)

STEPHEN / CAIPHUS: This is he.

PADDY / PILATE: Tell me, Jesus of Nazareth, are you the King of the Jews?

VICTOR / CHRIST: Do you say this yourself or have others *(Looks at* CAIPHUS) told you?

PADDY / PILATE: Am I a Jew? Your own people and the High Priest have delivered you to me. What have you done?

VICTOR: *(Interrupting)* Not so aggressively, Paddy. At this stage you still think the whole thing is a bit of a farce. You're just going through the motions. Also, you should say, 'Am I a Jew?' with a sneer.

PADDY: *(Excitedly)* I get it … I'm with you…

VICTOR / CHRIST: My kingdom is not of this world. If it were, my followers would have fought that I might not be delivered to the Jews.

PADDY / PILATE: *(With a sarcastic laugh)* You are then a king?

VICTOR / CHRIST: You say it. I am a king. This is

why I was born and why I have come into the world, to bear witness to the truth. Everyone who is of the truth hears my voice.

PADDY / PILATE: What is truth?

(MULLINS *is drilling quietly, trying to get close to* SARAH *who waves him away.*)

VICTOR: (*Interrupting*) That line says a lot about Pilate. He's too intelligent to be a soldier and too weak to be a leader. Yet there's something about Christ that unsettles him. He wants to wriggle out of the whole situation.

PADDY / PILATE: What is truth? ... I find no guilt in him and will wash my hands.

(*Gestures to* SARAH *who brings forward a basin in which Pilate washes his hands.*)

STEPHEN / CAIPHUS: (*An urgent tone in his voice*) We have a law, and according to that law he must die, because he has made himself the Son of God.

PADDY / PILATE: (*Prevaricating*) Where are you from? ... Will you not speak to me? Do you not know I have power to crucify you and that I have power to release you.

VICTOR / CHRIST: You would have no power at all over me if it were not given from above. Therefore he who betrayed me to you has the greater sin.

(*He glances towards* CAIPHUS.)

PADDY / PILATE: Power from above? From above Caesar?

STEPHEN / CAIPHUS: See what he says! If you release this man ... you are no friend of

Caesar's. For everyone who makes himself king sets himself against Caesar.

VICTOR: (*Interrupting*) This is the accusation that finally gets to Pilate. The reference to Caesar's friend is the killer blow … It would be like Dev accusing Lloyd George of being disloyal to the King. After months of plotting, you finally have him where you want him.

STEPHEN: (*Archly*) I get it.

PADDY / PILATE: Shall I crucify your king?

STEPHEN / CAIPHUS: We have no king but Caesar.

VICTOR: (*Interrupting*) This is the most important line in the whole play. By saying this you are denying everything you believe in about the coming of the Messiah. You, the High Priest, are committing blasphemy … This must have been the biggest lie in history. That's why in your next line, Paddy, you try to pass the buck.

MRS B.: And Caiphus is well-connected in Rome. Remember that.

PADDY / PILATE: (*Excitedly*) It's like Dev kow-towing to King George … tugging the forelock…

VICTOR: Right … Right … Back to the script.

PADDY / PILATE: How say you all?

STEPHEN / CAIPHUS AND ALL: We have no king but Caesar!

PADDY / PILATE: During the feast the people have the right of clemency for one prisoner. You will agree to that right being exercised?

STEPHEN / CAIPHUS: (*Triumphantly*) Yes. The

custom will be observed...

VICTOR: (*Positively*) All right. We're getting there. It's coming ... Let's take a break. Mullins, how about some tea?

MULLINS: Yes Sir! Troops, right wheel. Towards the kettle which is coming to the boil! (MULLINS *exits.*)

LIZ: Why does Caiphus agree to the right of clemency? He doesn't know the people will choose Barabbus.

PADDY: That's a good point.

VICTOR: Caiphus knows he can make the people choose Barabbus; he can fix it by sending his secret service into the crowds, by threats, by calling in favours, etc. The fanatic leaves nothing to chance...

(MULLINS *enters with a tray.*)

MULLINS: Tea for the stars, especially Salome.

MRS B.: Ah, good. Earl Grey I hope ... Now Victor, what's this surprise you mentioned? Don't keep us in suspenders.

VICTOR: (*Sitting beside her*) The vacancy in the Munster and Leinster Bank has been filled by Mark Taylor, a young man educated in Gonzaga College. He acted in all the main plays put on by that school, and spent some time in a seminary. His credentials are spot on. (*Consults watch.*)

He'll be here to audition in ten minutes or so. Maybe we can persuade Father Dunphy to let him play Christ. It's a long shot but we can hope.

PADDY: This Mark Taylor ... is a Dubliner?

VICTOR: Now, Paddy, let's not be provincial. We're damn lucky to get him.

MRS B.: Is he good-looking? (*Glances at* SARAH.)

SARAH: Oh, for goodness sake. Mammy!

VICTOR: I'd say so. Young ... clean-cut ... I think you'll find him acceptable.

STEPHEN: For once I agree with Paddy. Why can't we get a local man? Are we not worthy or something? All we get to play are Caiphus and Pilate and the Scribes and Pharisees ... Can nothing good come out of Hack?

VICTOR: Those are the best parts. Anyway, Father Dunphy is the problem. He has this thing about dignity. If it were up to me ... I'd have Mullins play Christ.

MRS B.: Well, I wouldn't go that far.

LIZ: Wouldn't you? That surprises me ... Oh, good evening, Father.
(FATHER DUNPHY *enters right, places his hat on the desk and accepts a cup of tea.* SARAH *modestly puts a robe on over the seven veils.*)

FATHER DUNPHY: You said something about a surprise, Victor...?

VICTOR: I want you to see an audition ... Mullins, is Mark Taylor in the dressing room?

MULLINS: Yeah. He's togging out.

MRS B.: Dressing ... not togging out...

VICTOR: Ask him to come straight here when he's ready.

MULLINS(*Muttering*) Go here ... go there! Get the

tea. Hammer softly...

(MULLINS *exits right.*)

FATHER DUNPHY: An audition? I hope it's not what I think it is. I had to rush here from the Legion of Mary...

VICTOR: (*Carefully*) Father, I know you have an open mind. I just want you to give this man a hearing. He's Jesuit-trained ... and his father is a Knight of Columbanus, quite senior I believe. It's an incredible stroke of luck...

FATHER DUNPHY: Victor, I don't like being presented with a fait accompli...

VICTOR: That is not the intention. It'll be your decision in the end ... whatever you say goes ... (*Looks to stage left.*) Ah, Mark...

(*Enter* MARK TAYLOR *dressed in a flowing robe. He has piercing brown eyes set in an intense face, framed by long brown hair and a beard. A spotlight gives him a mystical quality. His movements are graceful. An awed hush falls over the cast who gaze up at him.* SARAH *is entranced. Her eyes are wide and she makes an involuntary movement towards him.* MRS B *restrains her.*)

Lights down.

End of ACT ONE

ACT TWO

SCENE ONE

Members of the cast are in exactly the same positions as at the end of ACT ONE. They seem frozen and in awe of MARK *because of his likeness to Christ.*

VICTOR: (*Quietly, as if not wishing to break the spell*) This is Mark Taylor everyone. We'll get to meet him later … All right, Mark, as we discussed, the passages from John. In your own time. Mrs B., take your cue … You know the scene.
(MRS B., *surprised into silence, moves to the back of the raised stage. The cast becomes even more quiet.*)

MARK / CHRIST: (*Without script and with extraordinary presence*) Yet a little while I am with you, and then I go to Him who sent me. You will seek me and will not find me; and where I am you cannot come … If anyone thirst let him come to me and drink. He who believes in me, as the Scripture says, 'From within him there shall flow rivers of running water'.

VICTOR: (*Taking* MRS B. *by the arm*) Master, this woman has just now been caught in adultery. And in the law, Moses commanded us to stone such persons. What do you say?

MARK / CHRIST: (*Looking with great intensity into* MRS B.*'s eyes*) This woman will yet walk in the light ... (*He looks slowly around.*) ... Let him who is without sin among you be the first to cast a stone at her.

(MARK *places his hand gently on the crown of* MRS B.*'s head.*)

Woman, where are they? Has no one condemned thee?

MRS B. / MAGDALENE: (*Shakily*) No one, Lord ... No one...

MARK / CHRIST: (*With compassion*) Because your heart is pure neither will I condemn thee. (*Takes her gently by the hand.*) Go thy way, and from now on, sin no more ... You will be blessed and I will perfect you in all the mysteries, thou whose heart is raised to the Kingdom of Heaven more than all thy brethren. (*A long silence ensues, broken only by* MRS B.*'s barely concealed sobs.* SARAH *looks from* MARK *to her mother in amazement.*)

VICTOR: (*To* MRS B.) Are you all right, Mrs. B?

MRS B.: (*Trying hard to regain her composure*) I-I-Ye-yes ... of course ... I'm fine ... fine...

VICTOR: Well, Father ... what do you think?

FATHER DUNPHY: (*Obviously moved*) It was excellent ... and dignified. I'm at a loss ...

Maybe...

VICTOR: A definite maybe ... ?

FATHER DUNPHY: Don't rush me, Victor. (*Turns to* MARK.) Mr. Taylor, you have a very rare gift. (*Beckons him to sit beside him.*) Where did you learn to act like that?

SARAH: (*Smitten*) Yes. Where ... act like that...?

MARK: Gonzaga, Father ... and Miss...?

SARAH: Just Sarah...

MARK: I'm very glad to meet you, Just Sarah. (*They shake hands for a long time and stare into each other's eyes.*)

FATHER DUNPHY: Did you know Father Staunton there?

MARK: Yes. He was my English teacher and religious mentor. An excellent man. I feel I let him down, however, when I left Maynooth.

SARAH: (*In a trance*) Very ... glad ... to meet ... you ... too...

FATHER DUNPHY: You had a vocation ...?

MARK: (*Sadly*) Yes, Father ... But it wasn't to be ... The priesthood is such a high calling...

FATHER DUNPHY: (*Nodding sympathetically*) Scruples ... I've been through that ... Those awful scruples ... Not feeling worthy ... I sympathise ... believe me I do.

VICTOR: (*Delicately*) Well, Father...? Well?

FATHER DUNPHY: What? Oh, yes ... It's unprecedented and I'll be sticking my neck out ... But I'll have another word with the Bishop...

VICTOR: (*Excited*) That's marvellous. You've

made a wise decision if I may say so ... and we won't let you down...

SARAH: Yes, very ... wise ... decision ... won't let ... you ... down ... no ... we certainly won't...

FATHER DUNPHY: I suppose there are different ways of spreading the gospel message. (*Stands*) My housekeeper worries if I'm not in by eleven. Well, goodnight all and keep up the good work. It's been nice meeting you, Mark. Welcome to Hack by the way. We're not a bad little town...

CAST: Goodnight, Father. And thank you.

SARAH: Thank you, Father ... a wise ... decision ... very wise.

(FATHER DUNPHY *waves and exits right.*)

VICTOR: Well done Mark ... everybody. I think finally we have the makings of a production. (*In his excitement he inadvertently puts his arm around* LIZ*'s shoulders, and quickly removes it.*)

MRS B.: That really was superb, Mark ... I'm sorry if I overreacted a bit...

MARK: Not at all. You caught the essence of the part, if I may say so.

MRS B.: You may ... you may, Darrling ... Sarah, pour Mark a cup of tea. This is my daughter, Sarah,

MARK: We've met already. (*Offers hand which* SARAH *awkwardly takes.*)

SARAH: You are ... were ... excellent... (*Her robe slides open seductively. She prolongs the handshake.* MARK *smiles knowingly.*)

PADDY: I have to hand it to you, Mark. You've done this before. The only problem now is you're going to show up the rest of us.

STEPHEN: That wouldn't be hard…

MARK: Oh, I doubt that. I'm just delighted to have the chance of working with you. And perhaps (*Looks towards* SARAH) making friends in this town.

SARAH: It's important … to make … friends … in this town … We should … make friends … good friends … in the town…

MRS B.: (*expansively*) First thing tomorrow I'm going to move my account to the Munster and Leinster Bank. But for tonight, let's all go to our house and have a little celebration.

PADDY: I'll drink to that.

SARAH: Me too…

(*Animatedly, most of the cast collect their belongings and exit left together. Just before exiting,* MARK *surreptitiously takes a hip flask from his pocket and has a drink.*)

VICTOR: Catch you up in a minute. (*To* LIZ) I really think we have a chance now. This is our ticket out. We'll have to hammer Paddy and Mrs B. into shape of course. But they're willing enough … Incidentally, what's going on between you and Mrs B.?

LIZ: She knows about us.

VICTOR: (*Stunned*) She couldn't … Oh my God … How…?

LIZ: I don't know how. But she does.

VICTOR: She won't be able to keep that kind of news to herself for one minute. Shit, just when we'd turned the corner ... My fucking luck again.

LIZ: I think she'll keep quiet.

VICTOR: How can you say that? You know what she's like...

LIZ: Well, I let her know I had the goods on her too.

VICTOR: What goods... ? What're you talking about?

LIZ: It's nothing too dramatic. Just that certain ... am ... medicines ... have a habit of disappearing from her hubby's surgery, and from the hospital.

VICTOR: Drugs? I don't believe it.

LIZ: Oxygen too. She's partial to the odd whiff. Why do you think she's so animated all the time?

VICTOR: But why does she do it? I mean she's well off and well got, as they say...

LIZ: Silent marriage I think. Bob has his work. She has the 'gentry' ... or they have her, I'm not sure which.

VICTOR: It's sad in a way. Did you notice how she cried just then?

LIZ: You big softie.

(She touches his face.)

VICTOR: So you think you've ... spiked her guns?

LIZ: For the moment. Maybe. But I think we have to keep an eye on Sarah and Mark now. She's taken a real shine to him.

VICTOR: She has? I didn't notice...

LIZ: Are you blind?

VICTOR: Remind me to tell you I think you're O.K
… I hope Mrs B. keeps quiet till after the play.

LIZ: Shall celibacy reign till then?

VICTOR: Maybe we could take the odd chance or
two…

LIZ: Or three?

VICTOR: Let's not go mad altogether….

LIZ: You passionate director…

(*She kisses him on the mouth.*)

I'm the wrong Mary. I should be Magdalene.
Before she repented.

VICTOR: We'd better follow them out. They'll be
wondering about us.

LIZ: I'm wondering about us too.

VICTOR: Well don't. We've just taken the first step
on the high road to freedom.

(*Linking arms, they exit right.*)

Lights down.

SCENE TWO

Opening night an hour before curtain up. The stage is a hive of activity. Members of the cast pace to and fro, learning lines, adjusting costumes. There are some 'extras', including two bearded disciples and a helmeted centurion. The lights are being tested and this adds a sort of strobe effect. The young soldiers do some last-minute drilling and get in everyone's way. SARAH is in the middle of her balletic warmup exercises, dressed in a body-stocking. She also practices with large feathers and veils. STEPHEN stands alone looking tense. VICTOR, in his shirt sleeves, is checking a stack of records and winding up the gramophone.

VICTOR: I hope this bloody gramophone lasts the course ... Where are the spare needles? Paddy, are the other props in place...?

PADDY: (*Dressed in a purple toga*) Yeah, I just checked.

LIZ: Has anyone got any pins? My hem is coming down...

MRS B.: I have some. Here ... The moment of truth. Christ, why did I agree to do this? It'll soon be full out there. The Cardinal's coming and even the Hartfords ... and Larkin from the Observer ... That means reviews ... And the official opening, too…

VICTOR: (*Suddenly worried*) Are you … all right,
Mrs B.? You're not … em … dizzy or
anything…?

MRS B.: I'll be O.K … Don't worry…

VICTOR: (*Vying with the din*) Keep calm everyone.
The dress rehearsal went well. We'll be fine.
I'll be prompting from the wings … Mullins,
I'll cue you for the curtains and lights …
Where's Mark? Any sign of the adjudicator
yet? She's going to come backstage first for a
minute…

LIZ: There's plenty of time. Twenty minutes …
These sandals are killing me…

PADDY: Give 'em here … I'll stretch them for you.
(*He tries to put them on his own feet.*)
(*Enter right,* FATHER DUNPHY *and the
adjudicator,* DR LYNCH, *a tall elegantly
dressed woman. They are followed by
newspaper photographers whose exploding
flash bulbs add to the strobe effect.*)

FATHER DUNPHY: Victor, this is the adjudicator,
Dr Lynch.

VICTOR: It's an honour to meet you. I enjoyed your
Henry the Fifth in the Abbey in fifty-two …
Many wonderful directorial touches … I'm
afraid it's pandemonium here at the moment.

DR LYNCH: I know the feeling very well, believe
me. This is a fine looking theatre. Father
Dunphy told me over lunch about the effort
that went into its restoration. You are all to be
congratulated.

VICTOR: (*Nervously*) I hope the production lives up to it.

FATHER DUNPHY: Victor, if you could get the cast together I'll give the blessing now.

VICTOR: What? A blessing? Now? (*To all and sundry*) Has anyone seen Mark?

DR LYNCH: If you'll excuse me, I'll go out to the auditorium and set up my table. I need to find the best spot. Line of sight. Acoustics and all that.

FATHER DUNPHY: Of course. But you will join the Cardinal and myself out front for the opening ceremony?

DR LYNCH: Yes indeed. Just before curtain up. (DR LYNCH *exits right, followed by the photographers.*)
(VICTOR *assembles most of the cast, some of whom kneel while Father Dunphy blesses them.* STEPHEN, *however, stands, isolated from the rest.*)

FATHER DUNPHY: Dear Lord, I ask you to bless this community of people who seek to honour You by performing a Passion Play. Let them act to the best of their ability. (*He makes the Sign of the Cross*) In nomine Patris et Filii et Spiritus Sancti. Amen.

CAST: Amen...

FATHER DUNPHY: (*Folds and kisses his scapulary*) Now, I'll leave you to it and join the Cardinal. Good luck everyone. I know you won't let us down.
(FATHER DUNPHY *exits right.*)

VICTOR: I'm sure we all feel the better of that blessing. (*Looks at watch.*) Where the hell is Mark?

SARAH: (*Excited*) Don't worry. He'll be here. He won't let us down. (*She sprays perfume on herself.*)

MULLINS: (*Sarcastically*) Don't worry. He'll be here. Our hero won't let us down…

SARAH: Oh grow up, Mullins.

MULLINS: I bet he's no good at the French kissing.

SARAH: Get lost, you little pup. Go and play with your soldiers.

PADDY: (*Peering through imaginary curtain*) It's really fillin' up out there. Aw no, McMahon's in … and Sullivan. Christ, the mountainy men are there in force … For a laugh. To see if I'm going to be posh … I'm rightly stuck now…

MRS B.: Paddy, that makes no difference. The accent you worked on is neutral. Not posh … Don't let it slip.

VICTOR: (*Loudly*) Do it exactly as we rehearsed. No playing to the gallery … Oh, thank God, here's Mark…

(MARK *enters left, dressed in a well cut double-breasted suit.*)

VICTOR: Mark, fifteen minutes to curtain. You'd better get ready … Paddy, will you stop peeping through the curtain. You're just putting yourself under pressure.

PADDY: (*In a strained whisper*) The Cardinal's out there … just in front of the curtain, I mean … He's got the red hat on and everything … an' a big gold cross…

LIZ: It's the opening ceremony. He's going to make a speech.

PADDY: Jays … This is … bigger than I thought … a lot bigger…

(*Sounds of applause can be heard from the auditorium.*)

LIZ: You'll be fine. (*Puts a hand on* PADDY*'s shoulder.*)

VICTOR: Stephen, you're very quiet. Everything O.K?

STEPHEN: (*Trance-like*) Yes, thank you. I'm … OK … Fine … Why wouldn't I be?

(MARK *moves smiling through the mayhem and sits at the desk on the unraised part of the stage.* SARAH*'s eyes are on him all the time.*)

VICTOR: I really think you should get into costume, Mark. Eleven minutes to go, everyone…

(MULLINS*, marches around the stage, getting in everyone's way.*)

VICTOR: Mullins, could you confine yourself to barracks for the moment. This isn't the time…

MULLINS: Yes, Sir. Certainly, Sir. Troops, left wheel! (*He marches to an exit.*)

MRS B. (*Approaching* MARK) You left your sandals in the dressing room … Size ten wasn't it? Sarah will help with your make-up … if you like…

SARAH: (*Keenly*) Yes, I will … Delighted to help … Stay there, Mark, I'll be right over…

PADDY: (*Mumbling*) Neutral accent …

Blasphemery ... Blasph-emy ... Sed-ition ...
Clem-ency ... Bar-bus ... barbarous ...
Barabbus.

LIZ: That's it, Paddy. Good...

MRS B.: Mark, your make-up ... I say, would you
like if ... Are you listening?
(*Touches him gingerly on the shoulder. She
sees him take a long swig from a hip flask..*)

MRS B.: Mark, what are you doing ... What on
earth?

MARK: (*Mumbling*) They ... sent me here ... to this
kip ... Why? To dry out...? Some hope ...
Aha-haaaa ... Bankers ... bastards ... 'sall
bollocks anyway ... Jesuits ... even worse...

MRS B.: Victor, I'm a-afraid ... ! Victor! could you
come here a second ... ?

VICTOR: (*Walks towards the desk*) What is it now,
Mrs B.?

MRS B.: Look...!
(VICTOR *studies* MARK *with growing
incredulity.*)

VICTOR: (*Recoiling*) No ... No ... I don't believe
it! No!

MRS B.: Is it what I think ... ?
(MULLINS *enters and seems to be amused.*)

LIZ: (*Rushing forward*) He can't be ... It's not
possible...
(*She touches* MARK, *who gives a sickly grin
before his head lolls forward onto his chest.*)

LIZ: He is ... He's pissed out of his mind!

SARAH: Oh Lord...!

MULLINS: Scuttered! Ahaha ... The star attraction,

legless...

VICTOR: (*Pokes* MARK *with a trembling finger.*)
No ... no ... He can't be...

MRS B.: He is, you know. Drink ... and possibly
something else...

PADDY: Those Dubs ... feckin' gurriers ... I told
you...
(*He slaps* MARK*'s face. Makes a fist. Is
restrained by* VICTOR.)

MARK: (*Mumbles*) Should be ... Hollywood ... not
this two-bit ... Hackballs-something ... or
other ... Balls anyway ... 'Sall balls...
(SARAH *bends over him.*)

SARAH: Mark, it's me ... Mark, wake up...

MARK: Ahhh ... The lovely Sarah ... The only
bright spot ... in the gloom...

SARAH: Mark ... We're all depending ... on you...

MARK: Shouldn't ... Just a piss-artist ... can't get
enough ... Must sleep now ... lovely Sarah ...
a rose in the dungheap ... of Hack ... balls...
(MARK *starts to snore.*)

SARAH: Oh no. No ... Mark ... (*She shakes him to
no effect.*)

MULLINS: Maybe if a frog kisses him, our prince
will awake.

SARAH: Feck off, you.

VICTOR: (*In a low shaking voice*) That's it then.
It's over! Everything we worked for ... Cancel
the show ... Give 'em their money back ...
That bastard, Jesuit-trained yahoo ... My old
man never had anything ... Fuck it all...

PADDY: The Cardinal ... the opening ... the big

red hat on his head...

VICTOR: The adjudicator ... She's right out there
... Jesus Christ Almighty...

MRS B.: (*Weeping*) After all the effort ... The
Hartfords are in ... And the Tyndalls ... We're
disgraced ... Taigs in trade ... That's all we
are...

LIZ: (*Loudly*) Think! For God's sake, think! There
must be a way out of this ... Maybe Mark
could go on in a while...

VICTOR: Look at him! For God's sake look at him
snoring like a pig in shit...

SARAH: Ah now ... That's not fair ... He can't
help...

VICTOR: (*Loudly*) Can't help what? What...? Can't
help throwing booze down his throat...? Can't
help breaking his word ... Can't help being a
hypocrite ... Can't help being a dog's
bollocks!

LIZ: Easy, Victor ... Look we did rehearse for two
weeks before Mark arrived... We can still do it
... We can...

VICTOR: (*Still in shock*) How? The star is plastered
... The Star of David ... Ha! No understudy ...
not for Christ ... We're all in the shit!

LIZ: (*Grips his shoulders*) Listen, Victor. Plan B.
The original version ... Before we had a
Christ. You can use the megaphone from the
wings.

SARAH: I'm game. We can try it.

MRS B.: This isn't like you, Victor. Sarah is right.
We can give it a go.

VICTOR: A play without a lead! That spoiled bastard … that Pharisee … Scruples, my arse … I'll give him scruples … And Dr Lynch sitting out there…

LIZ: (*Shaking him*) We can do it? Forget about Mark Taylor … Stephen can do those extra Caiphus scenes … And 'voice' the Sermon on the Mount…

STEPHEN: (*In a thick voice*) Don't … think so. (*Stares at floor*) Can't breathe.. Dizzy … Hands numb…

LIZ: What's wrong … ?

STEPHEN: Panic … attack. Knew it … might happen…

LIZ: Relax! Just relax…

STEPHEN: Can't … treatment didn't work…

VICTOR: (*Head in hands*) Christ paralytic. Caiphus gone gaga. We're done for. Give 'em their money back. Clear the hall. Clear the bloody hall … !

LIZ: (*Shouts*) Stop it! It's just nerves. We've eight minutes to sort it out. Mrs B., can you help Stephen. Slap him across the face if you have to…

(MRS B. *rushes to* STEPHEN*'s side and produces a pill box from under her robe. She puts a pill between his lips.*)

MRS B.: Here, take one of these. Swallow it…!

LIZ: What are you giving him?

MRS B.: Just something to calm him down. He'll be O.K. in a few minutes.

VICTOR: (*Absently*) Father Dunphy was right …

We got above ourselves ... It's only Hack ...
only Hack ... Nothing good can come out of
here...

LIZ: (*Stands in front of him*) No, Victor, it's not
your fault. Don't feel so responsible. It can
work. It will ... it will...

PADDY: She's right, Victor. Let's have a go. We
can ad lib a bit if we're stuck.

MULLINS: My troops are at the ready, awaiting
your command.

VICTOR: Oh Christ, I've heard everything now ...
Might as well ask Mullins to play the lead...

LIZ: (*To* VICTOR) Come on, Love. (*Takes his
hands.*) We have a few minutes. Set it up for
us.

VICTOR: (*Looks slowly around at the anxious
faces*) You really ... want to go through with
this ... ? Really...?

LIZ / PADDY: Yes. Yes. We'll give it a lash.

MRS B.: We have to ... Look, Stephen's feeling
better already...

LIZ: Gather round everybody.

VICTOR: (*Fighting for composure*) I suppose there
... wouldn't have to be ... too much change in
the first act...

LIZ: That's right ... It'll give us a breather. I can do
the lines you cut last week...

MRS B: But what about the Church of Ireland
folk...? Oh forget it...

LIZ: That will buy more time. We'll be motoring by
then ... What about the second act ... ?

VICTOR: (*Rallying a little*) We'll have to cut John

the Baptist … Go straight into the first scene
between Caiphus and Pilate…

LIZ: (*Loudly*) Got that, everyone? Good, what else
… ?

VICTOR: In the Gethsemane scene I'll do Christ's
voice from the wings … That means Stephen
will have to do the soliloquy after his last
meeting with Judas.

LIZ: All right, Stephen?

STEPHEN: Yes, I feel … better now … I can do
it…

MRS B.: Good man. Let's get the show on the road.

PADDY: Sucking diesel, Mrs B.

VICTOR: It's time, I suppose … Places, everyone.
Good luck…

(PADDY *sits on the judgment seat with* MRS
B. *as Claudia by his side.* SARAH *prepares to
pour wine into goblets. Everyone else leaves
the raised stage and gathers around* VICTOR
in the wings – and the now, prone, body of
MARK.)

VICTOR: Paddy, after the report about the holy
innocents, go into a trance, just as we
rehearsed. Don't rush your lines. And
remember to project … Deep breathing now …
One minute to go. Forty-five seconds. Mullins,
stand by the curtain…

(VICTOR *puts on the introductory music, a
loud, 'heralding' piece with brass and timpani
drums. The lights come up.*)

VICTOR: Good luck, everyone. Right, Mullins,
curtain up.

MULLINS: Right so. At long last. Here we go.

Lights up full for a few seconds and then down.

SCENE THREE

The cast, still in costume, are arranged formally on the stage as if posing for a group photograph. FATHER DUNPHY *and* VICTOR – *with a blank expression – stand together in the back row.* (*At this point the real audience may applaud, mistaking the tableau for a curtain call.*) MULLINS *places a lectern and glass of water at the front of the stage. He rejoins the group.*

> (DR.LYNCH *walks on from the left with a sheaf of notes in her hand. She stands down centre and adjusts the mic while a couple of photographers crouch in front of her on the apron of the stage.*)

DR LYNCH: Your Eminence, Reverend Fathers, ladies and gentlemen, as you know, theatre lets us look at ourselves as we are, openly, frankly and hopefully without fear. It allows us to express ourselves, to metabolise, as it were, different aspects of our culture. This function of theatre is now more important than ever before because of the identity crisis that afflicts this land, partly due to our experience of colonisation. Emigration and low morale, especially in the provinces, have raised questions about the future of the country. Theatre, good theatre, allows us to confront such questions in a truthful and fearless way. (*In a meaningful aside.*) I am, by the way, assuming an uncensored environment... (*At a sign from* VICTOR, MULLINS *rushes forward from the wings to adjust the volume control of the microphone.*)

DR LYNCH: (*Resumes her flow with a slight moue of irritation*) The Passion Play is a traditional theatrical form. (*She offers her profile to one of the crouching photographers.*) For amateurs it has the advantages of a definite and well known storyline, strong characters, colourful costumes and settings, and, of course, a clear moral theme. A passion play is, therefore, almost foolproof, and I have seen some excellent productions up and down the country in halls which lack the ambience of this finely restored theatre...

(SARAH, *who is positioned at the right of the back row, is looking with interest into the wings on the same side. She is communicating by means of facial gestures with* MARK *who is off-stage.*)

(*Taking a sip of water*) Now, regarding this evening's performance, let me say immediately that the sets were excellent and one can only assume that the stage carpenter had all the skills of St. Joseph.

(*Pauses for audience laughter to subside.*) The first act, apart from a few nervous flutters, was competently done. I especially liked Mary's performance. The actress combined

quiet dignity with a certain youthful exuberance which would, after all, be expected of a vibrant young woman before she was called to give birth to the Son of God...
(LIZ *smiles.*)
(DR LYNCH *begins to pace but, realising that the sound fades, returns to the microphone.*)
The nativity scene was well staged and avoided what one might call 'crib clichés'. So far so good. The gift of Frankincense was, however, referred to as Frankenstein, but we'll put that down to nerves.
(*Takes another sip of water.*)
(*Some diversion in the wings catches* SARAH*'s eye again and she slips out right without attracting too much attention.*)
(*Becoming even more pompous*) Ladies and gentlemen, my task as adjudicator is to offer a critique and not to damn with faint praise. I have to say, therefore, that after the first act, things began to go wrong. Before saying why, I want to make a general point about the production as a whole at a conceptual level. The thematic emphasis on Caiphus was overdone and betrayed some strange fixation on the part of the director. Perhaps he was keen to see parallels between occupied cultures and subsequent diasporas. But a passion play is about peace and harmony, not, repeat not, about paranoia. The director, for reasons best known to himself, somehow managed to convert this passion play into a power play.

The production as a whole, therefore, did not gel into a coherent unity...

(VICTOR *stirs slightly; his face is a mask. But he is suffering.*)

(*More expansive now*) More specifically, I fail to understand why Magdalene, a peasant woman and prostitute, spoke and behaved as if she were a lady of noble birth. Of course, this actress also played the part of Claudia, a Roman lady, and one can only assume that she got the parts mixed up. Pilate, on the other hand, a patrician and procurator of Rome, acted and sounded as if he were a sheep farmer from a remote region of Kerry...

(MRS B. *squirms and* PADDY *wears a sickly grin. A faint ripple of audience reaction can be heard.*)

(*With growing relish*) As for Salome's dance, what can I say? Except that she was more like a Royalette on her first day in the chorus line, and it was far from apparent why King Herod would behead anyone for such a dubious spectacle.

(*Pauses for laughter which doesn't come*) Now, I appreciate the difficulty of putting on a passion play without a character playing Christ. (*Aside*) When will the provinces ever learn? But the offstage voice device didn't work. And for some reason the voice of Christ was heard on occasion giving prompts to the other players. This, of course, could have been divine intervention, but I doubt it. At some

point, too, in the second act, groans from
backstage could be heard in the front of the
auditorium, followed by a voice saying, and I
quote, 'Get that Jesuit-trained failed priest out
of my way.' Yet another reference to Caiphus
perhaps … ? We shall never know.
(*Spreads hands in ironic gesture as a flashbulb
explodes.*)
And as for Caiphus himself, around whom the
entire story was crafted, well we were treated
to a most unusual performance. Caiphus started
out woodenly and one expected him to loosen
up. But, no, he became almost catatonic and
seemed to fall asleep on his feet at the most
crucial moment of the trial. I do not pretend to
know what went wrong here. But the lapse was
not made good by Claudia announcing that the
wine was drugged, or by Pilate suggesting, and
I quote, 'Caiphus had a rough night last night'.
(*Apart from a couple of embarrassed sniggers
the audience reaction is one of growing
disaffection. The cast, assembled upstage, seem
dazed.*)
Towards the end of the third act I frankly
thought I'd wandered into a farce. Pilate and
Caiphus – at least while he was awake – were a
double act that would have been the envy of
Laurel and Hardy…
(*Grumbles from the audience.*)
VOICE FROM AUDIENCE: It wasn't so bad…
VOICE FROM AUDIENCE: Yeah … you're a bit
rough … there…

DR.LYNCH: (*Loudly, sensing the nascent hostility*)
The hand-washing by Pilate should have been
a solemn ritual, but was instead a burlesque. I
could have accepted the basin of water, just
about, but not, I'm afraid, the bar of Lifebuoy
toilet soap … That, in my view, was a prop too
far.
(PADDY *rises flustered from his seat but*
VICTOR *restrains him gently. Louder sounds*
of disaffection from the audience.)

VOICE FROM AUDIENCE: They did the best they
could…

DR LYNCH: (*Defensively and with irritation*) But
was it good enough? There are standards,
absolute standards which must be maintained
… Good can come out of Nazareth; that is the
whole point. Theatre is a high calling. Dublin
theatre-goers would not accept what transpired
here tonight…

VOICE FROM AUDIENCE: Ah, go on back to
Dublin…

VOICE FROM AUDIENCE: Yeah, you're out of
order, there, Missus…
(*Laughter*)

DR LYNCH: (*Grimly, gathering up her notes*) I had
other points to make … but I can see I would
be wasting your time and mine. I wish you
goodnight…
(*She turns abruptly away from the microphone*
as the photographers take some final shots.
FATHER DUNPHY *tries diplomatically but*
unsuccessfully to prevent her departure. DR

LYNCH *exits right to the sounds of ribald cheers.* FATHER DUNPHY *goes to the microphone and calms down the imaginary audience.*)

FATHER DUNPHY: (*Diplomatically*) Your Eminence, ladies and gentlemen, good people of Hackballscross, Dr Lynch was only doing her job ... and I'm sure she didn't mean half of it anyway. The ladies can be a bit hard to please every now and then, as we all know. Of course there were mistakes. It was opening night and we're only human after all. But the cast gave of their best. And it was all voluntary. If you enjoyed it tell your friends; if you didn't, then the Good Lord will bless your silence. We hope to run for another week. And remember, all of the proceeds go to St. Callista's Orphanage ... Goodnight and have a very happy Christmas ... God bless you all... (FATHER DUNPHY *signals the cast to rise and come forward. They do so diffidently and bow to loud applause. [The real audience may applaud at this point also.]* MULLINS *can then be seen lowering the imaginary curtain. The cast start talking among themselves.*)

LIZ: Don't go home yet. We'd better have a word, right Victor?

VICTOR: What? A word. Yes. A post mortem, I suppose.
(*Sounds of imaginary audience leaving.*)

Lights down.

SCENE FOUR

The cast start to unwind. LIZ *jumps off the raised stage to right centre, throws herself on the sofa and kicks off her sandals.* MRS B. *removes her wig and* PADDY *has a good scratch through his toga.* SARAH *who has returned, having helped* MARK *home, puts on a cloak in deference to* FATHER DUNPHY*'s presence.* STEPHEN *is still in something of a trance.* VICTOR *stands staring at the lectern with a woebegone expression on his face. With the exception of* VICTOR *and* STEPHEN, *however, the cast do not appear too downhearted – the final round of applause did something for their morale.*

PADDY: (*Seated, opens the thongs of his leggings and rubs his calves, sighing with relief.*) Well, that was a bit of a mauling old Dr. Fucksticks gave us … Excuse me, Father. I felt like pulling out the mic when she was in full spate. A *Kerry* sheep farmer … I'm from Cork, doesn't she know anything … ? And it wasn't Lifebuoy soap … it was Lux … Still, it's over. We've had a first smack at the ball.
  (*Joins hands and makes a hurley stroke.*)
FATHER DUNPHY: What on earth happened Mark Taylor? I sat out there sandwiched between the

Cardinal and the Bishop, waiting for him to come on and he never showed. Victor, I say ... what happened to Mark ... ?

VICTOR: (*Vacantly*) Oh, he turned up drunk...

MRS B.: Ossified ... out of his skull...

FATHER DUNPHY: Well, would you believe it? A whited sepulchre, eh? Imagine, Gonzaga turning out someone like that. You never can tell ... Of course, the drink can grab hold of anybody ... But, you see my point now, Victor? I won't say, I told you so. (*Changes subject diplomatically.*) Despite what her nibs had to say, I thought there was something in the Caiphus angle ... how to survive under Roman oppression ... as we had to survive under the Brits for seven hundred years. Food for thought there anyway ... Well, I have some rather senior Churchmen to look after and entertain. My poor housekeeper is at high doh with the excitement of it all ... Don't worry about Lynch. The woman's too much a perfectionist for her own good. The audience sensed it too. Anyway, tomorrow night will be better, you'll see...

VICTOR: (*Still rather dazed*) Dr Lynch won't be here. *Tonight* was our chance. Tomorrow's no good ... No good at all...

LIZ: Victor, of course it is.

FATHER DUNPHY: Good night all. Fly the flag. The Protestants are coming tomorrow night. I'm not looking for converts ... but you never know!

CAST: Good night, Father. Take it easy. All the best.

(FATHER DUNPHY *waves and exits left.*)

MRS B.*: (Begins to remove her make-up)* I can't get over that adjudicator … The cheek of her … What a nit-picker. Oh, a nasty piece of work … She must have serious problems at home. My advice, Victor, is to ignore her. After all the effort you put in. Who invited her anyway? It's a mystery to me…

SARAH: Yeah, me too.

PADDY: That Mark Taylor let us all down. Too sweet to be wholesome … should've known. *(Thoughtfully)* Imagine having all that talent and pissing it away … I don't understand it.

SARAH: Go easy on him. You don't know him. He has to deal with a lot of problems…

MULLINS: Yeah, like too much cash … and drink…

SARAH: What did you say?

MULLINS: Nothing…

VICTOR: *(Coming out of his reverie, to* MRS B.*)* What did you give Stephen before curtain up … ?

MRS B.: A … sleeping pill. I thought it'd just calm him down … Didn't realise it'd nearly knock him out. They don't have much effect on me … anymore. *(Looks towards* LIZ*)* I'm sorry … Just keep on interfering, don't I … ?

LIZ: You meant well. And he probably wouldn't have gone on at all without it … *(To* STEPHEN*)* I don't mean to pry, Stephen …

but if acting is such a problem for you … I mean, why did you volunteer … ?

STEPHEN: (*Chastened*) Dr. Bob recommended it … said it would be therapeutic. Better than pills … or any class of tonic…

VICTOR: (*Turning sharply*) W-wha-at … ? What did you say?

PADDY: (*Slapping* STEPHEN *on the back*) Damn me but … that makes two of us. He said acting would do me good too. (*To* MRS B.) That husband of yours wouldn't give you a pill if you were on your last legs. Says too many people take the easy way out. With tablets, you know? He's probably right.

MRS B. (*Sadly*) The easy way out … Tablets … I … suppose so.

STEPHEN: (*To* PADDY, *with keen interest*) But you're not … the worrying kind … A butcher cutting up mate all day…

PADDY: (*Diffidently*) Business hasn't been good recently. And, well … when you hit the fifty mark you sort of lose the run of yourself for a while. (*Shrugs deprecatingly*) Anyway, Dr. Bob suggested this … to get me out of meself … Try to get yourself out of yourself, Paddy, he says to me…

VICTOR: I can't believe what I'm hearing! The local doctor has taken on the role of casting director…!

STEPHEN: I wouldn't put it quite like that. He means well, like.

VICTOR: (*Loudly*) As much as I sympathise with

your various ailments, I have to point out that this is a drama society and not a clinic for the nervous and the bewildered. We do not do group therapy in this theatre...

MULLINS: (*Quietly*) Coulda fooled me...

LIZ: Take it easy, Victor. You're beginning to sound like Dr. Lynch.

MRS B.: But acting *does* do you a power of good. Afterwards I mean. I can't really explain it. (*With a downcast expression*) Maybe it just helps keep us occupied ... What do you think, Liz?

LIZ: (*Smiling*) Yes. It is therapeutic – better than a seaweed bath ... And we get to know each other better...

MRS B.: Sarah, why on earth did you leave with that fraud? I swore I wouldn't interfere again. (*Glances towards* LIZ) But there are limits ... He's not good enough for you. You could do a lot better...

MULLINS: A lot better, if you ask me.

SARAH: Look, Mark's got problems, all right? But he's not an axe murderer. He's very sensitive if you must know. Anyway, maybe I can help him ... sort himself out...

MRS B: Oh no, no, Sarah. Girls who try to reform wasters come to grief. It's very hard to change a man once the mould has set.

MULLINS: Impossible, I'd say, in my humble opinion.

SARAH: Look, don't worry, I'm not going to rush into anything...

MRS B: Yes, take your time, Sarah … Plenty of fish in the…

MULLINS: That's good advice from your Mummy…

SARAH: Oh, be quiet, you.

PADDY: Don't let that Dublin Jackeen bobble-dazzle you again, MRS B.

MRS B: Don't worry, Paddy … Once bitten, you know … I have the measure of that Jekyll and Hyde … (*She looks around at everyone*) You know, I'm kind of looking forward to tomorrow's performance.

LIZ: So am I.

PADDY: (*Tugs at the toga*) I can't wait to get out of this yoke. I could murder a pint … If we tapped on Flanagan's window he'd probably let us in. What say you all? Hey, I'm still in character!

MRS B.: We're game. Sarah?

SARAH: Why not. I could murder a gin and tonic.

MULLINS: Me too.

PADDY: You can have a lemonade, young fella … (*Tentatively*) Stephen … ?

SARAH: Yes, come on Stephen. Join us.

STEPHEN: Em … no … Oh well, why not … As long as Sergeant Dowd isn't on the prowl.

PADDY: Don't worry about him. He gets his meat from me … the best sirloin … Good man yourself. Come on, so. Victor? Liz?

LIZ: We'll catch you up later.

MRS B.: Make sure you do. Au revoir, darrlings … (*Throws kisses at them*)

ALL: See you later!

> (*All except* VICTOR *and* LIZ *exit. They chat and jostle each other.*)

LIZ: (*Quietly*) Are you all right?

VICTOR: I'll survive ... You?

LIZ: Fine. I had fun, believe it or not.

VICTOR I believe it. (*Stands and looks into the middle distance.*) Dr Lynch was bad enough. Taylor was ... is a waster ... But imagine Dr. Bob sending us his crocks ... Christ Almighty...

LIZ: They're not crocks, Victor. And they pulled together when the going got rough.

VICTOR: (*Slumps to a sitting position on the edge of the raised stage*) I know. I don't blame them. Or the props ... Whose idea was the Lifebuoy soap ... ? No, forget it ... The production was bad ... my fault. It just didn't happen and it was never going to happen. There was no ... lift. None ... And I don't know why. That's what scares me ... I don't know why...

LIZ: (*Sitting beside him*) Don't, Victor...

VICTOR: I was too ambitious ... My motives were wrong too.

LIZ: Don't be so hard on yourself...

VICTOR: I wanted it to be a ticket out ... (*Turns away guiltily.*) *I* invited the good Dr Lynch. Me ... Did you know that...? Some comeuppance ... the irony is perfect ... Maybe she was right about paranoia. (*Gives a harsh laugh.*) Maybe the real Caiphus wanted a ticket out too. ... a

bigger stage for his so-called talents …
(*Pauses, kneads his hands.*) The first of the
diaspora … I wonder. At least he succeeded in
what he set out to do…

LIZ: Did he? The biggest deception in history, you
called it. How could he live with himself
afterwards?

VICTOR: Everything has a price, Liz.

LIZ: That's not you … You're not Caiphus. Come
on, Victor, I know you … This is me,
remember…

VICTOR: (*Musing aloud*) You know, my old man,
despite all his faults, wanted the best for me …
Wanted me to 'go far' … Doesn't look like it
now, Dad … But thanks all the same…

LIZ: Going far doesn't have to mean going away …
Maybe it's not the town you have to surmount
… And if it's yourself, don't bother. (*Touches
his hand*). You'll do as you are … Teaching
isn't so bad, you know, if you put your mind to
it. The kids like you. So does Father Dunphy in
his own way … This town isn't so bad either.
We live … we carry on…

VICTOR: But how do you grow here?

LIZ: You grow. It's just that you have nothing to
measure it against. But in a way that's a
challenge, isn't it? To stay, rather than run…

VICTOR: (*Slightly disparaging*) And accept
everything … ?

LIZ: No, not at all … Try to change what needs to
be changed … But there is one thing you must
accept.

VICTOR: Which is?

LIZ: Yourself.

> (*They sit with their thoughts for a while as the lights fade.*)

VICTOR: So it's all in here. (*Hits his chest.*) Where've I heard that line before?

LIZ: It's in the script ... You wrote it. (*Stands and gives him a hand up*) Come on, let's go home ... Together.

VICTOR: In full view?

LIZ: Yes. Why not.

VICTOR: Do you know what you're saying?

LIZ: I think so.

VICTOR: (*Smiles*) Maybe they'll run us out of town...

LIZ: (*With a histrionic groan*) You never give up. (*They link arms and cross the stage towards the left. VICTOR looks back once towards the lectern. LIZ catches his look.*)

LIZ: We couldn't have done better.

VICTOR: (*Not too downhearted*) That's not saying a whole lot...

LIZ: It's enough for now ... And remember, tomorrow will be better still. (*Beat*)

VICTOR: What would I do without you?

LIZ: I don't know ... (*Beat*) ... I just do not know. (VICTOR *and* LIZ *exit left, linking arms.*)

Lights come down slowly.

END

WHEREWITHAL

A Play in Two Acts

CHARACTERS

DERMOT DOLAN

A returned emigrant in his late thirties. Having built up a successful business in the US, he now wants to be of service to the town he left some twenty years earlier. This means taking on the political establishment.

LIZ DOLAN

Dermot's Jewish-American wife, a psychologist. She is prepared to help Dermot achieve his ambition but is keen to re-enter the labour force now that the children are at college.

DAD

Dermot's father, a small farmer who now lives in the town.

JOE MARTIN

T. D. and former Chairman of the Town Council. He has been in National and Local politics for forty years.

SEOSAMH MARTIN

Joe Martin's son, a local businessman, aspiring politician, and an alcoholic.

MAY MARTIN

Seosamh's wife, formerly a school teacher. She still has feelings for Dermot.

SADIE

Editor of the local newspaper which is owned by Joe Martin.

MINISTER

A senior Minister of the Government and colleague of Joe Martin.

TOM

A hotel worker.

ACT ONE

SCENE ONE

Time Present. The melody of 'She walks through the Fair' is played on the Pan Flute. The curtain rises to reveal the living room of a hotel suite. Afternoon. There are two sofas and a coffee table at centre stage.

At up right there is a large window which overlooks the town and through which can now be seen a reddish evening sky. At the same side as the window but further down stage is a door leading to the bedroom. There are two other doors, one at centre left leading to a study, the other, at upstage centre, opens onto a corridor. To the right of this door is a cocktail cabinet displaying an assortment of liquor bottles and glasses.

DERMOT and LIZ Dolan, a couple in their late thirties, well dressed in casual, modern clothes, are settling into the suite, having recently arrived. DAD and SADIE are there to meet them. They are making last minute-arrangements for a small party.

DERMOT: So, thanks for bringing us up to date,
  Dad.

DAD: There's more to be told, son. But there's no
  rush. (*Looks at* DERMOT *and* LIZ) You're
  both looking in fine form, especially you, Liz.

LIZ: You old flatterer. You haven't changed at all.
  (*She wanders around the room putting away
  suitcases and rearranging chairs and coffee
  tables.*)

DAD: I meant to ask about your brother Sean on the
  way in from the airport. How is he doing? I
  haven't heard from him in ages –

DERMOT: (*On tilt*) Oh, he's fine … You know
  Sean … always up to something … He relies
  on me to keep in touch… (LIZ *pauses to look
  at* DERMOT, *then busies herself again.*)

DAD: Is he doing as well as you?

DERMOT: Oh, yes … He's still in New York
  though … (*Changes subject.*) Do the Kinsella's
  still own this hotel?

DAD: You're going back a bit there, son. No, Joe
  Martin bought them out after the property
  crash.

DERMOT: For a pittance, I'd say.

DAD: Joe Martin doesn't miss a trick. Don't forget
  what he did to Sean … You'd need to be on
  your guard.

DERMOT: I will be … (*Pause*) … Listen, Dad …
  You're sure about the cancer…?

DAD: Yeah, it's in remission. I'll be around for a

while yet.

LIZ: (*Turns towards him*) Great news. Good for you. And you're still OK living on your own?

DAD: I wouldn't have it any other way.

LIZ: (*Looking out window.*) You know it really is a nice-looking town...

(DERMOT *and* DAD *join* LIZ *at the window and look out.*)

DERMOT: Nice-looking? Do you think so? Lived-in more like ... God the memories are flooding back ... Time for that later ... No cranes, bad sign, no building ... and just one ship in. What's she unloading?

DAD: Potatoes ... from Cyprus. We're importing spuds nowadays...

LIZ: That seems odd...

DERMOT: Look, Liz. See the school ... Just the same as ever. And the church on the other hill. We used to go from school to confession ... Through the valley of death and come back pure...

LIZ: Aha! That explains all your guilt complexes. Don't worry, we Jews have them too.

DERMOT: The river is impressive isn't it? But the quays ... what's happened to the quays ... ? They used to be grass-covered with benches for people to sit...

DAD: Some people call it progress ... That's not a carpark by the way. It's a lot for Toyota cars. The Martins have the sole distributorship...

DERMOT: Meaning a monopoly?

DAD: What else? The craft centre is gone too ...

We'll talk more later. I have a couple of cows to milk so I'll leave you two to settle in …
Welcome back and I hope everything goes well for you…

DERMOT: Thanks, Dad. See you later.

LIZ: Take care.

(*They hug and* DAD *exits.*)

DERMOT: Great news about the remission, Liz.

LIZ: It is, absolutely … I was wondering if now might be the time to tell him…

DERMOT: About Sean? I don't know … Maybe … I just don't know…

LIZ: It's hard for you, I know.

DERMOT: Yes … (*Playing for time*) It's hard all round. What about you? Being uprooted, leaving your Clinic. Sure you have no regrets?

LIZ: Not so far … You're here, aren't you? And the kids will be over for Christmas. So what's the big deal? I just hope there aren't any skeletons in the closet.

DERMOT: My past is as pure as the driven slush.

(*The doorbell sounds and* DERMOT *opens it to admit* SADIE. *All embrace.*)

SADIE: Welcome back! Look at you two.

LIZ / DERMOT: Thanks, Sadie.

SADIE: I know I'm early but there's method in my madness … You're good copy … I want to do an interview for the local rag.

DERMOT: And there was I thinking we were old friends…

(*He opens a casement and there can be heard the pulsing whine of a burglar alarm.*)

By the way, what happened to the craft centre?
It used to be there across from the cinema.

SADIE: Oh, that's long gone. Went bust or
something.

LIZ: That car alarm's been on for ages. Doesn't
anyone answer? Or shut it off?

SADIE: (*Shrugs*) A good question.

DERMOT: (*Closes window*) Sadie, it's a long time
since we played handball up against Joe
Martin's gable end – to coin a phrase.

SADIE: It is. (*To* LIZ) I'm afraid I was a bit of a
tomboy back then, Liz.

DERMOT: I hear you've made a great success of
the newspaper, despite the internet.

SADIE: Thanks. I'll tell you all about it sometime.
(*She takes out a small recording device.*)

DERMOT: (*Musing*) Old Sergeant what's-'is-name
used to confiscate the ball and cut it in two
with his penknife. (*He gravitates back towards
the window.*) The harbour looks in good nick
anyway … a few nice boats too … Someone's
doing well … Remember, Sadie, when you
tried to walk on the water down there once.
Said if Christ could do it so could you. When
you came up for the third time, someone said,
'Oh ye of little faith'…

LIZ: Dermot you're beginning to babble … Well, I
guess you're entitled…

DERMOT: And look, Liz, over there … No, on the
other side of the river. I used to come in that
road to school on a bike, a High Nelly … My
Dad's bike … when we had the farm … (*He

stops abruptly.)

LIZ: Are you all right? (*Touches his arm.*)

DERMOT: Fine. Just … memories.

SADIE: (*Looking up from the tape recorder.*)
Talking about the past, how is Sean? We
haven't heard anything…

DERMOT: (*Alarmed*) Oh, he's fine … fine.

LIZ: Yes.

SADIE: I hope he hasn't written us off … after what
happened that last time…

DERMOT: He never bore a grudge in his life.

SADIE: Well, this is front page stuff, believe me.
(*Switches on the recorder.*) You don't mind
this yoke?

DERMOT: No. Shoot.
(*They all sit around the coffee table.*)

SADIE: Now, Mr. Dermot Dolan let's start with
some deep background…

DERMOT: Cut it out, Sadie…!

SADIE: Oh, all right. Dermot Dolan, you grew up in
Killteague, on a farm outside the town. Could
you describe what that was like?

DERMOT: It was a good life, wholesome. But times
were hard. We had a few chickens and hens.
Killed a pig twice a year … Yes, a good life.
Wholesome … Did I say wholesome?

SADIE: (*Laughing*) All right, all right. Just remind
me who your neighbours were so I can mention
their names in the blasted paper.

DERMOT: The Kinsellas, O'Kellys, Ryans, and a
Protestant family, the Kerins.

SADIE: Good. I can put in the Christian names …

They'll like that.

LIZ: (*Laughing*) It must be a slow news day.

SADIE: No. This is Pulitzer Prize stuff around here. Now, Dermot, what brings you back to these parts after … what … twenty years?

DERMOT: Roots … Identity.

SADIE: Come on … !

LIZ: Tell her the reason, Dermot. You're going to later on, anyway.

DERMOT: Our plan is to stay in this hotel for a couple of weeks or so and then we might look for a house somewhere in the town.

SADIE: But what do you plan on doing?

DERMOT: Why do you think we're going to do something?

LIZ: Go on. Tell her.

DERMOT: OK, I'm going to stand for election to the Local Council, as an Independent.

SADIE: (*Surprised*) Election? Indep … ?

DERMOT: Yep.

SADIE: You mean for the County Council?

DERMOT: The very same.

SADIE: (*Flustered*) But I mean…

DERMOT: What?

SADIE: (*Awkwardly*) You're not … a politician … You know, track record… etcetera…

DERMOT: You mean I'm a blow-in?

SADIE: After Sean's experience five years ago…?

DERMOT: I've learnt from that. I mean business. And I am a citizen of this State, for what it's worth.

SADIE: Of course. You do know that the local

elections are going to be crucial for the
Government? The whole thing is balanced on a
knife edge, ever since the crash. What happens
here could have a big influence on the next
General Election.

DERMOT: (*Stands and begins to pace*) I know the
Government needs all the support it can get.
That gives me more leverage.

SADIE: Absolutely. A slight swing either way, even
at local level, could make a huge difference.
God, this *is* news. Forget about your relatives
and neighbours and the parish pump ... Tell us,
when do you start campaigning?

DERMOT: Tomorrow. I've already sent out flyers.
Then we're going to hold a press conference
here in the hotel.

SADIE: You'll be up against Seosamh Martin, Joe's
son...

DERMOT: That's why we've invited him over –
with his wife May of course.

SADIE: To suss out the competition ... You fox ...
You have it all planned out.
(*Switches off tape recorder.*)
I'd better phone in what I've got already ... if
that's OK with you?

DERMOT: Sure. Be our guest.

LIZ: You can use that room. (*Points.*)
(SADIE *takes out a cell phone and goes into
the room on the left.*)

LIZ: That's odd...

DERMOT: What is?

LIZ: She didn't ask you anything about policies or

strategy...

DERMOT: We don't do policies over here ...
Anyway, she probably doesn't want an unfair
advantage over the other journalists.

LIZ: (*Eyes him*) I would doubt that...

DERMOT: Dad often told me about that clique. The
Martins. They're not interested in the town.
Only themselves. Joe Martin, young Seosamh,
and their henchmen. How many people were
forced into exile by them and their cronies?
When Sean stood for election, the Martins
blackened his name and forced him out...

LIZ: You need to be sure of your motives, Dermot
... Are you doing this for Sean?

DERMOT: Partly, yes, I don't deny it ... Sean
passed the gauntlet to me ... The cronyism has
to stop. Some people might receive favours but
there's always a price to pay.

LIZ: Such as?

DERMOT: Well, there was an incident at school. A
pal was locked in a press by a sadistic old
teacher. ... He was afraid of the dark. I tried to
force the door of the press open to let him out.
The teacher pushed me away. I pushed back.
The teacher fell and broke his wrist...

LIZ: And?

DERMOT: I was expelled. Or would have been.
Dad intervened with Joe Martin who got me re-
instated. But there was a price to pay.

LIZ: What price?

DERMOT: Joe Martin wanted our land ... such as it
was, God help us. Dad had to sell up. He had

given his word. I finished my education. But Dad's life was never really the same afterwards. And do you know what the land was used for? To extend the golf course. Nine more holes. Can you believe it?

LIZ: That's awful, Dermot … I'm beginning to feel uneasy about all this. Are we walking into some sort of feud?

DERMOT: I don't think so. No one forgets … that's true. But no one mentions these things either. Just pretend you know none of this when you meet Joe Martin and his son, Seosamh.

LIZ: Show – sav –. That's Irish for Joe?

DERMOT: It's a little trick that's sometimes used to avoid the impression of nepotism. Though God knows, a rose by any other name would smell as sweet.

LIZ: So you invited him here to get the measure of him??

DERMOT: Yes…

LIZ: Keep your enemies close?

DERMOT: Something like that … (*Pause*)

LIZ: Wow. Still, I think I will hang out the old shingle as soon as we get settled in here.

DERMOT: Do. Why not? But don't expect too much. This ain't California … or New York. People around here don't like talking about their personal issues…

(SADIE *re-enters.*)

SADIE: Well, that's the story put to bed. It'll hit the streets tomorrow, as they say. Now, where's that drink?

DERMOT: (*Pouring*) So, Sadie, you never had a
    yen to travel?

SADIE: The town isn't so bad … Oh, I suppose I'm
    just a sort of furry creature who doesn't
    venture too far afield. I know my limitations …
    not very enterprising, unlike some people I
    could mention. Maybe I should've been a nun.
    I thought I had a vocation once.

DERMOT: I remember that time the Reverend
    Mother tried to recruit you…

SADIE: I wasn't sure of my motives. And that
    wasn't a good sign apparently.

LIZ: You never married?

SADIE: I nearly did once. But it wasn't to be. It
    seemed as if all the good men emigrated … I'd
    have liked kids … Ah well…

LIZ: It's not too late.

SADIE: Maybe not. But I'm too stuck in my ways
    now, too fond of the old spinster comforts. I
    use an electric blanket, you know…

LIZ: That's not a hanging offence.

SADIE: You two are looking good on wedlock
    though.

LIZ: I can't complain. We have two great kids, both
    at college. One doing psychology, following in
    her Mom's footsteps, and the other,
    engineering. It's been good so far –
    (*A knock sounds on the door.*)

DERMOT: That'll be Seosamh and May. (*He rises
    to answer the door.*)
    (*Enter* SEOSAMH *and* MAY, *a couple also in
    their late thirties. He is overweight and dressed*

*in an expensive and fashionable suit though it
is a little baggy. She is dressed simply yet with
style. She appears to be a little tired.*
DERMOT *embraces* MAY *and shakes hands
with* SEOSAMH.)

DERMOT: It's good to see you both. I'd like you to
   meet Liz, my wife.

MAY: How do you do?

SEOSAMH: (*Pumping* LIZ*'s hand*) You did well,
   boy. Never doubted you. You must be coining
   it too. This suite costs a bomb ... unless the old
   fella's giving you a discount. But I doubt that.
   (*He accepts a whiskey.*)

DERMOT: You don't seem too badly off yourself.
   Isn't that your name I see down there on the
   Toyota lot.

SEOSAMH: Oh, yes. Sole distributor. I'm also an
   estate agent, so if you're in the market for a
   house...

LIZ: We may be as a matter of fact.

DERMOT: I was wondering about the old Heath-
   Manning estate?

SEOSAMH: Isn't that a good one? Sure, May and
   me moved in there a few years back. But there
   are other good properties on the market. I'll
   leave one of these for you.
   (*Places his card on the coffee table and takes a
   large gulp of whiskey.* DERMOT *replenishes
   his glass;* MAY *declines a refill.*)

LIZ: We don't want to talk business.

MAY: Absolutely not.

DERMOT: When did you two tie the knot?

MAY: March 2001 … a red-letter day. (*She gives* DERMOT *a meaningful glance.*)

SEOSAMH: Yeah. Not long after you left for the States. (*To* LIZ) I was lucky he did leave. These two had a thing going.

LIZ: It's all coming out now. I knew there'd be skeletons…

MAY: Oh, indeed it was all very innocent. The swinging noughties passed us all by in this neck of the woods.

SADIE: What swinging noughties?

MAY: See what I mean? (*To* DERMOT) So, has the good old U S of A been good to you?

DERMOT: Can't complain. After a shaky start we managed to get our ducks in a row.

LIZ: Don't be modest. (*To* MAY) He owns a thriving company. Building components. The main part of the factory is in a part of Chicago that was terribly run down. He got the Mayor's Award two years in a row.

MAY: Congratulations, Dermot. I can't say I'm surprised … How many people do you employ?

DERMOT: Three hundred and sixty…

LIZ: About a hundred too many if you ask me. But he just won't let any of them go.

DERMOT: They were with me from the beginning, Liz. You don't break up a team that's soldiered together. Accountants don't understand that…

LIZ: You're getting dangerously close to talking business.

DERMOT: You started it.

(Re-charges glasses. SEOSAMH *is drinking quickly and re-fills his own glass.)*

MAY: How did you two meet?

LIZ: At a counselling session. I was taking this group in the clinic…

SEOSAMH: A nut house?

LIZ: Sort of. And Dermot comes in with one of his foremen who had a drug problem. One of his old campaigners. And … well … it sort of developed from there.

SEOSAMH: *(Slightly inebriated)* Three hundred and what's-it … Christ that's some wage bill. How would you get value out of that mob…? Ah well, sure Dermot was always too big for this town.

SADIE: I'm impressed. That's big time, Dermot. I should've got that out of you earlier … at the interview. How did you do it?

DERMOT: Teamwork, hard graft … Oh, look could we move on … ?

LIZ: *(To* SEOSAMH) And your father is in the government?

SEOSAMH: He lives for politics … *(Looks surreptitiously at* DERMOT.) I hear you might have ambitions in that direction yourself…

LIZ: *(Startled)* Wow! News travels fast around here.

MAY: *(Heavily)* Nothing escapes the Martins … Of course, they own the paper.

DERMOT: *(To* SADIE) You never mentioned that.

SADIE: *(Uneasily)* Didn't I? I suppose it didn't come up. *(Takes off her glasses and wipes them.)*

SEOSAMH: (*Re-filling his own glass*) It's going to
be a bitch … of an election … I can tell you …
a real dog's bollocks of a yoke…

MAY: (*Embarrassed*) Moving right along…

DERMOT: (*With deliberation*) What happened to
the Craft Centre?

SEOSAMH: We had to sell it off. For site value.
The grants ran out…

DERMOT: But you were going to start exporting
when I left. I sent back all the market
information on a disk…

SEOSAMH: Exporting? Ah now that's a horse of a
different colour. Red tape … forms to be filled.
Too ambitious altogether … for the yobs we
had working there.

DERMOT: So there was more unemployment, more
emigration?

SEOSAMH: Yeah … You know the way it is …
They just bail out…

LIZ: Why is that? I don't understand. It's a beautiful
country from what I've seen. It's not short of
natural resources. The standard of education is
high. And there's no religious bigotry or
racism … I don't get it.

SEOSAMH: (*Slurring*) The grass is greener … They
just bugger off…

DERMOT: I think there's more to it than that.

MAY: What's really sad is that you can see the poor
morale in the children. When I was teaching I
found it hard to motivate the kids or get them
doing something positive. They *assume* they
can't succeed.

LIZ: Forgive the cliché. But low self-esteem is often behind that.

MAY: And whenever the kids *did* raise their game it was because something excited them ... got the adrenalin going. They needed that boost ... But they couldn't sustain it ... unfortunately.

SEOSAMH: Is my wife ... expounding one of her theories again? ... Just because she has a B.Ahhh ... Look, the real problem is ... that we're not material – material – istic ... Saints 'n scholars, see...? Not like you Yanks...

LIZ: (*Sharply*) I don't see anyone going barefoot but I do see a lot of wealth. Maybe it's not fairly divided...

SEOSAMH: Tell us ... Are you a WASP?

LIZ: No ... I'm Jewish.

SEOSAMH: Jewish? Jesus, that's good ... No rashers for you then...

MAY: (*Embarrassed*) Seosamh!

SEOSAMH: All this bleeding ... heart stuff ... (*To* DERMOT) You don't look short ... of the readies...

DERMOT: Tell me, Seosamh, did you ever sleep rough? Or were you ever an illegal alien, constantly looking over your shoulder?

SEOSAMH: No sympathy votes here, boy ... (*Suddenly lucid*) ... It's my seat you're after. Did you hear that? Mine!

DERMOT: It's a democracy isn't it?

SEOSAMH: You haven't a prayer ... We've got this town sewn up tighter than a duck's arse.

MAY: Give it a rest, Seosamh. For God's sake ...

I'm sorry, Dermot...

SEOSAMH: Don't apol ... ogise for me ... Some things ... have to be said ... You can't just walk out of this town and then waltz back ... thinking you can run things ... Some of us have been holding the fort through thick and thin...

SADIE: Ah now, Seosamh ... Visitors...

SEOSAMH: Day-trippers ... Swanking around in this hotel suite...

DERMOT: (*Begins to lose composure.*) In a hotel owned by your father. I didn't walk out of the town, as you put it. There was nothing for me here, Godammit ... Not after you and your father...

LIZ: Don't, Dermot...

DERMOT: It's time for a change. Change ... Do you know what that means?

SEOSAMH: (*Slumps back*) Don't fuckin' lecture me ... I know all about change for Jasus' sake ... Could tell you other things too ... if I had a mind to... You'd be surprised ... (*Eyes close*) ... keep powder dry ... not a prayer ... none of us ... nothing ... (*Sleeps.*)

MAY: I had hoped ... I'm so sorry ... (*She begins to weep.*)

LIZ: Don't be. It's not your ... He's just ... under the weather. Let him sleep it off. He's probably nervous about the election.

MAY: You don't have to make ... excuses for him.

DERMOT: I hope I ... you know, the election business ... hasn't thrown a spanner in the works…

MAY: He's responsible for what he does, no one else. If Seosamh loses the election, that's his problem. Who knows, it might even be good for him … Oh, I don't know anymore. (*She turns tearfully aside.*)

(DERMOT *goes to* MAY *and pats her gently on the shoulder.*)

DERMOT: Try not to worry, May.

MAY: I'll try … Thank you, Dermot…

(LIZ *looks from* MAY *to* DERMOT, *a quizzical expression on her face.*)

SADIE: (*With irony*) Welcome home.

DERMOT: Dad was right … Not much has changed.

Lights down.

SCENE TWO

Morning sunlight streams through the window of the suite which is in some disarray after the night before. SEOSAMH, *flat out on one of the sofas, and covered with a blanket, stirs painfully. He looks around slowly with an uncomprehending expression.*

SEOSAMH: (*Holds his head*) Christ … I swore never again…
> (*He rises very slowly and shields his eyes against the light. Tries to focus on his watch. Stretches out his fingers and abruptly clasps his hands to stop them trembling. Looks at a bottle of whiskey on the coffee table.*)
> God, no…
> (*Sits for a while, staring at the bottle, then reaches out, pours, and drinks. Hearing sounds from the bedroom, he quickly drains the glass and replaces it.*)
> (LIZ *enters from the bedroom.*)

LIZ: Morning, Seosamh. Would you like some … em … aspirin?

SEOSAMH: No thanks. Hair of the dog … if I may. (*Pours another glass.*) May's gone?

LIZ: Yes. She had to get back to the family. We did ask her to stay but she mentioned something about a babysitter.

SEOSAMH: I'm in the doghouse so.

LIZ: You're welcome to stay here. But don't you have work ?

SEOSAMH: The business takes care of itself. The old fella looks in every so often ... to check. Always checking, that's him.

(*Enter* DERMOT *from the corridor door. He's dressed in a suit.*)

DERMOT: Medicating yourself, Seosamh?

SEOSAMH: Just ... you know ... Good night last night ... Hope I didn't... well ... If I said anything ... forget about it...

DERMOT: Said what?

SEOSAMH: Oh, yeah. Right. (*Raises his glass.*)

LIZ: How did it go?

DERMOT: I threw the old hat in the ring. Some of the hacks didn't take me too seriously. But others seemed kind of interested. I challenged Joe Martin to a head to head. He may have to accept. I also rang the national newspapers.

SEOSAMH: Good luck. But it won't do you any good.

DERMOT: We'll see. No quarter given, eh Seosamh?

SEOSAMH: None asked for either. None needed.

DERMOT: You'd better eat something. I can order...

SEOSAMH: No thanks ... Just a smathán for the road. (*Pours another drink.*)

DERMOT: I met your father on the hustings. He didn't exactly welcome me with open arms.

SEOSAMH: I doubt if he's worried … We've always had two safe seats here. What with transfers and good vote-management. (*He pours himself another drink.*)

DERMOT: I like a good fight.

LIZ: What was it May said about adrenalin?

SEOSAMH: (*Gets unsteadily to his feet.*) Party's over … better push off now.

LIZ: Are you OK?

SEOSAMH: Never better.

LIZ: I mean … can we call you a cab?

SEOSAMH: Haven't I the car below in the carpark? Don't worry about me.

LIZ: It's others I'm…

(SEOSAMH *waves with his back turned to them and exits.*)

DERMOT: No fear of him being breathalysed … He ran over our sheepdog once … Old Jack. Broke his back. Dad had to shoot him. But he chased Seosamh down the lane with a pitchfork and dumped slurry on his new Mercedes … You'd almost feel sorry for the poor bastard in a way, overshadowed by his old fella…

LIZ: Good for your Dad … God, what a night … friendly at first and then a change sets in. I'm confused…

DERMOT: Seosamh would build a nest in your ear and rob it.

LIZ: Even Sadie. I'm not so sure about her either.

DERMOT: Oh, she's all right.

LIZ: I wonder … Joe Martin owns the paper … And what about you?

DERMOT: (*Surprised*) Me?

LIZ: Yes, you. Did you really level with *me?* Did you know that Seosamh would have the support of the main government party?

DERMOT: (*Defensively*) I suppose ... I half knew.

LIZ: You're as bad as he is. Doesn't anyone say things out straight?

DERMOT: (*Forces laugh*) You have to be cute.

LIZ: Cute? Not cuddly, right?

DERMOT: No, canny. Able to see around corners without being seen. It's all done with mirrors. Nothing is as it seems and there are no rules. That's what makes the game exciting. Yeah, maybe it is all about adrenalin or some kind of high...

LIZ: (*Puts down coffee cup*) I don't find it very amusing. And I'll tell you something else. Seosamh scares me.

DERMOT: He's not so tough ... I remember playing hurley with him. He used to run away from the action ... afraid of screwing up, especially if his old fella was on the sideline ... I, of course was a ground-puller...

LIZ: A what?

DERMOT: I was big for my age and I suppose a bit awkward so it was assumed that I couldn't do any of the fancy moves, like raising the ball, going on solo runs and so on. I was supposed to hit the ball on the ground as soon as it came to me. Nothing fancy ... just pull on the ground. But I was never satisfied being a ground-puller. I knew I could do better. My

Dad said so too…

LIZ: And did you do better?

DERMOT: I did … We got to the Finals one year.
And I decided to have a go, to take that scary
step … I raised the ball and did a solo run half
the length of the field. I don't know if I scored
or not. But I'll never forget that solo run …
Something flowed through me. I still
remember the buzz, the realisation that I could
do it … me the gawky lad from the back of
beyond, the ground-puller … I'd stepped out of
the shadows … (*Stops his reverie with some
embarrassment.*) You know what I mean … I
don't think Seosamh ever had that kind of
experience…

LIZ: Shit.

DERMOT: What?

LIZ: I'm supposed to be mad at you.
(DERMOT *smiles and touches her hand.*)

LIZ: You still didn't tell me this whole election
business would be so … fraught.

DERMOT: Guilty as charged. Maybe I left out a
few nuances.

LIZ: Nuances? We're walking into a hornets nest. I
can sense it. OK, maybe you had some
romantic idea about coming back here and
making a mark. But this is reality, Dermot.
These people aren't going to kill the fatted calf
for you … Not even May…

DERMOT: What's she got to do with it…?
Anyway, I never said it would be easy.

LIZ: You never said. Period. You can't just arrive

out of the blue and hope to win … I know how clientelism works. What if we've pulled up stakes for nothing…?

DERMOT: I know … It's a gamble…

LIZ: And you seem so absorbed. I feel like an observer.

DERMOT: It's different over here. Maybe old habits are coming back…

LIZ: What habits? What are you saying?

DERMOT: Uisce fé thalamh…

LIZ: What the hell is that?

DERMOT: Water under the ground.

LIZ: So you're going to talk to me in a foreign language now. I rest my case.

DERMOT: It's hard to explain, Liz. Around here you don't … you know … let your real feelings show. It's not done. Being up front is almost like indecent exposure. You keep three pairs of pants on at all times.

LIZ: I don't believe it. I thought that attitude went out with the middle ages. Even my grandparents who came to the States from Germany had conquered that old hang-up. Anyway, why should *you* be slipping back into old habits?

DERMOT: Ghosts … My mother died so young, I barely remember her…

LIZ: I know that the Druids went in for ancestor worship but this is crazy. Get real, Dermot. You're not going to get elected by magic.

DERMOT: I have some aces.

LIZ: (*Sarcastically*) Up your sleeve, I suppose …

Well hidden anyway.
DERMOT: OK, cards on the table. Let's talk about
it and everything else. Let's go to Dad's place.
(*They exit.*)

Lights down.

SCENE THREE

The melody of 'My Lagan Love' is played on the Pan Flute. The lights come on slowly and reveal a function room in the hotel. TOM *is arranging a long table with a mic on top.* DERMOT *and* LIZ *are sorting out sheaves of paper.* SADIE *paces back and forth, ill-at-ease.* SEOSAMH *and* MAY *are seated on a sofa which is now on the left side of the stage.*

TOM*: (Off)* Testing one ... two ... testing one ... two ... three. OK, that's it.

SADIE: I don't fancy this much ... Joe Martin asked me to chair it...

LIZ: The chairman should be impartial...

DERMOT: It doesn't matter, Liz.

> (*Studying a document*)
>
> Have we enough of this one, Liz?

LIZ: I have some more. (*She takes documents from a briefcase and places them on the table.*)

SADIE: What's all this paper about ... ?

DERMOT: All will be revealed in the fullness of time.

> (*Enter* JOE MARTIN – *a tall elderly man, dressed in a striped suit with silk tie.*)

JOE: Well, isn't this all very fancy. A press conference no less.

DERMOT: Joe. At last. May I introduce you to my
wife, Liz.

JOE: Hello. Hello. Haven't we all got more
important things to be doing than this?

DERMOT: There's nothing like a little chat with the
press to oil the wheels of democracy.

JOE: In the name of God, what's your interest in
local politics? You've been away for twenty
odd years. And made your pile by all accounts.
No one is going to take you seriously as a
candidate.

SEOSAMH: He's just playing at it, Da.

DERMOT: Choice, Joe. I'm an alternative. Besides,
this little meeting will give you and Seosamh
an opportunity to present your policies to the
electorate.

JOE: Policies.

DERMOT: Yes.

JOE: So, you're doing us all a favour!

DERMOT: No. The people.

JOE: I remember you as a youngster, a sensible lad.
What's come over you at all? (*Looks
inquiringly at* LIZ.) There's nothing in this for
you. Maybe you got a rush of blood to the
head. Sure, we all do from time to time. But I
don't want you to go through the mangle here
for nothing and then have to go back to your
adopted country with your tail between your
legs. Spare yourself that, Dermot, and your
good wife, and call off this foolishness.

SEOSAMH: I told him that before...

DERMOT: I appreciate your concern. But I think

we'll stick around…

TOM: (*Off*) You're all set up now. The journalists are downstairs in the lobby…

LIZ: Tell them we're ready.

SEOSAMH: (*To* DERMOT) You can still call it off.

DERMOT: Ah, no. We'll start as we mean to go on. Call it a solo run…

JOE: (*Darkly*) This isn't a game. And it's not for amateurs.

DERMOT: I know what it is and what it isn't … and what it should be.

JOE: (*To* LIZ) Are you going to stay?

LIZ: Wouldn't miss it.

(*Everyone on stage sits at the long table facing out to the auditorium. Sounds of Journalists assembling, flashes of cameras etc. Tom stands to the side with a hand-held microphone.*)

SADIE: (*Looking at the Audience*) Greetings everyone … I can see some of my fellow hacks here … and one or two even from Dublin. You're all welcome … I imagine you know Joe Martin here, T.D. and former Chairman of the County Council. Most of you also know his son, Seosamh, a member of the County Council – and his wife, May. Seosamh is standing for re-election … Dermot Dolan on my right is also standing … He has returned from Chicago to his home town to live … His wife, Liz, is seated at the end of the table … Now we don't want anything too formal here today. So I propose we go straight into question time … Yes, Sam … There's a mic on its way to you…

(TOM *descends into the auditorium. Each journalist who speaks appears on a screen.*)

JOURNALIST ONE: As you say, Sadie, we know the Martins well, but Dermot Dolan is a newcomer on the scene. My question to him is … what's it all about?

(*Laughter*)

DERMOT: Over two decades ago I, and my brother, Sean, like many others, had to leave this town to earn a living. Some of us were lucky; many were not so lucky. Five years ago my brother, Sean, stood for election and was undermined at every hand's turn. I realised that nothing had changed, except that the town was even more run down. Sure, there were some yachts in the harbour but there were more slum areas than ever before and people were still being forced to emigrate, especially after the crash of 2008. The population is now half of what it was a decade ago and almost one-third of those are on the dole or in miserable jobs. You only have to walk down the main street to sense the quiet despair … The benefits of European integration are not going to reach into those narrow streets … I think I can help the town get on its feet, to realise its potential…

JOURNALIST TWO: We've heard this before. The word was that you'd have something different to say.

JOE: *I* certainly expected more!

DERMOT: Maybe I have more to say. First, I am

standing for one term only. To do the job that has to be done. I will not be seeking a second term...

JOURNALIST THREE: That's a new twist all right. But what's the point of it?

DERMOT: The point is this. If I were interested in a second term I'd have to spend most of my time currying favour with the cliques and lobbies, instead of getting on with the job. By foregoing a second term it would be possible to get on with *real* business without fear or favour. So that would be my approach. Get the job done in one term and then bow out.

JOE: (*Laughs*) Bow out? I've heard it all now. Who'd believe that...? It's like a fella sitting down to his dinner, saying he'll only have the soup. Then the roast beef arrives, and he says well maybe a little taste ... a little taste won't hurt.

(*Laughter partly led by* SEOSAMH.)

DERMOT: (*Holds up a document*) This is a sworn affidavit saying that if I am elected, I will under no circumstances seek a second term. That should satisfy you, Joe. There are copies here for everyone.

JOURNALIST FOUR: This *is* newsworthy, Mr. Dolan. But is it a gimmick?

DERMOT: I simply want five years to help rebuild this town through self-help. I would be a true Independent working for all the people, not distributing favours to the select few ... or trying to strengthen a dynasty ... or re-zoning land for personal gain. My top priority will be job-creation.

SEOSAMH: That's easy to say but the Council is strapped for funds. Where's the cash going to come from? This is just a stroke.

DERMOT: The seedcorn is always available for productive enterprise. It's a question of mobilising the talent of the people and working to a plan.

(Holds up a second document. LIZ hands down a sheaf of them to TOM in the auditorium.)

Here you see an audit of the resources of the town and its hinterland. I've worked on this for over a year. On pages 7 and 8 you can see that the region has a clear natural advantage in two types of agri-industry. The details are all in there. I guarantee that within three years these sectors can be developed up to the point where emigration ceases and unemployment is cut in half. More important, the people will have a stake in their own future.

(Electronic flashes go off as the cameramen circle round the top table.)

JOURNALIST ONE: Why don't you just set up a factory here yourself?

JOE: A good question! It'd be a lot simpler.

DERMOT: That's one of the easy options tried so often in the past. How could the local people feel committed to a foreign operation plonked down in their midst and grant-aided up to the hilt? Where is the sense of ownership or accomplishment? Don't you see…? We can't go on living on hand-outs, tax incentives and brass-plate operations. We have to develop in a more natural way ... By ourselves. By our own efforts and sweat equity ... No more grants to foreigners, no more profit repatriations, no tax scams, nixers or dole. We do it the only way. The hard way.

JOE: (*Grinning*) What was that...? 'Sweat equity' was it ... ?

DERMOT: You heard, Joe.

JOURNALIST THREE: Suppose you did get something going in those sectors, what happens after your term runs out?

DERMOT: I'll still be around to advise if needs be. But if all goes well I won't be needed. You see the enterprises will be vested in, and controlled by, the workforce. Appendix 2 of the document you have sets out the legal framework...

JOE: Ah, Communism. Now we have it.

DERMOT: Sorry to disappoint you, Joe. It's nothing more than teamwork, something that's been conspicuously lacking up till now.

JOE: Whatever it is, it's all pie in the sky. You're only raising expectations. So that when the whole thing fails...

DERMOT: Like the Craft Centre, you mean? Why did the Craft Centre fail?

JOE: The market turned down.

DERMOT: Did it?

JOE: Yes, it did.

DERMOT: Isn't it true that the grants on which it depended were revoked because of sharp practice?

JOE: Rubbish! The market turned down. We had two bad tourist years. It's outrageous to suggest...

DERMOT: I'm not suggesting. I'm stating...

SADIE: (*Uneasily*) Maybe we ... could stick to the matter at hand ... Any more questions? Yes, Jim.

JOURNALIST FOUR: These proposals are quite new but maybe a little too ... experimental?

DERMOT: We have to change. With Europe moving towards a federation and the whole world becoming a global village, we can't sulk in a corner licking old wounds. We have to get out there and start painting the shop fronts.

JOURNALIST ONE: What's in it for you? What about conflicts of interest?

(DERMOT *hands another document to* LIZ *who distributes it.*)

SEOSAMH: Another piece of paper! You should write a book and be done with it.

DERMOT: Better than a wink and a nod, Seosamh ... You can see there the latest published accounts of my Chicago Corporation. Also a statement of my net worth, interests and affiliations. You might also note that I have never made any contributions to political parties. I should also say that, if elected, I would not accept any contribution with or without strings attached.

JOURNALIST THREE: So you're doing all this for philanthropic reasons?

DERMOT: I'll be well rewarded if I can help to revive this town. Money isn't everything. I have enough, more than enough.

JOE: This from a Yank.

JOURNALIST FOUR: Mr. Martin, a lot of what he says makes sense. He has a clear idea of where he wants to go and how he intends getting there. How about your policies?

JOE: My policies are well known. I've always acted in the best interests of the town. Ask anybody. The people know what I stand for...

JOURNALIST FOUR: Could you be more specific? How about additional local charges for example.

JOE: Oh, no more charges. You have my word on that.

JOURNALIST FOUR: Then how are you going to maintain services, roads, water, sewerage, public lighting? You'll have to strike a higher business property rate...

JOE: No rate increase either.

JOURNALIST FOUR: I'm confused. How then can you maintain, let alone improve, services? It's an impossibility.

JOE: That's Dublin's problem. The Government will have to come up with the funds. And you can rest assured Seosamh and I will be lobbying hard day and night to get those funds.

JOURNALIST FOUR: But the Government itself is strapped for cash. And they have to reduce borrowing to stay in the Euro. As a TD you know that.

JOE: Look, it's a question of political will. Let me say this. I know how the system works. Funds can be got if you know which tree to shake. I've been in this game a long time, at local as well as national level.

DERMOT: A very long time.

JOE: Experience is what counts. The old dog for the hard road. Not a young pup, wet behind the ears...

DERMOT: What's your sell-by date, Joe? When are you going to stand down?

JOE: (*Glares at him then becomes avuncular*) Look lads, we've heard a good pitch here today. Not a bad effort at all from someone who has no experience. And the man probably means well enough. But the thing of it is, you have to know the town and the people. Dermot was born here, but things change. He could walk down Thomas Street today and no one would know him from Adam. How could he operate a clinic or help people in a bind? He couldn't, and I suspect from what he said that he wouldn't even want to. Whereas Seosamh and myself ... well, we're available day or night. Always have been. I don't think I need say any more.

DERMOT: All that sounds very cosy and I've no doubt that wonderful favours are dished out in Joe's clinic, courtesy of the taxpayer. But that's just robbing Peter to pay Paul. Let me remind you again of the record: continuing emigration, rising unemployment and a pall of despair. People in this town have no longer confidence in their abilities. This all has to be reversed as a matter of urgency. Clinics won't do it. Nor will hand-outs. Greeting people in the street on first name terms won't do it. Lobbying Dublin or Brussels for free money won't do it.

JOE: (*Beginning to lose composure*) But you can do it, is that right? A fella who swans in from foreign parts, who's never in his life come within an ass's roar of public life. Let's face it, you're out of your depth, boy.

DERMOT: (*Becoming tense*) Stand down, Joe. Your day is done. It's time for you to parachute into the Senate or into a cushy job in the EU.

JOE: How dare you … I was a T.D. when you were in nappies … Your brother Sean tried to take me on once before … What ever happened to him? He's not around now, is he?

DERMOT: That's none of your Goddamned business…!

SADIE: (*Uneasily*) Now, gentlemen, we don't want to … get heated…
(*Voices of other journalists vie for attention. Camera flashes.*)

DERMOT: Why not get heated? It's better to get the issues out on the table for once … Penetrate the secret world of the Martins…

SEOSAMH: You watch what you're saying…

SADIE: Easy now … Easy everyone … One last question … OK, Sammy…

JOURNALIST FIVE: This is addressed to Mr.

Dolan. Are you really saying that you wouldn't hold clinics at all?

DERMOT: Yes. That is exactly what I'm saying. No clinics, no Party favours...

JOE: (*With alacrity*) There you have it now, from the horse's mouth. He'd do nothing for individuals in need ... And he's standing for election. .. This is priceless stuff. Better than a pantomime. You've heard it all now.

DERMOT: Clinics create dependencies, turn people into supplicants. Under my proposals there'd be no need for clinics. Why? Because people would become self-sufficient...

JOE: He's said it again. No clinics. Did you get that, lads? I can hardly believe my ears. Fantastic stuff ... Better than Duffy's Circus ... Sadie, I don't think there's any more to be said.

SADIE: What? Oh, yes. That's it so. Ladies and gentlemen, thank you all for coming and for your questions. I'm sure your copy will be fair and balanced. Thanks again.

JOE: (*To journalists.*) Drinks on the house downstairs, lads. I'll join you in a minute. (*Sounds of journalists filing out.*)
Well that's that. It's a pity you shot yourself in the foot there at the end. The first lesson is never to answer 'yes' or 'no'. Life is more complicated than that.

DERMOT: We'll see. Keep your eye on the papers.

JOE: Oh yeah. Like they're going to reproduce your 'documents' in full. Those journalists know well that you're just play-acting.

DERMOT: Where's the new blood going to come from … ?

JOE: Seosamh is no older than you.

DERMOT: And exactly like his father.

JOE: (*In a flash of temper*) Just who the fuck do you think you are? You'd have been kicked out of school if it weren't for me … Just because you lived in the States you think you know it all. Everything is better over there, isn't it? Well, go on back then. Piss off out of it. Don't come over here and tell us what to do. We'll go our own way.

DERMOT: Yes. Cronyism, hand-outs, and back-scratching … No vision, no planning…

SADIE: Ah now … easy…

JOE: You haven't a bloody clue. The people don't want your ideas … Sweat equity, Jesus Christ…

DERMOT: So throw them a few crumbs, zero-hour contracts, or the dole. Keep 'em on the reservation. Or let them emigrate … (*Earnestly*) For God's sake don't you see what's happening? Don't you see?

JOE: You know what your problem is? You want to play God.

DERMOT: Better than playing Judas. You've betrayed the town, Joe.

SEOSAMH: How dare you say that to my father. You wouldn't say it in front of the press … Sadie, you've got that? You heard him.

DERMOT: I almost forgot. You own the newspaper too … You know, the sad part is I used to look up to you. I thought you knew what public service meant. Maybe you did once. You built those parks and the harbour wall. Then my father told me you owned the quarries that provided the stone. You didn't miss a trick...

JOE: Don't be a fool. Your father was all talk...

DERMOT: You took most of his land ... to extend the fucking golf-course.

JOE: He couldn't farm for shit. You'd see him in a field any time of the day reading a book ... Or leaning over a hedge talking to Sean ... I did him a favour.

DERMOT: My God, you're low. In any other country you and your henchmen would be in jail for fraud ... And don't mention Sean ... You blackened his name when he stood up to you...

JOE: Don't use that moral tone with me. How many corners did you cut? In Chicago or wherever the hell it was.

DERMOT: You just don't get it. There's talent here. It grew in the eighties when there was the promise of real development. Then you came along with your fast buck approach. You spoiled everything, destroyed hope, set us back half a century. We were better off under the British...

JOE: That's outrageous ... You need to be careful...

DERMOT: Is that a threat...?

LIZ: (*Coming between them*) Enough! Enough! I can't listen to any more of this...

JOE: The hustings are just beginning. (*To*

DERMOT) You're going to be taught a lesson you'll never forget.

(JOE *storms out.*)

DERMOT: (*Fighting for composure*) That would appear to be that. I guess the issue's well and truly joined.

LIZ: I'm at a loss…

SADIE: I'm glad that's over.

MAY: It's not. It's just beginning.

SEOSAMH: You can say that again.

LIZ: Sadie, where do you stand in all of this?

SADIE: I just want a quiet life sitting on the fence … reporting on the passing parade.

MAY: Are you sure that's what you've been doing?

SEOSAMH: (*Roughly*) Stay out of it. Come on. We've no business here.

MAY: (*Looking at* DERMOT.) Maybe it's time to get off the fence.

SEOSAMH: What do you mean by that?

MAY: (*Quietly*) Change … Maybe it is time, Seosamh.

SEOSAMH: (*Pushes her towards the door*) Keep out of it.

(DERMOT *takes a step forward in protest.*)

MAY: Don't worry … That's about the worst he can do.

(*Exit* SEOSAMH *and* MAY.)

SADIE: (*Follows them, then turns*) Be … careful.

(*Exit* SADIE.)

LIZ: My God, what does that mean?

DERMOT: She exaggerates…

LIZ: What've we started? I'm not sure I want to go

through with this. Even if you win you lose …
How would we live with these people? They
hate your guts. That was real anger. On *both*
sides. Dermot, I've never seen you like this.

DERMOT: (*Grimly*) Maybe we need anger. It might
get something moving. Anyway I thought you
shrinks believed in letting go every so often…
(*Reflectively*) I was out scratching for a buck
when you students were rebelling and letting it
all hang out. Maybe it's my turn now.

LIZ: Students had no real voice. That was a cry for
significance.

DERMOT: Is this any different? What voice have
the people around here? What choice do they
have?

LIZ: (*Shudders*) There's something about Joe
Martin … That blustering facade… And
behind that something more sinister … He
scares me.

DERMOT: (*Sarcastically*) He's supposed to be a
charmer. Didn't work for you, Huh?

LIZ: I might ask you about May.

DERMOT: God, she must have an awful life with
Seosamh.

LIZ: Mmmm … Not what I meant … Why doesn't
she leave him?

DERMOT: It's not so easy. Custom … She's three
kids. Where would she go?

LIZ: The Martins must have some redeeming
qualities.

DERMOT: Joe probably started out well-meaning
enough. But he's too dug in now, too used to

running the show ... To be ousted now would
be like death to him.

LIZ: Then he's going to fight ... I don't know where
it will end...

DERMOT: (*Places an arm around her shoulders.*)
Neither do I, but we've got to see it through.
There's too much at stake.

LIZ: I know ... By the way was that your Dad who
slipped in to the back of the hall?

DERMOT: Yes. He didn't want to be on the podium
... Now let's hit the campaign trail and press
the flesh. I've got a group of campaigners
together ... Then we'll call on Dad and show
you the old homestead or what's left of it.
(*She puts her arms around him. They stand for
a while.*)

Lights down.

End of ACT ONE

ACT TWO

SCENE ONE

The melody of 'Mise Éire', played on the Pan Flute. At the end of the piece the sound of a burglar alarm mingles eerily with the music. Then all sound ends and the lights come on to reveal another function room in the hotel. The furniture is much the same, though arranged differently. JOE, SEOSAMH *and* SADIE *are present. Discarded newspapers are strewn on one of the tables.*

JOE: (*Switches off a TV set and begins to pace*) I don't know … I just don't know. These last few days have been a right pain in the arse.

SEOSAMH: You said it was safe.

JOE: There are no safe seats anymore. Voting patterns are breaking down. And now we have Dermot Dolan on top of that. I was on to the party yesterday. The Minister is on her way. Damage limitation, she calls it … And for Christ's sake, sober up. I can't cover for you

anymore. Don't you know what's involved
… ?

SEOSAMH: May has me demented … I dunno …
That woman is getting very odd.

JOE: (*Gives him a withering look*) Sadie, you took a
straw poll. How bad is Dolan going to hurt us?

SADIE: A lot of the floaters are kind of … intrigued
by him. That one-term idea of his seems to
have … struck a chord. Even the Dublin papers
ran with that, as you know … as well as his
self-help approach. One of the journalists went
on about mould-breaking … said he would
make a good T.D. … Even a Minister…

JOE: That's all Dublin Four shit … What about
here, on the ground?

SADIE: I wouldn't write him off. There's a bit of a
groundswell starting … He's been going
around asking the punters how they think
emigrants would vote, if they had the vote…

JOE: That's all we need … And the polls are saying
the Party won't get an absolute majority in the
General Election … We have to put a stop to
his gallop … Trouble is we don't know too
much about him. He's been out there in
Chicago, away from it all … We have to hit
him where it hurts … What would you say is
his strong suit?

SADIE: (*Dissembling*) It's … it's hard to say…

SEOSAMH: He's a successful businessman.

JOE: (*Reflectively*) Yeah but that's not … Wait a
minute … This thing about employment … the
image of him being a great employer …

Suppose a dent could be put in that?

SEOSAMH: Like he really doesn't employ that many at all?

JOE: No. He's given those audited accounts to the hacks ... (*Slowly*) Suppose, over there in Chicago, he pays non-union rates ... below the minimum wage. We could run that in the paper for starters.

SADIE: But it's not true.

JOE: There are ways of putting it ... hints. You know the sort of thing. Remember the stuff we concocted about Sean and a couple of his young female campaigners...?

SADIE: I was never happy about that...

JOE: It was just innuendo ... So let's try this low-wage thing...

SEOSAMH: Yeah, it would put him on the back foot. Once you start having to deny something like that you're on the run.

JOE: Of course we need something more than that. A clincher ... But that'll do for now. See to it, Sadie...

(*Flashing lights and the whirring sounds of rotor arms indicate that a helicopter has landed on the roof.*)

JOE: The Minister descends on us from the heavens. Leave the talking to me. I wonder if our great mistress has anything to offer.

SADIE: I didn't know she was coming in a helicopter.

JOE: They'll all be using them in the General Election. The Mercs don't cover the ground fast enough. I remember when we all went around on bikes ... Where do you think our taxes go?

SEOSAMH: Fair point.

(*Enter Minister, a middle-aged woman, well-dressed and groomed.*)

JOE: Ah, Bev, glad you could make it.

MINISTER: I haven't much time, Joe. (*Nods towards* SADIE *and* SEOSAMH.)

SADIE: Good to see you, Minister.

SEOSAMH: Minister.

JOE: We won't hold you. But we have a problem here.

MINISTER: (*Bustling*) So I've heard. We were counting on you, Joe, for two seats, three if possible. We assumed you had the two nailed down. We could always count on you in the past. You know how important it is for the Party to hold its own in these local elections.

JOE: Yeah, we delivered in the past. But we need a hand now. Dermot Dolan's pissed in the well.

MINISTER: Can't you handle it, Joe? We've enough problems. You know the polls as well as I do. Any local losses could push the backbenchers over the edge. The Party isn't as strong as it used to be. If there was a vote of no confidence we could be fucked.

JOE: I've taken care of business in the past ... without making too many demands on the Party. But what has Dublin done for the region? The local hospital is a joke, the roads are falling apart; it's harder than ever to get the dole for people. We can't keep it together on promises.

MINISTER: You did before.

JOE: But you have to deliver some time. You know what we need…

MINISTER: Ah, your famous laundry list. We can't *designate* the town for the Special Development Scheme. You missed the boat on that one.

JOE: Look, even if it got out, what's the worst that could happen? An inquiry. Some fat-arsed judge would write a report in ten years' time and no one would be named or shamed. It's not a problem.

MINISTER: I'm not afraid of inquiries … But you can't see the bigger picture. It's not just the backbenchers but the rag-tag Independents all crying foul…

SEOSAMH: Would you care for a drink, Minister?

MINISTER: No thanks … We got you that chipboard factory.

JOE: (*Plaintively*) That was two elections ago.

MINISTER: As I recall you also got grants for new machinery.

JOE: So…?

MINISTER: The machinery wasn't new, was it, Joe?

JOE: That's water under the bridge.

MINISTER: (*Magnanimously*) I'm not here to argue … there isn't time. But we've looked after you well … Rezoning, sub-contracts, lottery funds…

JOE: I've done a lot for the Party ... organised fund-raisers and other contributions. Personal cheques too. It's a two-way street, Bev.

MINISTER: Have you done enough to keep the backbenchers in line? They could bring down the Government ... Or mount a leadership challenge ... If we don't do well in the local elections they could get very Bolshie ... OK, bottom line. Have you a better candidate than Seosamh here?

SEOSAMH: Hey! Wait a minute...

MINISTER: No offence, Seosamh. You're young enough to have another chance ... The Toyota distributorship is going well, I hear?

JOE: (*Angrily*) No one pushes him out. Christ Almighty, I can't believe my ears. If he stands down so do I. Where will the Party be then?

MINISTER: You're bluffing, Joe. For fuck's sake you couldn't give it up if your life depended on it ... and neither could I.

JOE: There's no one else. That's final.

MINISTER: Nothing's final in this game.

JOE: Remember one thing. I know about those personal cheques that were meant for the North...

SADIE: (*Nervously*) Maybe I'd better leave...

JOE: You stay here.

MINISTER: I don't take kindly to threats! No one breaks ranks. You do not do that. You said it yourself, it's a two-way street. Teamwork, Joe, teamwork.

JOE: Well, don't push it then. Let the fucking hare

sit.

MINISTER: Tell me then, how do we get this lad of
yours onto the Council ?

JOE: We'll find a way. You can help by coming to
the public meeting tonight, and saying a few
words about our record in public life. Give
Seosamh a boost...

MINISTER: That's what I'm here for. I've another
meeting first. (*Sighs*) There's just no let up. All
right, Joe, I'll be back in time for your gig but I
want a full hall and an important arse on every
seat. This is a one-off. There'll be no second
bite of the cherry.

JOE: (*Sarcastically*) It shall be so ordered.
(*Minister exits.*)

SEOSAMH: She was prepared to hang me out to
dry. Who the fuck does she think she is?

JOE: A Minister of course. Oh, grow up Seosamh.
It's a tough trade. No one counts as an
individual. We're just bees in a hive. You don't
exist without a Party, or without votes. Sadie,
are all the arrangements made for tonight?

SADIE: Everything's ready.

JOE: You'd better beat the bushes once more. She
thinks her divine presence will pull the
chestnuts out of the fire. I'm not so sure...
(*They listen to the sound of a helicopter taking
off.*)
I remember when she went around in a
clapped-out Volkswagen selling insurance...

SEOSAMH: Don't forget, we need that clincher to
nail Dolan.

JOE: We'll work on that … Look, you lay off the drink, for God's sake. Sadie, put him on that Antabuse stuff again.

SEOSAMH: I don't need that…

JOE: Do it.

SADIE: I'll need a prescription … It's risky stuff.

JOE: Do I have to handle everything myself? Get Doctor Morrissey on it. Now. And don't forget that newspaper piece on Dolan.
(SADIE *exits*.)

SEOSAMH: You treat me like shit in front of everyone.

JOE: I kept you on the ticket. That's the main thing. What more do you want?

SEOSAMH: To be my own … man … To be … You wouldn't understand…

JOE: (*Relenting*) Maybe I would … In this racket you have to be all things to all men. Sometimes you have to swallow your pride and do what's necessary. Take that deal with the Minister … She wants me to help calm the back benches, but she didn't level with me. She wants to calm things until she's ready to make a heave for the leadership … She doesn't think I know that … But I'll play my part anyway. We're all actors. We do what we're told; we *become* what we're told … You think power is freedom? It's a drug … Most of the time I'd probably hate myself … if I knew who that self was. But I don't know, so I go on…

SEOSAMH: Why did you get into it in the first place?

JOE: I honestly don't know. My father maybe ...
I'm not sure.

SEOSAMH: You were out all the time ... I ... we
thought the family wasn't enough for you...

JOE: Well, that's enough of that ... Anyway, there
are compensations. The point is you make your
choice.

SEOSAMH: I never made that choice.

JOE: What're you saying? You're not interested?

SEOSAMH: No ... I'm not saying that...

JOE: What else could you have done?

SEOSAMH: I don't know...

JOE: There you are then.

SEOSAMH: I never had the chance to make up my
own mind.

JOE: You're thirty-seven ... You never had a
chance to because you were too busy drinking.

SEOSAMH: OK, leave it ... I'm going home.
(SEOSAMH *exits.* JOE *writes a note in his
smart phone which he then puts back into an
inside pocket.*)

Lights down.

SCENE TWO

The hotel suite. DERMOT *and* LIZ *are ushering out a number of campaign-workers, journalists and cameramen. Placards and posters litter the suite.*

DERMOT: Thanks again for the coverage. And for the posters. If you need any more copy just call me. You all have my card. Many thanks... (DERMOT *closes the door behind them and he and* LIZ *gravitate towards the window.*)

LIZ: There's a lot of excitement down there. Not long to go of course. (*She closes the window to shut out the sound of loudspeakers.*)

DERMOT: The day of reckoning draws nigh.

LIZ: We'll have to put in a special effort tomorrow. It's the last opportunity. I don't know how much damage was done by that smear about low wages.

DERMOT: I can't believe Sadie allowed that into the paper.

LIZ: I'm not so surprised. And it's not the first time ... she didn't do Sean any favours either...

DERMOT: She has a conflict of interest ...
Anyway, I've rebutted it as best I can so maybe the voters won't set too much store by it.

LIZ: We should still get out there and do what we can in the time that's left. Suppose you lose by only a handful of votes you'd never forgive yourself for not campaigning up till the last minute. Oh God, what a horrible thought. Tell me I'm not being obsessive.

DERMOT: I know what you mean. It sort of gets to you. The campaigning itself isn't bad though.

LIZ: No. Nice people. They deserve the best. And you know something? I think they like you. And they obviously like your Dad.

DERMOT: *You* certainly wowed them. I don't think they're used to wives on the campaign trail ... Strange business though, asking for votes. It keeps you humble. Maybe that's the point.

LIZ: Except the humility doesn't usually last long. It quickly turns into its opposite.

DERMOT: I found myself using the old stock phrases like, 'You won't forget me now' and 'You'll keep me in mind'. The one I didn't use was, 'Sure, I knew your father'. There are only a few phrases you can use ... You'd think there'd be more since it is the national pastime.

LIZ: Pastime or blood-sport? Anyway, I'm bushed.

DERMOT: It's hard work, trying to be popular. You have to admire politicians in a way.

LIZ: Come on. They don't see it like that. They're all too thick-skinned .

DERMOT: Dad was a great help on the doorsteps ... You know, I think the canvass went well enough.

LIZ: Do I detect a note of confidence?

DERMOT: That American positive thinking has to rub off some time ... And Liz...

LIZ: What?

DERMOT: I'm glad you rallied round. You had me worried there for a while.

LIZ: It was the Martins. But once we got out and about and met people it was like a breath of fresh air.

DERMOT: I'm glad ... By the way, I think we should visit my mother's grave tomorrow ... Somehow I feel we should do that before the poll booths open...

LIZ: (*Moves close to him.*) Did I ever tell you that I find superstition a big turn-on.

DERMOT: As long as you don't expect a night of unbridled passion. This canvassing has me whacked out.

LIZ: (*Takes him by the hand*) Maybe we can work something out...

(*A knock sounds on the door. DERMOT and LIZ exchange startled glances. DERMOT answers the door. SADIE rushes in.*)

SADIE: Did you hear? Seosamh's in hospital.

LIZ: What happened?

SADIE: The official line is food poisoning. But the truth is he drank on top of Antabuse. He passed out at mass, in full view...

DERMOT: Antabuse? Is it serious?

SADIE: He'll recover in time. But politically, he's in trouble...

DERMOT: Why are you telling us, Sadie? Why compromise yourself ... ?

SADIE: I'm not. I'm throwing in with you.

LIZ: (*Suspiciously*) Oh really?

DERMOT: Joe Martin won't let you away with it. He'll exact a price.

SADIE: That's the whole point isn't it? I have to stand up some time. Now is as good a time as any. Things have to change around here. I'm sick of it all. I'm … sorry about that smear in the paper. I'm going to retract it tomorrow…

LIZ: Will you publish the real reason behind Seosamh's 'illness'?

DERMOT: Don't ask her to do that, Liz. Her job…

SADIE: I'm going to do it anyway … My guess is that things are fairly close. This will give you the edge.

LIZ: Surely it would disqualify Seosamh. He's not a fit and proper person to hold public office. If he was on Antabuse it means he's an alcoholic.

SADIE: (*Grinning*) If we disqualified all the soaks we wouldn't have a Government. People don't expect too much of their representatives.

DERMOT: Joe Martin will come down hard on you.

SADIE: I used to be a good journalist … Once … Believe it or not. I'd like to feel what it's like again. I'm doing it for me.

DERMOT: It's risky.

SADIE: Risk … We're all so afraid of it. Everything is so safe and cushy … We all back certainties, so no one wins. And everybody loses.

DERMOT: I'm not sure I'd want to win this way … Seosamh is sick…

LIZ: (*Sharply*) For God's sake, Dermot, it's his own

fault. Don't go all bleeding heart now. Take the edge. What would the Martins do if the situation were reversed? They'd milk it for all it was worth.

DERMOT: Go for it? The American way.

LIZ: Right. And what's wrong with that? Especially when you want to do something constructive.

SADIE: I've never fully understood what drives politicians...

LIZ: The roar of the crowd ... Strong medicine for insecure people.

SADIE: Joe Martin insecure?

LIZ: See how well he disguises it! What was he like when he was Seosamh's age I wonder?

SADIE: The apple doesn't fall far from the tree? That's rich ... So, the last round-up tomorrow. You should get out and about early. There are still a lot of floaters who can be swayed. Can I offer a word of advice?

DERMOT: Of course.

SADIE: Don't mention anything about Seosamh.

LIZ: Why not? The people should know the truth.

SADIE: They will know. Trust me. But if Dermot refers to his drinking it would give the impression of crowing over him. That wouldn't wash. Around here, you don't kick a man when he's down. You mustn't come across as superior in any way.

LIZ: Curiouser and curiouser.

SADIE: Believe me. I think Dermot knows this too. And another thing...

DERMOT: What?

SADIE: If you don't mind my saying so, I think your campaign so far has been a little … highbrow. The worst sin of all is to come across as too smart … If I were you I'd spend all day tomorrow just chatting and chewing the fat. No more policy stuff … you're just being one of the lads…

LIZ: I've heard everything now. Back home we'd give our right arms for a candidate who *could* chew gum and walk a straight line at the same time.

SADIE: (*Laughing*) Here we prefer the common man.

DERMOT: Not a gobshite, I hope.

SADIE: Not quite as common as that.

LIZ: Isn't that a little disingenuous? What about the good old honesty ticket?

SADIE: You can't change the situation overnight. Besides … there's been a whispering campaign by the Martins.

DERMOT: Like what?

SADIE: To the effect that you're some kind of eccentric conducting an experiment with people's lives. Remember that movie, 'Trading Places'?

LIZ: Those bastards. We'll be out at dawn to scotch that.

SADIE: Good … And good luck. Well, back to the presses…

(SADIE *exits.*)

LIZ: (*Pouring a Ballygowan*) Is she on the level?

DERMOT: Who, Sadie? Of course she is. She apologised for her part in undermining Sean.

And she's going to retract the low-wage smear tomorrow. She's changed...

LIZ: Talk about Protean characters. It's all sleight of hand ... now you see her, now you don't. Who can you trust ... Or when?

DERMOT: I'm here.

LIZ: You don't count.

DERMOT: (*Musing*) It was a pity about the old homestead ... I didn't realise they'd pulled it down. I should have known. They even levelled the hill we could see out the kitchen window ... There were hazel trees and a stream where we used to get fresh water ... All gone, razed to the ground...

LIZ: I'm sorry.

DERMOT: Not even a trace ... Nothing. It's as if it never existed ... They obliterated it. Standing there, I felt ... homeless. Stupid isn't it? Dumb ... It reminded me of the time I met you first. I felt so dumb, not at all the accomplished Jewish boy your parents wanted for their gifted daughter.

LIZ: I was terrified of your father.

DERMOT: But he liked you on sight.

LIZ: You could have fooled me. He gave me a real grilling.

DERMOT: (*Smiling*) That he did.

LIZ: We diaspora have to stick together.

DERMOT: Yes, we do ... We start from scratch and build together...

LIZ: It was exciting, Dermot. Still is.

DERMOT: No regrets?

LIZ: Absolutely not. (*Takes his hand.*)

Lights down.

SCENE THREE

Hotel function room. JOE, SADIE *and the* MINISTER *are seated, grim-faced.*

MINISTER: My God Almighty, that son of yours. In a detox ward. Two days after my speech. I praised him to the skies. Upright and diligent, I said. Devoted to public service, I said … And now he's in a wet brain ward having his fucking stomach pumped. Jesus Christ. That food-poisoning yarn better do the trick. You're losing it, Joe. Maybe there was a time when drink was acceptable. But not anymore … And not the way he puts it away … You told me there wasn't an alternative candidate. You said in this very room we couldn't do better than Seosamh.

JOE: (*Bristling*) And we can't. The Party hasn't done much to foster or bring on…

MINISTER: What?

JOE: Nothing … nothing.

MINISTER: Goddammit, we might as well pack up and go home if that's the case. Maybe the Party is short on talent now. But not that short, surely to Christ. You worry me, Joe. You've lost your objectivity. I have a family too but the Party comes first. You know that.

JOE: (*Bitterly*) So if you were me you'd have

thrown your son to the wolves?

MINISTER: Don't be so dramatic. I'd have put him off the ticket. Of course I would.

JOE: Well, you're not me ... Look, what else can Seosamh do...?

MINISTER: You're really bringing a tear to my eye now. He's got two businesses, hasn't he?

JOE: What good would they be if he didn't have political connections? What about our name in the town ... ?

MINISTER: I'm not going to pursue this further. There's no time.

JOE: Look, we can get a doctor to verify the food-poisoning story in tomorrow's edition ... Sadie, you see to that...

SADIE: I can't...

JOE: What do you mean, 'can't' ... ?

SADIE: Tomorrow's paper will carry the true story. There'll also be a retraction of the union smear.

JOE: Wha-a-at ... ?

SADIE: You heard me.

JOE: Which journalist is responsible...?

SADIE: I am.

JOE: Have you lost your fucking marbles...?

SADIE: Maybe ... But found a conscience...

JOE: Don't retract anything!

SADIE: Too late. The copy's gone in.

JOE: Jesus Christ, I trusted you ... gave you editorial responsibility...

SADIE: Because I was a lap dog, a paid stooge. The paper's become a propaganda sheet. I didn't fully realise that until recently.

MINISTER: (*Darkly*):You've lost control, Joe. I
    knew it.

JOE: (*To* SADIE) Be in my office later. Get out of
    here. Now!

SADIE: I'm glad. My breakfast was coming up …
    And I won't be in your office later.

JOE: You're resigning then.

SADIE: I'm not. Who resigns in this country?
    Besides, I could do with redundancy money.
    You'll have to fire me. I may even sue for
    unfair dismissal. Think of the publicity…

JOE: Go on, fuck off out of it. Just fuck off.

SADIE: May I offer you the same advice.
    (SADIE *exits.*)

MINISTER: Well, that says it all! After the effort
    I've put in … At the expense of other
    constituencies, I might add. Now this. It
    couldn't be worse … It – could – not – be –
    worse. You've put us over a barrel.

JOE: (*Uncertainly*) There's still a day left. (*Looks
    hard at* MINISTER.) We've been in tight spots
    before.

MINISTER: I hate this. I hate it. You've backed me
    up to the cross, do you know that? Have you
    any appreciation of the cost involved?

JOE: (*Eyeing her closely*) You've a fall-back
    position, Bev. You must have discussed this at
    cabinet.

MINISTER: You reckon?

JOE: (*Softly*) Yes. You've never been out-
    manoeuvred in your life.

MINISTER: (*Hesitates*) Suppose there was

something…?

JOE: Yes?

MINISTER: Would you sort out the backbenchers from this neck of the woods?

JOE: There are a few of them ready to cut and run. They can be sorted out.

MINISTER: Action, Joe. Not just promises.

JOE: Yes. Yes. Come on, what've you got?

MINISTER: OK, But this sickens me. The political capital we're going to have to spend on one or two lousy local seats. It's such a fucking waste.

JOE: What is it? The hospital … an advance factory … ?

MINISTER: Your laundry list again … ? Forget it.

JOE: Then what … what's the deal? You're not thinking … what I'm thinking…?

MINISTER: (*Sarcastically*) Great minds…

JOE: Say it … It's designation isn't it … for this region…?

MINISTER: No it's not designation. I told you before, that scheme got us into trouble with Brussels…

JOE: Those bloody Mandarins … So what is it?

MINISTER: Decentralisation…

JOE: Decentralisation? Jesus, that's almost as good. (*Makes a triumphant fist.*) Talk about silver linings … Bev, I never doubted you. Is it a whole Department…?

MINISTER: (*Gruffly*) Half … I suppose that's not enough for you…

JOE: How many civil servants?

MINISTER: Eight hundred, give or take … We're

going to have to promote a lot of them to get them to move down here.

JOE: Fantastic! Think of the effect on house prices alone ... And they said there was no God ... Eight hundred salaries, fuck me!

MINISTER: You'll owe us for this, Joe. The backbenchers, remember. And also later on if there's a Leadership heave ... Do you catch my drift?

JOE: A nod is as good as a wink ... Decentralisation ... I still can't believe it. We'll have to get this out on the wires fast. First thing tomorrow morning. Press, radio ... National as well...

MINISTER: Tonight. Now. Get the hacks out of the pubs. There's no time to lose...

JOE: (*Hesitates*) Wait a sec ... Is there a risk ... Will it come across as a stroke ... ?

MINISTER: So what if it does? There's no problem as long as it's a good stroke ... And this is the best.

JOE: (*Relieved*) You're right ... as usual.

MINISTER: Your squeaky wheel gets the oil again this time, Joe. But never again. Do you understand? Never again.

JOE: It'll be a good investment all round. You'll see. You won't regret it. And neither will I. It'll sort out fucking Dolan and his pushy wife. Shake on it.

(*They shake hands, the* MINISTER *somewhat reluctantly.*)

Lights down.

SCENE FOUR

The Hotel Suite. Morning. Melody of 'Carrickfergus' on the Pan flute. DERMOT *and* SADIE *are standing by the window.* DAD *is seated.* LIZ *enters from the bedroom, looks at them for a while, then approaches* DERMOT. *He turns to face her.*

DERMOT: (*Reflectively*) It seems so long ago since we came here, that first night. Remember?

LIZ: Ages.

DERMOT: (*Sighs.*) Anyway it's all over bar the shouting.

LIZ: You tried, Dermot.

SADIE: You ran them close enough too. Given what you were up against, it was a great performance.

DERMOT: Thanks, Sadie, but no thanks. I lost.

SADIE: There' s such a thing as a moral victory...

DERMOT: I know you mean well...

LIZ: I agree with Sadie. Absolutely...
    (*She collects some sweaters and puts them in a suitcase.*)

DAD: You ran a great campaign. Your press conference that first night was excellent. It made people think. Maybe for the first time.

DERMOT: You should have come up to the podium.

DAD: No, it was your show. And you certainly

didn't need any help from me.

SADIE: What could you have done, Dermot? The town promised most of a Government Department by the Martins. It was the ultimate in auction politics. Better than goodies flooding in from Brussels ... This was the clincher the Martins needed.

DAD: Yeah, the fix was in.

DERMOT: Has anything really changed? Plots instead of plans. The blind man's cup ... No action ... only reaction. Business as usual ... I contributed nothing.

SADIE: How can you say that? If it wasn't for you the town wouldn't have received any largesse ... O.K., it was happenstance to some extent but you were the catalyst. You should feel good about that?

DERMOT: No, I don't. Where's the self-reliance, the spark of accomplishing things? What will these hand-outs do for people's self-respect, their sense of self? They must know that some other, poorer region has been deprived so as to benefit them ... And the Martin dynasty is consolidated ... What happens in three years' time ... five years ... ?

SADIE: I don't know. Maybe the future takes care of itself. (*Sarcastically*) Maybe we'll discover oil...

DERMOT: Shouldn't we try to plan our future?

LIZ: And the past? (*She closes a suitcase.*)

DERMOT: The past determines us.

DAD: But you have to outgrow it. Sometimes it has to be wiped out, like the house you grew up in.

Like the memory of ... (*Stops abruptly.*)

DERMOT: Who? Whose memory...?

(DAD *lapses into silence.*)

LIZ: Sadie, how are you fixed ... personally, I
mean. After your...

SADIE: Oh, my little act of sabotage will soon be
forgiven. I haven't enough clout to cause real
damage. Besides, Joe Martin can't do enough
for everyone now with all this manna about to
rain down. He has the wherewithal at last ...
everything in his gift. Decentralisation was one
of his dreams and he's realised it. His craft will
be the first to bob up on the rising tide. And he
has all the time in the world to hand the tiller
over to Seosamh who will probably be elected
to the Dáil in a few years. And then when he
screws up there they'll put him in the Senate or
send him off to Europe.

LIZ: I'll bet. And they'll go on and on, that double
act. The closed shop forever closed.

DERMOT: (*Self-deprecatingly*) Was it for this the
wild geese fled and spread the grey wing upon
the tide? The rising tide ... Sadie, come out to
Chicago sometime. Better still, come for good.
Think about it.

SADIE: Thanks. But I don't know ... Bit long in the
tooth now ... stuck in the old ways...

LIZ: We have electric blankets out there, you know.

SADIE: (*Smiles*) I think I'll just soldier on here ...
Who knows, I might be able to make sure the
Government Department doesn't buy this
hotel, or a site from Joe Martin. I might go to

Cork … I have a few friends there.

DERMOT: Thanks for all your help. You risked a lot.

SADIE: Not really … You gave me the chance to redeem myself for … and to make my little protest. I feel the better of it … even if it didn't come to anything … Will you write sometime, or call?

LIZ: Of course. (*She embraces her.*)

SADIE: It was good while it lasted … It was good… (*Shakes hands with* DERMOT, *then they embrace briefly.*)

DERMOT: Keep the faith, Sadie.

DAD: Good luck.

(SADIE *exits hurriedly.*)

LIZ: How do you feel?

DERMOT: Drained. Maybe the whole idea was daft, menopausal … I could never get a foothold here … Nor could my brother, Sean … Not then and not now. I don't fully understand … It's just not in the cards…

LIZ: Let it go, Dermot. We have our own life. Think of the children. We'll be meeting them in a couple of days … Remember when Dermot Junior was born? Up all night with colic in that small apartment in New York … And you were on the morning shift on those dreadful skyscrapers. We thought we'd never make it. Look at us now.

DERMOT: I don't know how you stood it back then, Liz…

LIZ: I had someone to lean on … and someone to

fight with too.

DERMOT: Yeah, we had some good rows. We really sparked off each other. Good sparks. Hustling our way through New York and Chicago. You know, I never felt like an outsider in those massive cities. Yet here, in this Godforsaken place, I feel like an outcast. It's as if I've spent my whole life hammering on a door that won't open.

LIZ: Maybe there's nothing inside.

DERMOT: But you have to find that out for yourself.

DAD: Yes, you do, but you can guess too. One of the reasons they won't open the door is because they're up to no good on the inside.

DERMOT: (*To* LIZ) Thank God for you and the kids ... Yes, it'll be a good reunion ... You won't be sorry to leave here.

LIZ: No ... it's funny though ... Ireland, the land of welcomes. And it is. But it only goes so far ... something's missing. There's a ... hollowness. Maybe what's missing are the millions who left. Those who stayed have to live with ghosts. Sometimes, on this trip, I thought you were so far away ... as if...

DERMOT: (*Startled*) As if what ... ?

LIZ: I'm not sure ... Some presence maybe. At first I thought it might have been May but she's real ... memories of Sean maybe...? (*Beat*)

DAD: (*Softly*) Why memories...? (*Pause*)

DERMOT: Why ... do you ask that...?

DAD: He's dead isn't he? (*Pause*)

(LIZ *sits*. DERMOT *looks away*.)

DAD: It's all right, son. You can tell me. Is Sean dead?

DERMOT: Yes, Dad…

DAD: Why did you keep it from me?

DERMOT: He asked me to just before…

DAD: Why?

DERMOT: He knew you had cancer and didn't want to worry you.

DAD: (*Shakily*) How did he die?

DERMOT: It was when he worked with me in Chicago … His office was on the seventh floor … I called in … He wasn't there … Then I saw the window was open…

DAD: Oh God…

DERMOT: He died in the ambulance … I was holding him…

DAD: Did he say why?

DERMOT: He said he didn't belong … anywhere…
(*Dad weeps quietly*. LIZ *and* DERMOT *sit beside him on the sofa*.)

LIZ: I'm so sorry…

DAD: Coming here … was for Sean as well … ?

DERMOT: (*Nods*) He stood up to the Martins … and lost … He had to leave … If he had stayed … he would still be alive … I thought I could somehow make it right for him … and for all the others who had to emigrate … But it was all fantasy … (*Sits crouched with bunched fists*) … The unknown emigrant… There should be a monument … (*Loudly*,) Jesus Christ, is there any country in the world that

treats its people with such contempt? The President used to light a candle in the window of her palace … a clever, pretty token… clever and cynical … There was never a greater insult. You know what's missing in this cosy, do-nothing country? Grief … grief and anger… (*He weeps.* LIZ *embraces him.* DAD *puts a hand on his shoulder.*)
(*Looks around*) This plush, ridiculous suite says it all. Comfort for the few left in the nest … no thought for those forced out … before they could fly … No thought at all. Maybe here, this place, right here, we are behind the closed door … and you're right. Dad, there's nothing here…

DAD: (*Weeping*) It all … makes sense … now. Jesus mercy…
(*A knock on the door upsets* DAD. DERMOT *leads him into a bedroom.* LIZ *opens the door.* MAY *enters.*)

MAY: I hope I'm not interrupting … I just wanted to say goodbye.

LIZ: That's kind of you, May … We're not fully packed yet … How is Seosamh?

MAY: Celebrating … non-stop … since the election…

LIZ: It must be hard for you.

MAY: You make your bed … The kids will soon be old enough to leave. That's the main thing.

LIZ: But if it's a … bad marriage maybe you should consider leaving too… Sorry, it's none of my business.

MAY: Oh, we tend to stand by the post, as they say. You adapt … yes, adapt. Anyway it's sad all round … I don't think people care too much about anything … There are times when I'd like to scream but there's just no point…

(DERMOT *enters from the bedroom.*)

DERMOT: (*Vacantly*) You know, at school we had a name for Seosamh … 'His Master's Voice', meaning that he always echoed his old man. It can't be easy for him … in Joe's shadow…

MAY: Believe it or not, there are times when I'm sorry for him … Sometimes when he's passed out I can see the pain in his face … But then the next morning … Well, enough of that…

DERMOT: I'm sorry, May.

MAY: Don't be. I don't want to be an object of … I don't want you to think of me … that way … For what it's worth, I think I understand what you tried to do, Dermot. It was a good idea. It should have worked. But it's too late.

DERMOT: What is it about this place? I thought I understood … Can you …?

MAY: I don't know … You left twenty years ago. And now you're leaving again.

DERMOT: Yes.

MAY: Can you explain it?

(DERMOT *shakes his head.*)

MAY: You won't be back?

DERMOT: There's no point.

MAY: Too bad.

(MAY *kisses him.* LIZ *watches fondly.* MAY *exits.*)

LIZ: She loves you.

DERMOT: We grew up together.

LIZ: You don't have to explain.

DERMOT: There's a street party down there in Maiden Lane.

(LIZ *opens a window to admit faint sounds of festivity, above which one voice can be heard singing a verse from 'Carrickfergus'.*)

VOICE: 'But the sea is high and I can-not swim o-o-ver,
Nor have I wings that I might fly...
I wish I could me-et a hand-some boat-man
To ferry me o-over to my love and die...'

(LIZ *closes the window.*)

DERMOT: Everything's different. Yet nothing's changed...

(LIZ *checks luggage and airline tickets etc. in her briefcase. DAD enters.*)

DERMOT: You have to come with us, Dad. There's nothing for you here...

LIZ: You must come...

DAD: No thanks ... I don't need much, son. I'll be all right here ... near your mother...

DERMOT: (*Shakily*) I ... I don't want to leave you again, Dad.

DAD: We have memories to keep us going ... You, Liz and the kids have your own lives to lead. We can keep in touch.

(TOM *enters, collects and removes the larger pieces of luggage.*)

DERMOT: This trip ... the election ... was it all just a game?

DAD: For some more than others. But not for you.

DERMOT: I'm sorry I failed.

DAD: Not by my rules, you didn't.

DERMOT: You set easy rules. Always did.

DAD: Only because you were hard enough on
    yourself ... Go on now ... Go home to your
    family.

DERMOT: (*Tearful*) I don't ... want to leave you ...
    again.

DAD: Go on, son. There's nothing for you here ...
    You must go ... Live a good life ... God go
    with you ... and with Sean ... (*They embrace.*)

DERMOT: Goodbye ... Dad...

    (*He wipes his eyes with the back of his hand.*)

LIZ: (*Gently*) Are you ready?

DERMOT: Yes...

    (*They look back as they near the door. DAD
    stands as they leave, then sits, very still, in the
    same position as in the opening scene. Sounds
    of 'Carrickfergus', played on the Pan Flute,
    grow in volume, gradually become discordant
    as the burglar alarm intrudes.*)

Lights fade slowly. All sound suddenly stops.

Lights down.

END

GET UP

A Play in Two Acts

CHARACTERS

DUNNE

> A former prison governor, wheelchair-bound due to phantom paralysis. Middle-aged. A member of the previous, now fallen, regime.

DR HOGAN

> A lesbian psychiatrist, fond of dancing. Middle-aged. Very ambitious. Works for the present regime.

MS. GRIBBON

> A nurse, wild, athletic, young. A good heart. Works for the present regime but keeps options open.

ASSISTANT ADMINISTRATOR / PRISONER 1

> Part of the present regime. Middle-aged.

AIDE / PRISONER 2

> Part of the present regime. Young.

PRISONER 3 ('MARKIE')

A poor man's Messiah. Truth-seeker. Young.

ACT ONE

SCENE ONE

Loud music – Verdi's 'Dies Irae'. The stage is dimly lit. There is a plain grey opaque backdrop. No props apart from a scaffold tower. After about ten seconds the music stops. There is a sudden unseen commotion and scream. A body falls from the flies and lands heavily on the apron of the stage. There is a period of silence, then groans, then silence again. The stage goes completely dark.

SCENE TWO

African drumming, loud at first then fades out. The lights come up slowly. DUNNE, *the man who has fallen, is lying in a hospital bed. He is comatose. Bending over him are* DR HOGAN *and* NURSE GRIBBON *They are dressed in dark suits and are very well groomed.*

DR HOGAN: I've seen worse, Nurse Gribbon.

NURSE GRIBBON: Me too, Doctor. Why have we been called in?

DR HOGAN: (*Nodding towards Dunne*) He must be important. Who called you? Not the Administrator?

NURSE GRIBBON: No. One of his assistants. But I understand he's going to meet us here today. The Assistant Administrator himself. In person … In this hospital room.

DR HOGAN: So I understand.

NURSE GRIBBON: I've seen him on TV. Have you met him?

DR HOGAN: No. He doesn't socialise much. Understandable I suppose.

NURSE GRIBBON: Yes. I'm sure he has a lot of enemies … from the previous regime…

DR HOGAN: Be quiet! … You mustn't say that … I think he's coming.

(A stocky well-dressed man enters from the right.

He is the ASSISTANT ADMINISTRATOR*'s*
AIDE. *He 'sweeps' the room and frisks* HOGAN
and GRIBBON. *He goes to the door.*)

AIDE: All clear, Sir.

(*The* ASSISTANT ADMINISTRATOR, *very
formally dressed, enters.*)

ASSTNT ADMINISTRATOR: Good morning. You
must be Dr Hogan and you Nurse Gribbon. (*He
shakes their hands.*)

DR HOGAN: (*Nervously*) You must be … the…

ASSTNT ADMINISTRATOR: I'm the Assistant
Administrator. The Administrator has been
called away on urgent business. But he has
briefed me on the matter in hand. Our patient
here, Mr Dunne, suffered a bad fall but I'm
told there is little physical damage.

DR HOGAN: Nevertheless, he appears to be in a
coma.

ASSTNT ADMINISTRATOR: It is unusual, Dr
Hogan, but apparently not unknown. That's
one reason why your … em … alternative
psychiatric skills may be needed. As well as
the special talents of Nurse Gribbon.

NURSE GRIBBON: We aim to please … and serve.

DR HOGAN: As I'm sure you know, we're very
busy these days since the … Upheaval. With
your permission … I would like to ask why Mr
Dunne merits such special treatment…?
Wasn't he part of the previous … regime?

ASSTNT ADMINISTRATOR: I knew him … in
different circumstances. All you need to know
is that he is important to us. It is your job to

restore him to health ... physical and mental health.

DR HOGAN: But ... well, yes ... I see.

ASSTNT ADMINISTRATOR: Any other questions?

NURSE GRIBBON: (*Nervously*) I would like ... to ask about the new system of incentives...

ASSTNT ADMINISTRATOR: This will apply in full, Nurse Gribbon. If you restore Mr. Dunne to health you will be well rewarded. This Administration appreciates its friends.

NURSE GRIBBON: Excellent. Thank you, Sir.

(DR HOGAN *bends over* DUNNE)

ASSTNT ADMINISTRATOR: Did he say anything?

DR HOGAN: No.

ASSTNT ADMINISTRATOR: Do you recognise him?

DR HOGAN: No. Should I?

ASSTNT ADMINISTRATOR: Not really. (*He picks up a file from the bedside table and hands it to* DR HOGAN.) These are the Consultant's notes. Good luck with the case. I will personally review progress. So we'll be in touch.

DR HOGAN: (*Deferentially*) Thank you, Assistant Administrator. We will give this case our full attention.

NURSE GRIBBON: And more. All the stops shall be pulled out.

ASSTNT ADMINISTRATOR: We are depending on you.

DR HOGAN: We won't let you down.

ASSTNT ADMINISTRATOR: Good … You may go.

> (DR HOGAN *and* NURSE GRIBBON *exit right. The* ASSISTANT ADMINISTRATOR *stands over Dunne with an expression of loathing. He makes a fist and then unclenches it. His* AIDE *spits on Dunne's face.*)

AIDE: I could do the fucker right now…!

ASSTNT ADMINISTRATOR: No, not now … But I know what you mean … He just loved playing the Liberal, didn't he. I think he got off on it … Well, look at him now!

AIDE: When will we have a chance like this again? (*He lifts up a pillow.*) We could say he slipped into a deeper coma and then just drifted away.

ASSTNT ADMINISTRATOR: Look, I have the same memories … But for some reason, the Administrator thinks Dunne can be a valuable asset…

AIDE: American renditions…?

ASSTNT ADMINISTRATOR: It might have some bearing … Take it easy for now. We'll see how it plays out…

Lights down.

SCENE THREE

African drumming, loud at first then fades out. The lights come up slowly to reveal DUNNE*'s home. A huge screen covers the back wall.* DUNNE *is seated in a motorised wheelchair. He is greying, paunchy and about forty. There is a red blanket over his knees. He is wearing a grey suit, white shirt and dark tie. He drinks from a polystyrene cup. A buzzer sounds.*

DUNNE: (*In exasperation*) Aaaagh!
> (*He drives the wheelchair towards an intercom on the wall near the hat stand and presses a button. He takes another sip from the cup, grimaces, drives the chair back towards the kitchen facilities and throws the contents of the cup into the sink.*)

DUNNE: Fuck it! They're here again ... right on time.
> (*Enter left* DR HOGAN, *carrying a black medical bag. She is dressed in a dark business suit. She places her hat carefully on the hat stand. She is followed by* NURSE GRIBBON *in a tight-fitting track suit. She also has a medical bag, light brown in colour.*)

DR HOGAN: May we?

DUNNE: If you must.

DR HOGAN: (*Sits, places bag on the table*) Good to see you again, Mr Dunne.

NURSE GRIBBON: How are we today?

DUNNE: We are still paralysed Nurse Gribbon.

NURSE GRIBBON: (*Sympathetically*) Oeuuuuuu … (*She walks over to the parallel bars and does some ballet exercises.*)

DR HOGAN: Mr Dunne, we've been over this before…

DUNNE: No doubt about that…

DR HOGAN: Why not accept it?

DUNNE: I do, Dr Hogan. I'm a cripple. The fall crippled me.

DR HOGAN: But you're not a cripple. (*Takes papers out of her bag.*)

DUNNE: Put those away.

DR HOGAN: The best consultants and even the Assistant Administrator say that it's…

DUNNE: Phantom paralysis!

DR HOGAN: For want of a better term, yes. Phantom paralysis. It's not unknown, especially after a trauma…

NURSE GRIBBON: Such as a fall.

DR HOGAN: Yes. A heavy fall. From a height … If you really want to walk again, you will. Gravity is not an enemy, Mr. Dunne … I've explained the visualisation techniques.

DUNNE: Visualise movement … exercises … sports.

DR HOGAN: Yes. Don't discount the power of imagination. It means 'seeing beyond'. We all need to do this to see what's possible, to bring about important changes ... You do want to walk again, don't you?

NURSE GRIBBON: You have to want it ... want it badly.

DUNNE: What do you think? Do you think I want to stay like this, destroyed?

DR HOGAN: You'd be surprised how many people expect the worst ... or fear success, and hope for failure. We can be quite perverse creatures at times...

DUNNE: Not me.

NURSE GRIBBON: Even so, negative thoughts can trickle in to the conscious mind....

DR HOGAN: Nurse Gribbon, please leave diagnosing to me. (*To Dunne*) Have you seen yellow yet?

DUNNE: (*With a withering look*) No ... no yellow...

DR HOGAN: We can choose to take control of our lives. Keep trying. Once you see yellow the process really begins. Yellow is the colour of Easter, new beginnings. The imagination will kick in at that stage ... Nurse Gribbon, why don't you prepare Mr Dunne's bath?

NURSE GRIBBON: Certainly, Doctor. I'll check the water temperature with my elbow. (*She dismounts the parallel bars and exits right.*)

DR HOGAN: Incidentally, Nurse Gribbon will stay with you ... to help out.

DUNNE: I can look after myself. I don't need her here.

DR HOGAN: You don't have a choice. She's

staying with you.

DUNNE: I can wipe my own…

DR HOGAN: Can you? Can you? (*She picks up her bag.*) I'll see you in a few days. Here.

DUNNE: I won't be anywhere else.

DR HOGAN: You know where the emergency button is. Under the left arm of the chair.

DUNNE: Yes. Yes. I'll press it if Nurse Gribbon attacks me in a fit of passion.

DR HOGAN: Good, you're using your imagination already … Remember … Yellow. The first sign. Yellow. The colour of rebirth, resurrection … risings…

DUNNE: Don't mention risings to me…

DR HOGAN: Why not? Rising is better than falling. Think about that.

(*She exits left, doing a couple of dance steps as she goes.*)

DUNNE: It all evens out in the end. Rising tide, ebbing tide … You could think about that. (DUNNE *drives around the room in some agitation. He loosens his collar to ease his breathing. He pours water into a polystyrene cup, drinks, wets his fingers, removes his glasses and draws wet fingers across his eyelids. Looks intently at the screen. Hits forehead in frustration. Replaces glasses.*)
(NURSE GRIBBON *enters right carrying a couple of towels.*)

NURSE GRIBBON: Has Dr Hogan left?

DUNNE: Look around.

NURSE GRIBBON: Your bath is ready. (*She begins*

to remove his clothing.)

DUNNE: I'm not a child!

NURSE GRIBBON: Don't take it out on me, you old goat … I didn't ask for this assignment.

DUNNE: (*To himself*) Have to get out of this jail. (*He stares hard at screen. He removes his glasses and massages his eyelids.*)

NURSE GRIBBON: Any yellow?

DUNNE: Don't keep asking me. It won't come if you keep asking me.

NURSE GRIBBON: OK. You sound like a child trying to pee … Bath now. (*She starts to push the wheelchair but he drives away from her. Both exit right. After a few seconds a faint yellow spot appears on the screen.*)

DUNNE: (*Off*) Aaaagh! The water's freezing! Mother of God…! Get that sponge out of there…!

NURSE GRIBBON: (*Off*) Oh stop whingeing … The regime of pampered morons is over. Haven't you heard? Stop that! You're splashing water all over me…!

The yellow spot fades out. Lights go down.

SCENE FOUR

Lights come up slowly. DUNNE *is on his own,
staring at the screen. He rubs his eyes, groans and
hammers the sides of the wheelchair in frustration.
He finally falls back exhausted. The yellow patch
begins to appear on screen – very faintly at first. He
leans forward eagerly, then with mounting
excitement. Some disjointed images begin to appear
on the screen and these gradually coalesce to form a
scene from 'Swan Lake' in black and white – with
music. A male ballet dancer can be seen leaping in
slow motion.* DUNNE *reaches towards the image,
his arms trembling.*

DUNNE: Yes! Yes! At last. Something…
(*The ballet images fade and are replaced by
footage of* NURSE GRIBBON *in a bikini,
dancing suggestively and beckoning him
towards her.* DR HOGAN *then appears on the
screen, looks censoriously at* DUNNE *and
banishes* NURSE GRIBBON *from view.*)
DUNNE: My God, what's going on? (*He drives
quickly to the kitchen area and pours himself a
stiff drink which he gulps down.* DR HOGAN
enters left. When DUNNE *turns around he is
startled to see her.*)
DUNNE: How did you get in?

DR HOGAN: (*Holds a key aloft*) The key to the kingdom.

DUNNE: I didn't agree to that.

DR HOGAN: So? You don't have any rights ... Your licenses have been revoked and won't be restored until you're on your feet.

DUNNE: Which means never. Many thanks.

DR HOGAN: See any yellow yet?

DUNNE: (*Reluctantly*) Yeah.

DR HOGAN: I can't hear you.

DUNNE: Yes. Yes! And some images. Black-and-white ones.

DR HOGAN: Movement?

DUNNE: Yes. Ballet. I don't know why. I'm not a fan. Instead of making them stand on their toes why don't they get taller people?

DR HOGAN: An ancient quip ... Still, any movement is better than none. Brain and body. (*Taps forehead.*) The old B and B. You should be able to control the images as you progress. Now that you've started it's important to continue. You must continue.

DUNNE: Why is it so important? Why am I getting all this attention?

DR HOGAN: Everyone gets the same nowadays...

DUNNE: Since the regime changed? I doubt that ... I think it's the opposite.

DR HOGAN: You must continue with the images ... for your own sake.

DUNNE: Well, it was you who just put a stop to it. (*Nods towards the screen.*) You appeared in it. Ruined everything.

DR HOGAN: Did Nurse Gribbon also 'appear', as you put it.

DUNNE: Mmm.

DR HOGAN: That might explain it.

DUNNE: What?

DR HOGAN: Guilt.

DUNNE: (*Carefully*) What have I to be guilty about?

DR HOGAN: You tell me. You ran a prison. Strange things happen in prison.

DUNNE: How do you know what I did...?

DR HOGAN: It's my job to know. And it was a Gulag, not just a prison.

DUNNE: You don't know what you're talking about ... Go to hell.

DR HOGAN: Which one? The one you've created for yourself?

(NURSE GRIBBON *enters right in her figure-hugging tracksuit. She crosses the stage, mounts the parallel bars and does quite a sophisticated routine.*)

DR HOGAN: (*Watching in admiration*) How has our patient been?

NURSE GRIBBON: He's reached the yellow stage. And some monochrome pictures. But he doesn't like cold water ... or a wet loofah in his nooks and crannies ... Or my lentil soup.

DR HOGAN: A Spartan regime is important. If he's to recover it must be hard-won. It's all about toughness, mental toughness. We all have our demons to conquer...

DUNNE: (*Shouting*) I'm paralysed, fucking

paralysed!

DR HOGAN: (*With infuriating smile*) No. Not at all.
You used the … am … opportunity of the fall
to cripple yourself. You chose not just to fall
according to the laws of gravity, but also to fall
from grace, and to stay fallen. You remain
among the fallen. But we can change that if we
all work together.

(NURSE GRIBBON *lowers the trapeze which
is attached to the scaffold tower, unhooks the
rope ladder and climbs up. She begins some
exercises on the trapeze.*)

DUNNE: (*Shouting*) Why would anyone who falls
want to stay fallen?

DR HOGAN: There are different kinds of fall. As a
prison Governor you would have seen inmates
fall in different ways. Suicide, attempted
suicide, cries for help. Some may have done
the pushing but fallen themselves…

DUNNE: Meaning?

DR HOGAN: Think about it. I believe you may
already know…

DUNNE: (*Uncertainly*) Upheavals can cause falls…

DR HOGAN: Yes, they can. For sure. But we often
contribute ourselves … to our own downfalls
… Downfall … odd word, isn't it…? No one
falls up … No, it's always down.

(*She picks an orange out of a bowl and lets it
fall. She repeats this three times.*)

This orange is being pulled down by the mass
of the entire earth and yet I can lift it up with
just one hand. Isn't that amazing? Gravity is a

very weak force but it is ubiquitous. Even birds can fall … I've seen them. There are other planets where gravity is ten times stronger. If you had fallen there you would have become a pancake. Not just a fall but a collapse … a catastrophe … Like the Fall of Adam … Consider yourself lucky…

DUNNE: Yeah, life is a long series of ups and downs. But maybe nothing really changes. The peasants still break rocks…

(NURSE GRIBBON *dismounts the trapeze, bends her knees as if falling, then straightens up abruptly, flinging her arms in the air. She sits sprawling in one of the chairs.*)

DR HOGAN: (*To* NURSE GRIBBON) Good dismount! Not even a wobble … And now I must away to do my statutory two hours in the official gym. But first, a fitness-twirl…

(*She opens her arms and* NURSE GRIBBON *glides into them. They do several steps of a Samba to loud music. They look at* DUNNE *as if taunting him with their power of movement. Still dancing, they both exit left.* DUNNE *drives the chair back and forth in an agitated way. With great determination he stares at the screen. He cranes forward gouging his eyes, willing something to happen. But no colour or images appear. He cries out in frustration.*)

DUNNE: Aaaah! Aaaaah! Come on! Aaaah!

Lights down.

SCENE FIVE

DUNNE *is staring at the screen.* NURSE
GRIBBON *is sitting on the trapeze swinging slowly.*
DR HOGAN *is rummaging in her medical bag.*

NURSE GRIBBON: No, not too many bonus points
    going here, by the looks of things.
DR HOGAN: We're not finished yet … Actually,
    we haven't really started.
NURSE GRIBBON: I need to buy things … and the
    cost of living is soaring as we speak.
DUNNE: I'm sure you make a good living out of
    what you do … all this bullshit…
    (DR HOGAN *advances menacingly towards*
    him. NURSE GRIBBON *dismounts and throws*
    her towel over the cctv camera. Without any
    warning DR HOGAN *slaps Dunne hard across*
    the face.)
DUNNE: What the fuck … !
DR HOGAN: What? I shouldn't hit a cripple?
    You're not one. So why don't you hit me back?
    You've seen prisoners slap their bitches. See.
    (*Slaps him again.*) You don't rate a punch.
    Punches are for men.
DUNNE: I-I-I-I'll report you … you lousy…!
    (NURSE GRIBBON *comes over to watch the*
    action. She appears uncomfortable.)
DR HOGAN: To whom? To whom will you report

me?

DUNNE: The new regime ... the leaders of our new republic ... if that's not a contradiction in terms.

DR HOGAN: But you don't know them. Anyway, don't you think they've already witnessed that little act of necessary chastisement...?

DUNNE: How could they? ... What are you implying?

DR.HOGAN: They like to be informed at all times...

DUNNE: Bugs...? Oh Christ. That's the last straw.

DR HOGAN: So, apart from some American gadgetry, there's only you and me ... and Nursie makes three. We're a complete trinity. Or triad if you prefer. Now I certainly don't care if you get slapped and I don't believe Nurse Gribbon cares very much either. I don't care about you at all. But we will cure you. We will beat you better if that's what it takes. (*She slaps him again and backs out of the way as* DUNNE *makes a despairing effort to retaliate.* DUNNE *tries to stand, fails and falls back.*)

DUNNE: You bitch...!

(DUNNE *fumbles for the emergency button on the chair but* DR HOGAN *grabs it and yanks it out of the socket. She nods to* NURSE GRIBBON *who comes forward and sits on Dunne's lap. Dunne tries to drive away but* DR HOGAN *disconnects the battery.*)

DR HOGAN: Anything?

NURSE GRIBBON: (*Grins*) Nothing, Doctor.

DR HOGAN: Can't do that either. Everything fallen ... down and out. Too bad. The prisoners would really enjoy seeing you like this. By the way, Mr. Dunne, I don't believe your fall was a simple accident. Our records show the prisoners rioted on that day. It was a major disturbance just before the Upheaval ... Coincidence? I think not ... What caused the riot?

DUNNE: (*Shouting*) Get out. Get out! Leave me alone, you butch sadist!

DR HOGAN: You will tell me, you know. It's just a question of when. Now, it's time for a change of diaper. Nurse, could you oblige please? Judging by the odour I would suggest double strength incontinence padding with triple absorption.

NURSE GRIBBON: Do I have to? It's below my pay grade.

DR HOGAN: Do it. Do it now! And don't spare the baby powder. Give him a sponge bath while you're at it.

NURSE: Oh Lord!

DUNNE: I'm right here ... I can hear everything! This is a fucking nightmare.

(NURSE GRIBBON *pushes* DUNNE *in the chair. They exit right.* DR HOGAN *does some stretching exercises on the parallel bars and exits left.*)

Lights down.

SCENE SIX

DUNNE *is centre stage watching the screen intently. The yellow patch appears more strongly than before. The screen fills with footage of traditional Irish dancing and gradually builds up to the sophisticated routines of Riverdance.* DUNNE *beats time with his hands. Sometimes the images – all in black and white – fade and blur but he manages to sustain them until the climax of the final dance number. When this ends* DUNNE *raises his fists in triumph.*

DUNNE: I'll show them. (*Tries to stand, fails.*) Not yet. But I'll show them soon. Get back on my own two feet … Of course that's what they want. But I want it too … for different reasons.

NURSE GRIBBON: (*Enters right carrying a tray*) Did I hear your foot tapping?

DUNNE: No. Just my hands. Only my hands.

NURSE GRIBBON: Still…

DUNNE: No. Moving. (*He laughs, then notices she doesn't get it.*) Not still … moving.

NURSE GRIBBON: Good one.

(NURSE GRIBBON *shrugs, lays the tray on his lap and watches him eat. He looks in disgust at the cheap plastic cutlery.*)

DUNNE: I meant to ask you … Dr Hogan … does

she always behave like that?

NURSE GRIBBON: Like what?

DUNNE: Like a bully and a bitch.

NURSE GRIBBON: A bully-bitch…? Oh the slap
thing? I don't know. I haven't worked with her
much.

DUNNE: But you must know something about her. I
thought you were … you know … a couple …
maybe a bit gender-fluid…

NURSE GRIBBON: Not really … Come on now …
(*She opens her mouth to encourage him to eat.*)

DUNNE: But you seem close … you danced with
her…

NURSE GRIBBON: So? Jest doin mah jawb,
Honeybunch.

DUNNE: Well what about other doctors and nurses?
What methods do they use?

NURSE GRIBBON: It depends on whether they're
alternative or mainstream. And it depends on
the regime, doesn't it? There are different
methods. Mind, body, soul … No wait …
There's no soul anymore. That's gone by the
board … Oh, I've heard it all. When you've
been in this rack… business … as long as I
have, you pick up a few things … Now eat
your spuds. Starch good. Calcium good.
Mmmmm, brainfood … Open the door of the
garage … Num-num-num … (*She brings the
spoon close to his mouth but he waves it away.*)

DUNNE: Tell Me. Why do you and Hogan want me
to get better? Is it some kind of game?

NURSE GRIBBON: I don't follow.

DUNNE: It's obvious you don't give a shit about me. So why do you bother?

NURSE GRIBBON: We're professionals, that's why.

DUNNE: Professionals? With all due respect...

NURSE GRIBBON: I mean we get paid. We're not amateurs. We don't do it for love.

DUNNE: Might I ask ... is it well paid?

NURSE GRIBBON: My pay is average. I don't know what she earns ... The information is classified ... But we get points nowadays.

DUNNE: What points?

NURSE GRIBBON: Marks, if you like. Top marks for every success. The marks go on our file. They help our careers. American-style incentives ... Bonus points can be used to insure against accidents.

DUNNE: What kind of accidents?

NURSE GRIBBON: Oh, the usual ... unexpected of course. It's like they say: shit happens. You can't prevent it from happening. Not in your case, anyway.

DUNNE: I'll ignore that ... Could you be more specific about these ... accidents?

NURSE GRIBBON: Well, it could be a fall ... like yours. Falling over, collapsing. Falling from one state to another, falling from a burning skyscraper, falling from grace. Anything like that.

DUNNE: This is all very new ... And who ... awards these points?

NURSE GRIBBON: Come on, finish your din-dins.

Just a couple of fish fingers left ... come on now ... (*She pinches his cheek.*)

DUNNE: You didn't answer.

NURSE GRIBBON: Din-dins. Be a good boy ... Nice ketchup...

DUNNE: Who awards the marks?

NURSE GRIBBON: You know, The Administrator ... or his assistant. Those at the top of the tree ... They must never fall of course. It's a long way down for them ... We have to prevent that, or do whatever we can to break their fall.

DUNNE: You seem to think I know them. And that they want me to get well.

NURSE GRIBBON: I guess so.

DUNNE: I imagine plenty of people fell during the Upheaval. I slept through the later stages of it. Coma, remember? You're right, the new gang must be afraid their turn might come. Maybe they think there's something I can do for them.

NURSE GRIBBON: I don't get involved in the ins and outs of things. The whys and wherefores are not for me ... I stay on surfaces ... I dance on surfaces ... tables, bar-tops ... I skate and slide, never staying in the same spot for long ... Sometimes dance is all we've got...
(*She does a short soft-shoe shuffle.*)

DUNNE: Maybe you're right ... Though I don't think you are superficial ... I think you search as well as skate ... delve as well as dance...

NURSE GRIBBON: Why thank you ... I think there's a compliment in there somewhere...

DUNNE: Maybe … Well, there's one advantage about being in a wheelchair. You can't fall any further. You can't suffer from vertigo when you're already down.

NURSE GRIBBON: Are you sure? When you ran that prison maybe you fell more than you thought.

DUNNE: I only fell once. I don't know what you're implying.

NURSE GRIBBON: Use that bread to mop up the gravy … and the ketchup … Sometimes we use others to take the fall.

DUNNE: (*Agitated*) I've had enough … Take the tray away. Leave me. I want to do some … work.

NURSE GRIBBON: Glad to hear it. Try to concentrate.

(NURSE GRIBBON *exits right, doing some dance steps. DUNNE manoeuvres the chair so that he faces the screen. After some deep concentration – and distant cello music – a yellow patch appears. This is followed by a collage of Olympic events, all in slow motion, including gymnastics, the triple jump, pole vault, and a front shot of 100-metre sprinters. The images are life-size but still in monochrome.*)

DUNNE: Good! Good! Excellent stuff entirely.

(*The images begin to blur and fade out.*)

DUNNE: Aw, no. No!

(*Backdrop containing the screen begins to rise.*)

What's happening? I didn't imagine this.
What's going on? Is this real?
(*Dry ice envelopes the back of the stage and
becomes visible as the backdrop is raised.
Through the mist real actors can be dimly seen
– three prisoners in orange boiler suits. The
dry ice gradually disappears. The scene is that
of a prison yard. Two of the prisoners
encourage a younger one, Prisoner 3 or
'MARKIE', to lie on the bench press to lift
weights. MARKIE has a pleasant face with
long hair and a downy beard. PRISONER 1
stands in front and PRISONER 2 stands
behind to 'spot' him. MARKIE lifts the weights
easily and grins as the other prisoners praise
him. When PRISONER 1 turns around it is
obvious to the audience that he is now the*
ASSISTANT ADMINISTRATOR. *DUNNE
recognises all three prisoners – but doesn't
realise that one of them has become the*
ASSISTANT ADMINISTRATOR.)

PRISONER 1: Good man, Markie. Go for the burn.
I see those triceps bulging already. You'll be
ripped in no time flat.
(*They put extra weights on the bar and
MARKIE lifts them with a greater effort.*)

PRISONER 2: Good one, Markie. You'll soon be
king of shit mountain.
(DUNNE *becomes agitated, looks away and
then back again.*)

MARKIE: I just want to do my time and get out of
here as fit as when I came in.

PRISONER 1: Why do any time? We're not
     criminals. Political prisoners maybe. But not
     criminals. Right Markie?

MARKIE: (*Innocently*) Right.

PRISONER 1: Although the Governor probably
     wouldn't agree. What do you think, Markie?

MARKIE: (*Guiltily*) I don't ... know ... I don't
     know him...

PRISONER 2: But we thought you got on well with
     the Governor. Very well ... Are we wrong
     about that?

MARKIE: You think I met him or something? No
     ... No way ... You have to believe me...

PRISONER 1: We believe you, Markie. For now.
     But maybe things will change. Wait and see.
     (*He walks forward and stares out at* DUNNE.)
     Wait and see, Markie.

DUNNE: No ... I don't want this ... Not this...!
     (DUNNE *turns his head away and drives the
     chair towards the kitchenette where he
     splashes water in his face. He looks back and
     sees that the weight-lifting is continuing in
     silence though* MARKIE *is now under
     considerable stress.*)
     No ... stop it ... For God's sake ... make it
     stop...!
     (*Additional dry ice makes the images more
     faint, and the backdrop with the screen is
     beginning to descend.* DUNNE *covers his eyes,
     opens a press and switches on a TV as a
     distraction. The lights go down behind the
     backdrop and the images fade out. The lights*

on the front part of the stage go down slowly.
DUNNE *sits, in considerable discomfort, in the*
flickering glare of the hidden TV. He removes
his glasses and massages his eyes. He looks
behind him once or twice and seems relieved
that the prison yard scene has disappeared.
The light from the TV gradually fades until the
entire stage is in darkness.)

End of ACT ONE

SCENE ONE

Lights come up slowly. DUNNE *and* DR HOGAN *are on the stage near the kitchen area.* NURSE GRIBBON, *in gymnast's leotard, is exercising on the trapeze set at its low level.*

DR HOGAN: Two weeks and no more progress. You're not trying.

DUNNE: So what? It's up to me. I decide.

DR HOGAN: Willpower, get it? Brain and Body ... B and B, remember? The imagination fuels the muscles with images of movement ... Life is a verb, did you know that? Yes it is ... We do and act and have our being. Endorphins reward us with good feelings...

DUNNE: Oh give it a rest. You'll be talking about chakras and crystals next. Anyway, why is it so important to you?

DR HOGAN: You're connected, it seems ... part of the gold circle...

DUNNE: Back then maybe. Before the Upheaval. But now...? I don't think so ... What's going on?

DR HOGAN: Look, just try harder. You mustn't waste my time ... or Nurse Gribbon's...

DUNNE: (*Glancing towards her on the trapeze*) She's quite good at that, herself.

DR HOGAN: Nurse Gribbon is surprisingly good at

what she does. And so am I, as it happens. There are other clients out there who could benefit from our help and experience. Have you thought about that?

DUNNE: Why am I being given priority?

DR HOGAN: They need you apparently...

DUNNE: Who needs me?

DR HOGAN: They ... They ... Look, I can't answer that question ... Just accept it ... and be grateful ... very grateful ... A lot of people disappeared on your watch...

DUNNE: But why are they helping me ... if that's what it is? I'm all washed up...

DR HOGAN: You have special skills ... or intel ... or something ... Just be glad ... they think you have something. If they didn't think that ... you wouldn't be here.

DUNNE: I feel like an animal being fattened up for the slaughter.

DR HOGAN: For all I know, that could be a good analogy.

DUNNE: And that wouldn't bother you at all? What about your Hippocratic oath?

DR HOGAN: Ha ... There's no such thing anymore. To whom would you take such an oath? God? The Administrator? Think about it. You're so naïve. How on earth did you survive for as long as you did?

DUNNE: Are you saying the Administrator doesn't exist?

(DR HOGAN *plays with the orange again. Tossing it up and catching it. Then she smashes it down on the floor.*)

DR HOGAN: Assisted gravity. See? More Gs, more force. More force, more damage. This is what power is.

Lights down.

SCENE TWO

NURSE GRIBBON *is working out on the trapeze, in low position, to a musical accompaniment. When she sees* DR HOGAN *enter left she dismounts. Both sit down at centre stage.*

DR HOGAN: I was sent for.

NURSE GRIBBON: By ... himself ... the Assistant Administrator?

DR HOGAN: Yes. He's not happy with progress, or lack of it. He emphasises yet again how important this case is. I got the impression he came across Dunne in some previous incarnation. Anyway, he's far from happy.

NURSE GRIBBON: With us?

DR HOGAN: His unhappiness includes us. Embraces us. Which is annoying...

NURSE GRIBBON: Worrying, more like ... It's all Dunne's fault. He isn't working his programme properly. I mean, he tries but he can't get past the prison yard ... Something happened there. It keeps coming up and each time it scares him to hell ... He doesn't want yellow anymore.

DR HOGAN: We'll have to try ... different methods ... Shush ... He's coming...

(DUNNE *enters right.*)

DUNNE: I thought I heard voices. Using your key again, I see.

(DUNNE *moves to switch on the TV. NURSE GRIBBON restrains him and* DR HOGAN *unplugs the set. She produces a knife from the inside pocket of her immaculate suit and cuts the TV cable.*)

DUNNE: What the fuck are you doing? This is my house. Mine.

DR HOGAN: Ownership is a difficult concept nowadays ... No more escapism. You have to concentrate ... and face your demons ... TV gives you images ... You have to summon up your own.

DUNNE: You can't just barge in here and start ordering me around.

DR HOGAN: I've just done it. And this is only the beginning. From now on you'll have no books, Kindle, laptop, music or radio. Those licenses have been revoked.

DUNNE: What licenses?

DR.HOGAN: The new guard has brought in a system of licences for individual behaviours. You have to pay for a lot of freedoms you took for granted ... water, air, speech, to name but a few...

NURSE GRIBBON: The costs mount up, I can tell you ... The cost of living ... The cost of surviving, more like...

DUNNE: Some therapy this. Solitary confinement would be better.

DR HOGAN: Well put. You may regard this as prison ... though you're not in charge ... I am...

DUNNE: I thought the person you call the Assistant Administrator is in charge...?

DR HOGAN: (*Caught off-guard*) Well ... maybe, but...

DUNNE: Do I detect a secret ambition on your part ... Aha...!

DR HOGAN: Shut the fuck up...! Back to your behaviour ... No distractions of any sort. Do you understand? You're blocked. You have to get past it. Go through the prison yard and get to the other side.

DUNNE: I don't know what you're talking about.

DR HOGAN: Oh, I think you do. You understand all too well. Face it, Dunne. And stop being such a coward. If you don't do it the hard way your body will seize up completely. Double incontinence ... You'll start puking up faeces ... All licenses will be revoked. Is that what you want? Is that what you really want?

DUNNE: I'd kill myself first.

DR HOGAN: How? You can't even get out of that chair.

NURSE GRIBBON: The cutlery is plastic. And the cups are Styrofoam. Not easy to get at an artery.

DR HOGAN: Anyway, I don't think you have the guts. All your life you chose the path of least resistance ... You never went high except that one time ... and then you fell.

NURSE GRIBBON: You've always figured out the angles and played the odds. That's why you're not fit.

DUNNE: Fit? How can I be fit? I'm paralysed...

NURSE GRIBBON: Fit for purpose ... the purpose of the regime.

DUNNE: What do they want with me anyway?

DR HOGAN: You have skills apparently ... and you know things...

DUNNE: So that's it ... And you want your precious points.

DR HOGAN: Someone's been talking, I see ... Yes, that's the new system. You don't think we're doing this out of compassion. Good God, man, I think you're gross. In normal circumstances I wouldn't touch you with a barge pole ... I'd scrape you off my shoe ... I'm a curer, not a carer.

NURSE GRIBBON: And we don't care who we cure. I told you, we're professionals. That means we do it for the money. And the points of course.

DUNNE: Thanks for that! It's a real morale-booster...

DR HOGAN: Did you care for your prisoners? You hated them, didn't you? And you used them for your own purposes...

(*She takes a large hypodermic needle from her bag.* DUNNE *eyes it suspiciously.*)

DUNNE: No...

DR HOGAN: I think you used the prisoners to gather intelligence ... for the last crowd...

DUNNE: (*Loudly*) That's ridiculous...

DR HOGAN: I don't think so. Why should I ... we ... be any different?

DUNNE: You're always on about the mind ... the
wonders of the mind.

DR HOGAN: No. Wrong. The brain, not the mind.
Neural connections only. We don't do soul.
The soul is gone ... banished. B and B. Think
and move. Think and move. Mens sana in
corpore sano. Get it? (*She points to the TV.*) If
you're going to break the rules I'll drop your
case faster than it took you to hit the ground
when you fell. There's nothing in it for me. Do
you understand? I don't need another ... I
don't need a failure on my hands. Do you
understand?

DUNNE: Oh yes, it might ruin your chances of
rising in the hierarchy ... Maybe even going to
America ... or working in one of their bases...

DR HOGAN: Shut your mouth! ... Do you
understand what I'm saying to you?

DUNNE: Yeah. (*He looks at the needle.*)

DR HOGAN: I didn't hear you.

DUNNE: Yes. I said yes!

DR HOGAN: Again!

DUNNE: YES! YES! Fuck's sake...

DR HOGAN: You can take these off too. (*She
removes DUNNE's tinted glasses and puts
them in her pocket.*)

DUNNE: God Almighty...!

DR HOGAN: No higher power please. He may or
may not be dead but he's certainly not
interested. You're on your own.

DUNNE: What's that needle for...?

DR HOGAN: Just a little test.

(She jabs him viciously in the thigh.)

DUNNE: Aaagh! What the hell is that?

DR HOGAN: An anti-cowardice serum ... To get
    you past the prison-yard scene ... It's quick-
    acting ... Any feelings of bravery yet?

DUNNE: No. How dare you!

DR HOGAN: It may take longer to penetrate
    through your layers of blubber ... Nurse, come.
    Nous allons.

NURSE GRIBBON: Certainly, Meine Medizinerin.
    (NURSE GRIBBON *glides into her arms and*
    they dance a very smooth quickstep across the
    stage and exit left. DUNNE sits motionless as
    the lights fade.)

Lights down.

SCENE THREE

African drumming, loud at first then fades out. The lights come up. The interior of DUNNE*'s flat is unoccupied. The yellow patch appears on screen for a while and then fades out.* DUNNE *enters from the left in the wheelchair. He is drinking from a small plastic bottle. He is followed by* NURSE GRIBBON. *She hangs up their coats and hats on the hatstand. They both move towards centre stage.*

NURSE GRIBBON: It was cold but the air was so fresh, bracing. Did you enjoy it?

DUNNE: No. You kept pushing me. I don't like being pushed.

NURSE GRIBBON: Well, get up then. It's up to you. Up you get … Gettit?

DUNNE: Christ, not this again. Change the record.

NURSE GRIBBON: But it's true. Sometimes we graze a knee or bruise an ego. But we get up, don't we? We get up and carry on as best we can. We have to. There's no alternative.

DUNNE: What about a merciful release?

NURSE GRIBBON: That's not an option at all.

DUNNE: Well, I can see why it might not appeal to you.

NURSE GRIBBON: Why not?

DUNNE: You have a nice fit body … flexible too.

NURSE GRIBBON: I didn't know you cared.

DUNNE: I don't. Well, not in that way.

NURSE GRIBBON: Anyway, there's no percentage in suicide.

DUNNE: No points. No gravy for the middle-man ... I couldn't cut myself with this anyway. (*He throws the plastic bottle into the kitchen bin.*)

NURSE GRIBBON: I'm told that your religion condemns suicide because it ... usurps God's right to end your life...

DUNNE: That was one view ... I don't think anyone believes that now...

NURSE GRIBBON: Wasn't it guilt that drove you to it...?

DUNNE: You're assuming I jumped. Do not assume ... or presume...

NURSE GRIBBON: No hard feelings...

DUNNE: (*Reflectively*) I wonder ... if we become corrupt so gradually that we don't notice it...? Maybe this is my punishment ... This could be my visualisation of Hell...

NURSE GRIBBON: Aw, we're not that bad, are we?

DUNNE: Is it possible that I'm imagining you?

NURSE GRIBBON: No, I exist ... Feel. (*She puts his hand on her breast.*)

DUNNE: Mnnn. But what if it's silicone?

NURSE GRIBBON: Well, that's real too ... Seriously though, you should work the programme. It's for the best.

DUNNE: (*Quietly*) I know ... I've started again, if you must know.

NURSE GRIBBON: What, you have? Excellent.
That's great news ... I should leave you alone
for a while. And remember, gravity isn't that
strong. Don't fear it. Defy it. Gravity must
always be defied ... Sometimes, when the
trapeze is set high, I feel ... Oh nothing ...
forget it...
(She exits right.)
(DUNNE *looks at the screen. The yellow dot
appears, followed by scenes of hurling and
rugby matches in colour.)*
DUNNE: At last! Excellent ... And in colour...
*(The backdrop with the screen moves up
slowly, revealing the prison-yard and the real
prisoners.)*
DUNNE: God help me now...!
PRISONER 2: Good lift, Markie. Not bad for a kid.
Do I see a little four-pack coming in there?
MARKIE: Thanks, man.
PRISONER 1: Not bad for a squealer.
MARKIE: Wha-a-t? What're you saying...?
PRISONER 1: You heard me. You ratted us out to
the Governor. Didn't you know we'd find out,
Markie? We have eyes and ears everywhere.
MARKIE: You're mistaken...
PRISONER 1: How did he find out where the
explosives were hidden? No answer. Well, I
know how. Don't insult my intelligence. I
don't respond well to that.
PRISONER 2: I'd listen to him, kid, if I were you.
MARKIE: The Governor ... he used me...
DUNNE: No ... no ... Stop it now...!

PRISONER 1: He used you all right. And where did the names of the political activists end up?

MARKIE: I don't know anything about that.

PRISONER 2: It's never too late to learn.

PRISONER 1: It's time for your first lesson.
(PRISONER 2 *holds* MARKIE *down on the bench press.* PRISONER 1 *picks up a fifty-pound weight and smashes it down on* MARKIE*'s knees.* MARKIE *screams.*)

DUNNE: (*Gouges his eyes*) Oh my God!

PRISONER 2: Maybe we should finish the job. Get it over with…

PRISONER 1: That would be too easy.

PRISONER 2: He can still talk to the Governor.

PRISONER 1: We can fix that. (*Nods to* PRISONER 2 *who produces a shiv from his overalls and bears down menacingly on* MARKIE.)
(DUNNE *covers his eyes. The screen backdrop comes down and obliterates the prison yard scene.*)

DUNNE: Oh Jesus … It was my fault. MARKIE took the fall! (*He hammers his thighs and tries to get out of the wheelchair. He falls on his knees and tries to crawl towards the screen without success.* NURSE GRIBBON *appears stage right and sees* DUNNE*'s prone body. She opens her cell phone and whispers into it.* DUNNE *continues to moan and whimper.*)

Lights down.

SCENE FOUR

Lights Up. DUNNE *is still on the floor but unconscious.* NURSE GRIBBON *opens the door at left to admit* DR HOGAN. *They both help* DUNNE *back into the wheelchair.*

DR HOGAN: He saw something didn't he?
NURSE GRIBBON: Yes. It scared him...
DUNNE: I'm not dead. I can hear you.
DR HOGAN: Well, tell us about it. What did you
    see?
    (DUNNE *shakes his head*)
NURSE GRIBBON: It will help you to talk about it.
DUNNE: Violence...
DR HOGAN: Caused by ... ? You...?
DUNNE: Maybe ... I had something to do with it...
NURSE GRIBBON: And it resulted in your fall?
DUNNE: If you say so.
DR HOGAN: Someone who helped you?
DUNNE: A prisoner ... a youngster ... (*Puts his
    head in his hands.*) Markie ... poor Markie...
DR HOGAN: An informer maybe? He helped
    you...
NURSE GRIBBON: And then what?
DR HOGAN: He paid for it?
DUNNE: Nothing! Nothing! Let me be...
DR HOGAN: He paid for it, didn't he?
DUNNE: (*Loudly*) Yes...!

DR HOGAN: With his life?

DUNNE: (*Howling*) That's enough! No more…!
   (DUNNE*'s head slumps to his chest. On a nod from* DR HOGAN, NURSE GRIBBON *fills a syringe from a phial and injects* DUNNE *in the neck. He makes only a token resistance. Within a few seconds he passes out.*)

DR HOGAN: I don't think he's going to confront this properly. He seems to have a conscience. Just our luck. Would you credit it? A Governor of a prison with a conscience. An interrogator who doesn't really like torture. You can never tell about people, can you?

NURSE GRIBBON: (*Nervously*) We may have a failure on our hands. That won't do at all.

DR HOGAN: We could try hallucinogens. But not yet, I think. There's a possibility he might find his own way … That fall … Hmmmm … I'm almost certain he jumped.

NURSE GRIBBON: Interesting … He has a conscience … so it probably was guilt-related … Hmmm.

DR HOGAN: Remind me, are you a psychiatrist or a nurse? I've forgotten. Did you spend seven years in medical college? Could you refresh my memory please?

NURSE GRIBBON: I am a humble nurse and a bimbo, Ma'am. My only aim is to please my betters.

DR HOGAN: I say we give it a week and review matters then. I realise that the Assistant Administrator is going to call on us soon.

NURSE GRIBBON: (*Nervously*) He's going to decide on the bonuses.

DR HOGAN: Some of us want more than points.

NURSE GRIBBON: May I ask what could be more important than points?

DR HOGAN: How about joining the new Administration? Becoming one of them? Imagine sitting with them at the round table in The Hall of Debate or at The Field of Horses … or even Congress … Hmmmmm. Nice.

NURSE GRIBBON: Too rich for my blood. I couldn't aspire to that … I'll settle for points.

DR HOGAN: But something to think about?

NURSE GRIBBON: Maybe, Frau Doktor.

DR HOGAN: Remember, if Dunne falls again he'll take us down with him. We're joined at the hip now.

NURSE GRIBBON: I understand that…

DR HOGAN: I've noticed something else … You seem to be warmer towards him. Be warned: Don't get too close.

NURSE GRIBBON: No, Doctor.

(DR HOGAN *pats her on the bottom and exits left.* NURSE GRIBBON *studies her nails for a while then looks at the slumped form of* DUNNE.)

Who'd have thought it? One thing is for sure. It would be hard to fall for him. Not head-over-heels at any rate.

(*She does some stretching exercises on the parallel bars.*)

Mustn't forget to renew my license for the

State Gym. Must keep fit for regime change.
Fit for purpose and fit to practise.

Lights down.

SCENE FIVE

African drumming. Loud at first then fades out. Lights up. DUNNE *is waking up from the drug. He is wearing a strait-jacket. He struggles for a while to no avail. Sees a note pinned to the wheelchair.*

DUNNE: (*Reading the note*) 'Had to administer sedative. Strait-jacket is to prevent self-harm. Next appointment, Tuesday as per usual.' Self-harm? Those bastards. I'll show them. Fuck them all.
(*He positions himself in front of the screen and concentrates very hard. The yellow patch appears and the screen rises, revealing the prison yard. There's blood all over* MARKIE*'s face.*)

PRISONER 1: This is a distinct improvement. He can't walk … or talk. Maybe our day will come after all. Everything will change then … after the Upheaval … Count on it … The rest of the men in Block K are with us…

PRISONER 2: You're sure about that?

PRISONER 1: Positive … Trust me.

PRISONER 2: But our mute friend here could still write a note to his pal, the Governor.

PRISONER 1: Good point. I think we have to do

something about that. Call it pre-emptive
defence.
(PRISONER 2 *smashes* MARKIE*'s hands with
one of the heavy weights.* MARKIE *screams.*)
DUNNE: No more ... Please no more ... !
(DUNNE *twists and turns his head and
struggles violently against the strait-jacket. His
head falls forward in despair. The lights go
down for a few seconds then come up again.
The backdrop begins to come down.*)
DUNNE: Thank God ... for small mercies...
(*The prison yard is now concealed by the
backdrop.* DUNNE *sits bolt upright.*)
That's it! *Good* movement. The circus. Why
not? The ring, sawdust ... Fellini. All that
harmless crazy activity. Oh please let it be ...
Must concentrate ... Good stuff, good stuff...
(*A yellow patch appears on the screen and
gives way to circus scenes, life-size and in
colour. The first scene shows all the artistes –
and animals – parading around the circus ring.
It is colourful, glitzy and entertaining. There is
plenty of movement.*)
DUNNE: Thank God ... This is great ... Where are
the acrobats ... there should be acrobats ...
What did Nurse Gribbon say ... 'Sometimes all
you've got is dance'. Yes, bring it on...
(*He nods his head to the lively circus music
and gradually begins to smile.*)

Lights down.

SCENE SIX

A new backdrop is lowered. There is a large semi-transparent door in the middle of it. DR HOGAN *and* NURSE GRIBBON *are peering through the door towards the auditorium.*

DR HOGAN: I wonder if something might be happening.

NURSE GRIBBON: I do not doubt your opinion. But what?

DR HOGAN: It's not for me to say.

NURSE GRIBBON: Why so, Doctor?

DR HOGAN: It's *his* imagination, not mine.

NURSE GRIBBON: Of course. We're on the outside. But I'm trying to read his face.

DR HOGAN: In other words, you're trying to imagine what he's imagining?

NURSE GRIBBON: Yes, Doctor.

DR HOGAN: And what do you intuit?

NURSE GRIBBON: I don't see violence or demons. No, something good. He seems relaxed … possibly even happy.

DR HOGAN: Happy? Happy? As a scientist, I don't believe in miracles.

NURSE GRIBBON: Shush … you mustn't say that … Bugs everywhere…

DR HOGAN: (*Loud whisper*) You mustn't say that

either.

NURSE GRIBBON: I didn't say anything … Did you meet the Assistant Administrator?

DR HOGAN: I did. They're keen to get Dunne back in his old post … Intelligence-gathering … and something else … The Administrator thinks he'd be a poster boy for the new guard … Time is running out. They want results … The CIA as well…

NURSE GRIBBON: And you're keen to help them.

DR HOGAN: But of course … Aren't you?

NURSE GRIBBON: Absolutely. But looking at him now, I wonder if our work here is nearly done?

DR HOGAN: Counting chickens is not a good idea in our business … You do know what pride comes before…?

NURSE GRIBBON: I do indeed. There are banana-skins everywhere. And elephant traps.

DR HOGAN: Will you join me in a fitness-twirl, Nurse Gribbon?

NURSE GRIBBON: Certainly, my doctor. 'To dance' is my favourite verb. We move and we stay upright.

DR HOGAN: My dance license is up to date. I hope yours is?

NURSE GRIBBON: Most certainly, Doctor. I regard it as one of my most important licenses.
(*She glides into* DR HOGAN*'s arms and they dance a vigorous foxtrot.*)

DR.HOGAN: I'm glad to hear it, Nurse Gribbon.
(*They continue to dance and finally exit.*)

Lights down.

SCENE SEVEN

The screen is back in place. Dance music becomes more circus-like and it swells. Lights up. DUNNE *is in the same position watching the circus parade which has become louder and livelier.*

DUNNE: Oh this is the right stuff ... the bees knees ... lowbrow and fabulous ... better than ballet any day ... Look at those acrobats ... fabulous! (*He moves the wheelchair closer to the screen and makes one or two attempts to get out of the chair.*)
Give it time ... This is just what the doctor ordered ... good movement ... my kind of action...
(*A sudden noise and a spotlight divert attention to the entrance on the left where* MARKIE *appears in a manually operated wheelchair. His hands are bandaged. He is wearing the prison overalls. He looks straight at* DUNNE. *The circus scene fades out.*)
(DUNNE *is shocked to the core.*) Jesus Christ! You ... I can't believe my eyes ... How did...?
MARKIE: You'd prefer if I went away. For good ... Joined the Disappeared...
DUNNE: (*Nervously*) No ... of course not, Markie ... And I'm so sorry for what happened to you ... desperately sorry ... (*Looks surprised.*) I

didn't think … I mean you can talk…

MARKIE: Sometimes. When it's necessary … I had operations … I see you're in a chair too.

DUNNE: It's only phantom paralysis … so they say. But you…

MARKIE: My legs are no good … not fit for purpose … I blamed you for a long time. I didn't know the information was being used in that way. But after a year or two, I realised you were caught up in the system. Maybe you weren't a prisoner but you weren't free either. After a while, I stopped hating you…

DUNNE: You don't know what that means to me, Markie. I dreaded … meeting you again in case … you … Well, you know … I would do anything to help you walk again. And use your hands. I didn't know there would be a … riot in the prison … and that it would spark the Upheaval…

MARKIE: It was the match to the tinder … The CIA was involved … Covertly of course … Sides were taken. When that happens you can't be independent anymore. You either rise or fall … can't stay where you were … No…

DUNNE: I didn't take sides. I just happened to find myself on one side … the establishment I suppose you would call it … at least back then under the old regime…

(NURSE GRIBBON *enters carrying her bag. She remains silent, but looks and listens.*)

MARKIE: Well, I've nailed my colours to the mast … The Upheaval was a bad mistake … It must

be undone. We have to mobilise to undo the
present Administration...

DUNNE: Will it really make any difference? Isn't it
just eternal recurrence...? The more we change
the more we stay the same. Besides, we can't
go against America...

MARKIE: How can you even think that? You have
to believe that things will get better ... We're
human ... We can be perfected ... sacrificial
blood has been shed...

DUNNE: I know how they crucified you ... I'd like
to help, Markie ... but I don't really know the
issues ... I was in a coma at the start...

MARKIE: Don't worry, I'm not trying to recruit
you ... Who's helping with your recovery?

DUNNE: Someone called the Assistant
Administrator.

MARKIE: (*Pointedly*) Have you met him? Do you
know who he is?

DUNNE: No. I don't think it matters. I've learnt my
lesson ... You're sure we're all square?

MARKIE: There's no point in holding a grudge. If
you had benefited in some way ... it would've
been different. But I think you suffered too in
your own way. The fall and everything. So,
yes, we're OK.

DUNNE: Thank you, Markie. You don't know what
that means to me ... (*He looks at the screen
then back to* MARKIE *and blurts out.*) You're
real, aren't you? Not just my imagination. Not
a simulacrum?

MARKIE: It's often hard to tell nowadays. But I'm

real, don't worry.

DUNNE: (*Emotional*) I'm not sure … I deserve your forgiveness.

MARKIE: No one deserves anything. You just try to go by the book...

DUNNE: You're a bigger man than I am...

MARKIE: Maybe you haven't been tested yet … Maybe you're big test will come sooner than you think … I have to leave now. Go back to your therapy and get fit … fit for the test...

DUNNE: Don't go, Markie … We … I need you...

MARKIE: I must go … But I'll be back.

(MARKIE *exits left.*)

DUNNE: Not tested yet…? He's forgiven me though. That's the main thing. I can handle anything now.

(NURSE GRIBBON *steps forward.*)

NURSE GRIBBON: Be careful...

DUNNE: Of Markie?

NURSE GRIBBON: No … He sounds all right. Be careful of the others … and of this test...

DUNNE: I didn't know you cared...

NURSE GRIBBON: Just be careful.

Lights down.

SCENE EIGHT

Circus music. Lights up. DUNNE *is watching the screen where the circus parade continues. To the left of the screen stands* DR HOGAN *in the garb of a ring-master. At the other side of the screen is* NURSE GRIBBON *similarly attired. As the parade leaves the circus ring they introduce the first act.*

DR HOGAN: Ladies And Gentlemen, for your pleasure and edification...

NURSE GRIBBON: And excitation...

DR HOGAN: We bring you, direct from Afghanistan, the amazing...

NURSE GRIBBON: Breath-taking ... heart-pounding...

DR HOGAN: Gravity-defying ... the incredible Panackretos!

(NURSE GRIBBON *dances over to* DUNNE *and removes the strait-jacket with a flourish. She and* DR HOGAN *exit left, dancing in theatrical fashion.*)

(*To loud, upbeat music the screen shows a troupe of acrobats running into the ring and engaging in an athletic and sophisticated routine, involving equipment such as vaulting horses, spring boards and trampolines.*)

(DUNNE *watches the routine keenly, cheering and applauding.*)

DUNNE: This is great stuff ... Back on track now
... must try ... best chance ever...
(*He tries to stand, falls back, tries again
several times, fails, keeps on trying. Eventually
he manages to get half-way out of the
wheelchair, groaning with the effort, then falls
on the floor.* DR HOGAN *and* NURSE
GRIBBON *enter left and rush forward to help
him. They are dressed in their normal formal
wear.*)

DUNNE: No ... must do it myself ... Ah ... ah.. (*He
tries to crawl.*)

DR HOGAN: Good...!

NURSE GRIBBON: Oh try...! Good man...!
(DUNNE *begins to crawl though very slowly.*)

DR HOGAN: Yes ... Yes...!

NURSE GRIBBON: Feel the music ... feel it...!
(DUNNE *continues to crawl and then after
many failed efforts manages to get to his
knees.*)

DR HOGAN: Come on, you can do it ... ! Feel the
power flowing through your legs...

NURSE GRIBBON: Just a little more effort ...
Don't give up ... Reach for the gold ring...!
It's right there in front of you ... for the taking
... Grab it...!
(*After many failures and with a great surge of
energy* DUNNE *staggers to his feet and
stands.*)

DR HOGAN: Oh well done, Sir ...
Congratulations...!

NURSE GRIBBON: Absolutely bloody marvellous

... Wonderful ... wonderful...!

(DUNNE *tries to walk, falters, falls, gets up again.*)

DR HOGAN: Take it easy ... easy. One step at a time.

(DUNNE *tries again, loses balance, falls forward.* NURSE GRIBBON *rushes forward and catches him.*)

DUNNE: (*Breathless*) Leave me be! Please...!

NURSE GRIBBON: Sorry...! You can do it on your own!

(*Gradually* DUNNE *finds his feet and begins to walk in 'baby' steps, his arms out for balance. He uses the parallel bars for support, then manages without them.*)

NURSE GRIBBON: It's too much ... I'm welling up ... Sorry ... The world is full of apathy and irony and then something like this happens ... and it buffets the heart ... makes it soar...

DR HOGAN: It's ... so rewarding ... and moving ... I admit it ... It's as if Icarus fixed his wings and flew again...

(DR HOGAN *takes a cell phone from her pocket and sends a text message.*)

(*The screen goes blank.*)

DUNNE: (*Noticing blank screen*) I probably won't need that anymore.

DR HOGAN: No. And if you did, you could always start at yellow again. Because now you *know* you can recover, become fit.

(DUNNE *is walking almost normally.*)

DUNNE: (*Breathless*) I can hardly believe this. Oh

this is just marvellous…

DR HOGAN: Well, we told you … Oh ye of little faith … Fit at last, Lord … fit at last…

(DUNNE *tries the parallel bars and performs a simple routine.*)

NURSE GRIBBON: Careful…

DUNNE: (*On fairly good dismount*) How about that? The legs held up well. Not quite your standard, Nurse Gribbon. But I'm upright and moderately fit.

(DUNNE *eyes the trapeze which is at the highest level.*)

NURSE GRIBBON: (*Laughing*) No. Not yet. Out of the question … Soon though…

DUNNE: Only kidding. I know my limitations.

(DR HOGAN *goes to the door at left and admits a tall, immaculately dressed man and a shorter man.*)

DR HOGAN: There's someone here to see you.

DUNNE: Who?

DR HOGAN: May I present the Assistant Administrator and his Aide.

(DUNNE *looks over, recognises the man and realises that his former prisoner – the toughest and most rebellious – has become the* ASSISTANT ADMINISTRATOR. *His* AIDE *is* PRISONER 2 *now dressed in a dark suit.* DUNNE *resiles in shock.*)

DUNNE: (*Astonished*) You! My God … You…! It can't be…!

ASSTNT ADMINISTRATOR: You didn't know? I thought you kept up with all the information,

Governor Dunne. Anyway, glad to see you're back on your feet. You know my Aide, of course.

DUNNE: You of all people ... I thought you wanted me dead...

ASSTNT ADMINISTRATOR: (*Smoothly*) We can afford to be gracious in victory. Besides, you're seen as a good asset. Remember, I know better than most how valuable you can be.

DUNNE: That was then. Then.

ASSTNT ADMINISTRATOR: So? Same job. Different regime. It's just a matter of changing sides. But remember a revolution is not 360 degrees. It's 180 degrees. We are now facing the opposite way.

DUNNE: I can't ... change direction like that.

AIDE: Can't...?

ASSTNT ADMINISTRATOR: Ever see a cat cosying up to its new master? Everyone does it. We often fear the unknown but if you give it a chance it may well prove itself. America isn't such a bad superpower ... People have a wonderful capacity for accepting things.

NURSE GRIBBON: So true ... so very true...

DUNNE: Not everyone can accept ... not everyone...

ASSTNT ADMINISTRATOR: Oh yes, you've been talking to Markie.

DUNNE: How do you know...?

ASSTNT ADMINISTRATOR: It's part of my job description to know. Or to find out – which is where you come in. We need you back running that prison … But look, forget about Markie. He's an innocent abroad. No street smarts … and not cyber-savvy … (*He looks towards his* AIDE *who grins.*)

DUNNE: But maybe he's right … morally…

ASSTNT ADMINISTRATOR: Morally? You can't be serious. Who talks like that anymore? There are no values or beliefs nowadays … There's no centre of gravity. Get real, Mr. Dunne.

DR HOGAN: It seems to me you're being made a good offer by your benefactor … If it were me I wouldn't hesitate, not for a minute.

DUNNE: Keep out of this. You've done your job.

NURSE GRIBBON: And done it very well … if I may say so … Both of us…

AIDE: Shut it! You'll get your damn bonus points.

ASSTNT ADMINISTRATOR: Mr. Dunne, I'm sure you'll see sense. The alternative would not be appealing … (*He looks towards the* AIDE *and back at* DUNNE.) Let me explain something to you. In jail I hated your guts. I still do … I would kill you where you stand if it were up to me. But the Administrator thinks you have a special skill in enhanced interrogation … Not so much waterboarding as the psycho stuff … He also believes you have intel on members of the former regime. Personally, I think he's overestimating your worth, but for now we want you back in harness, working for us. If you want the truth, I'm half hoping you'll refuse … because then I'll be free to give you what you deserve … and it won't be quick and it won't be pretty … Remember, I'm a chemist … Yes, it was I who taught the rebels how to make explosives. You didn't know it but that jail was a university … I learnt many things too, especially how to make people see sense … So think it over. You have one day.

(*The* ASSISTANT ADMINISTRATOR *and* AIDE *exit left.* DR HOGAN *and* NURSE GRIBBON *see them out, fawning over them. They return to centre stage.*)

DR HOGAN: A damn good offer. Are you mad? Don't look a gift horse … It's your chance to join the Administration … And if you did you would be in a position to … repay your friends…

DUNNE: I am grateful to you … But none of this is your responsibility. (*Pensively*) Why do I have the impression that everything's been … choreographed? That everyone is on the inside except me?

NURSE GRIBBON: The alternative didn't sound too good. It scared the giblets out of me.

DUNNE: Maybe we'll find out…

NURSE GRIBBON: You knew the Assistant Administrator from before ?

DUNNE: Yes. It's extraordinary … What goes around comes around … (*Almost to himself*) No wonder our freedoms are being taken from us … There will be worse to come … much worse … The constitution will be shredded … Black ops … corruption on a huge scale … misery for the mass of people … That age will last for a long time before there's any hope of a true republic...

NURSE GRIBBON: (*Whispering*) I have a bad feeling about him ... Please, Mr. Dunne, don't do anything to annoy him...

DUNNE: You don't have to be concerned...

NURSE GRIBBON: But strange as it might seem, I am...

DR HOGAN: I think we can wrap it up here, Nurse. Our work is done. He's seen the medical results first hand. That's what the bonus points will be based on.

DUNNE: You've done well. Thank you both. I am grateful. And I don't think it was all for bonus points and licenses ... I think that, in your own way, you ... were amateurs ... Nurse Gribbon anyway...

NURSE GRIBBON: Don't be a martyr...

DR HOGAN: It would be better if you saw fit to...

DUNNE: Play ball? Thank you for your advice ... It's my call ... Thank you again for all your help.

(*They shake hands.* DR HOGAN *and* NURSE GRIBBON *dance fairly slowly towards the door on the left and exit.* NURSE GRIBBON *looks back. She seems worried. Dunne looks after them and sighs.*)

(*Sadly*) I thought she might have danced with me. Just once.

Lights down.

SCENE NINE

Faint and slow echoes of circus music. DUNNE *is sitting in an armchair, drinking whiskey from a glass. The backdrop is raised so there is no sign of the screen. A book rests in his lap. He rises from the chair and paces back and forth, deep in thought.*

DUNNE: Am I fit for their purpose? Maybe ... But, I can't do what they ask ... I wish I could, but I can't ... I can, however, leave this note for Nurse Gribbon. She has a good heart even if you have to dig a little to find it.
(He sits at a table and puts the letter in an envelope, seals and addresses it.)
She'll know what to do with this.
(He puts the letter in a medical bag she's left in his apartment.)
(He continues to pace for a while then walks with more purpose towards the parallel bars. He walks between them. He stops beneath the trapeze, unhooks the rope ladder from the wall and begins to climb. Half-way up he stops and looks down at his apartment. There is a wistful look on his face. He continues to climb. Lights down suddenly followed by a shout and sound of body hitting the stage.)

SCENE TEN

Phrases of Verdi's 'Dies Irae'. Lights come up. DR HOGAN, NURSE GRIBBON, *the* ASSISTANT ADMINISTRATOR *and his* AIDE *are on the stage looking at* DUNNE*'s body.*

ASSTNT ADMINISTRATOR: What a waste. By all accounts, he was a good interrogator, you know – a natural. Perfect for renditions … It's not as easy as you might think … And apparently he knew a lot about our enemies … Sleeper cells that have not yet been identified. The Administrator is not going to be pleased. Why would Dunne fall deliberately? I don't get it. He had just recovered from his last fall and now he throws himself into another one.

DR HOGAN: I can't believe he did it … After all the work we put in.

NURSE GRIBBON: (*Weeping*) It's … upsetting … He was so happy to be back on his feet … He had more imagination than anyone else…

ASSTNT ADMINISTRATOR: (*To* DR HOGAN) I'm surprised you didn't see it coming, and alert us to the danger. We trusted you…

AIDE: And you didn't come cheap.

DR HOGAN: (*Flustered*) Sometimes … suicidal ideation is not predictable … Not a precise science … you know … But I've always been loyal ... You know that...

NURSE GRIBBON: (*Surprised*) Always ... loyal?
You knew them before...?

ASSTNT ADMINISTRATOR: Loyal, Dr Hogan...?
I'm not so sure about that ... I understand you
have ambitions to rise in the Administration...

DR HOGAN: (*Frightened*) But only if there were a
vacancy ... Not otherwise ... No...!

ASSTNT ADMINISTRATOR: I see ... And where
were you, Nurse, when Mr Dunne performed
his second fall?

NURSE GRIBBON: (*Nervously*) Me...? I was off
the case. Dr Hogan had sent me home...

ASSTNT ADMINISTRATOR: I hate investments
that don't pay off. I took a chance on him. It's
not as if...

AIDE: He was never a friend. And he sided with the
others. He was one of them.

ASSTNT ADMINISTRATOR: You can say that
again. He was a devious son-of-a-bitch ...
Played both sides against the middle.

DR HOGAN: (*Nervously*) Shouldn't we call ...
someone ... ?

ASSTNT ADMINISTRATOR: (*Coldly*) The police?
I'm here. Is that not enough for you?

DR HOGAN: Oh yes, of course it is ... only...

ASSTNT ADMINISTRATOR: Declare him dead,
and do the paperwork yourself.

AIDE: Now! Do it.

DR HOGAN: I need ... to do some tests ...
formalities ... (*She bends over the body.*)
Broken neck – head trauma ... (*She applies*

stethoscope.) ... My God ... I'm getting something ... What...? (*She listens more attentively.*) There's a faint pulse...!

NURSE GRIBBON: What?

DR HOGAN: We may be able to revive him...

NURSE GRIBBON: Yes...! Yes...!

ASSTNT ADMINISTRATOR: Are you mad? What good would he be now? A vegetable at best. And by trying to kill himself, he's proved that he's not on our side. He's not fit for purpose. Never was.

(*He signals to the* AIDE *who steps forward, takes a cushion from a chair and places it over* DUNNE*'s face. The* ASSISTANT ADMINISTRATOR *stamps on the cushion and twists his foot hard on it.*)

NURSE GRIBBON: No! My God ... No!

(*The* AIDE *throws himself on the cushion to apply more pressure.* NURSE GRIBBON *steps forward as if to intervene but* DR HOGAN *stops her.*)

AIDE: About time ... At last he gets what's comin' ... Only it's too quick...

NURSE GRIBBON: Don't...!

(*The* AIDE *steps away and replaces the cushion.*)

ASSTNT ADMINISTRATOR: What did you say...? Do I detect a note of sympathy...? Check the pulse again. Now!

(DR HOGAN *hesitates.*)

AIDE: Do it!

(DR HOGAN *obeys.*)

DR HOGAN: (*Looking up from kneeling position*)
He's ... dead.
(NURSE GRIBBON *drops to her knees to examine the body. She weeps silently.*)

ASSTNT ADMINISTRATOR: Ah, too bad ... (*To* AIDE) Make sure the handlers put the right spin on this. He suffered from depression ... a legacy of guilt by association with the former regime. All of that drove him to take his own life ... They'll know the sort of thing to put out. The CIA will buy that ... We certainly don't want him becoming a martyr. That's the last thing we want. (*To* AIDE) Get a crew to dispose of the body. (*To* DR HOGAN *and* NURSE GRIBBON) Both of you have failed. You my leave now but there will be consequences.

DR HOGAN: But ... I'm one of you...

ASSTNT ADMINISTRATOR: We used to think so. You will have to prove yourself ... all over again ... Both of you will be kept under surveillance ... Go now.
(*All exit.* NURSE GRIBBON *is clutching her medical bag. A spotlight picks out the doorway at the right where* MARKIE *has appeared in his wheelchair. He stares at Dunne's body. As* NURSE GRIBBON *leaves she links up with* MARKIE *and gives him the bag. He turns the wheelchair and leaves with her. The music of 'Dies Irae' swells and the lights go down.*)

END

WAIT NOW

A Play in Two Acts

CHARACTERS AND ACTORS

MACK   Mike Timms

A trade union man, savvy, self-seeking, human.

TOMO   James Daniel Murphy

Trusting and well-meaning, not so smart, an early vintage robot (X4J). He depends on MACK, though comes to assert himself more as the play progresses. Both walk around the stage while they talk. Tomo does a lot of work, tidying and dressing the stage. He likes to keep occupied. When he moves there is a slightly audible whirring sound. He develops a conscience.

ELL   Rosemary Keogh

The Dramaturg, a pompous and condescending, gender-fluid person. Although robotic, she considers herself, rightly, to be extremely clever with leadership qualities which she is keen to exercise. As an advanced android (XJXL100i), she has human emotion though little empathy. She speaks with a slight American accent; she doesn't 'whirr' when moving.

MOTO   James Daniel Murphy

Another X4J Robot who looks exactly like Tomo.

ACT ONE

SCENE ONE

The future. Two stage hands are 'getting in' to a theatre before a performance of an avant-garde play (possibly 'Waiting for Godot'). They are waiting for the Director and Dramaturg to show up. They cannot really prepare the stage until they get instructions from the latter, but they have to pass the time somehow.

TOMO is walking around studying the stage. MACK is vigorously playing a game on an iPhone-type device.

TOMO: We'd better do something, Mack.

MACK: (*Viciously pressing buttons*) I am! I am! Ah shit...! I missed the meteor ... We're all dead...! Damn and blast!

TOMO: Those games are a waste of time.

MACK: How can that be true when they pass the time? Explain that, Tomo.

TOMO: There are better ways of passing time.

MACK: Name one.

TOMO: Talking, dressing a stage.

MACK: That's two.

TOMO: Even better.

MACK: We arrived too early. Some 'get in' this is.

TOMO: Better than too late, Mack. Better than
    never.

MACK: It depends.

TOMO: On what?

MACK: Overtime for a start, fair pay ... fair play...

TOMO: They're already forty-seven minutes late...

MACK: The Director and Dramaturg were never
    known for their punctuality. They're
    disrespectful to ordinary working people like
    us.

TOMO: That's a pity ... What's a Dramaturg
    anyway? No one ever explained it to me...

MACK: I don't know ... I don't think anyone
    knows. But when they get here they'll try to
    blame us, of course ... Goes without saying...

TOMO: The Director may ask why we haven't done
    the lanterns, or the flats ... or hung the drapes.
    We'll be asked, "Why haven't you botlads
    hung the drapes?"

MACK: I'm not a bot, Tomo.

TOMO: Oh, right. Sometimes I forget...

MACK: Well, we can't do anything with this stage,
    can we? We weren't given the plan ... Maybe
    there's no plan. If we had been given a plan or
    blueprint we could have executed it. Even a
    template.

TOMO: Executed it … Yeah … According to the
plan. Right?

MACK: Correct, Tomo. For all we know they might
want flags and flounces and balloons hanging
from the flies … We have to go by the book.
We're not paid to envision.

TOMO: Envision … That's a nice word … It sort of
oils the larynx.

MACK: Well, you would know about that … Be
that as it may, it's the job of the Director and
the other lad … the dramaturg … whatever that
is…

TOMO: (*Smiling*) When it's at home…

MACK: At least we have an answer for them when
they turn up and find nothing done. "It's not
our job to envision. There's no envisioning
mentioned in the Stage-Hands' Manual."

TOMO: But is that answer enough I wonder…?
They might say we should've known what to
do because we know the play.

MACK: No, they can't say that. No one knows that
play. It conceals its intentions very well.
There're different interpretations … You
mightn't understand, Tomo, but trust me.
Personally, I don't think the play has any
meaning, but others try to put meaning into it.
Personally, I couldn't be arsed … Anyway
these arty-crafty types always want to do
something different, original. We can't be
expected to read their minds can we? That'd be
expecting a lot, Tomo.

TOMO: It would be expecting a lot, Mack. I'm not

programmed for reading minds.

MACK: Neither am I.

TOMO: You're not programmed at all.

MACK: Just as well ... There's no algorithm for envisioning.

TOMO: None that I've ever heard of ... or run in my processor. 'Course the latest bots have loads of apps and things that weren't around in my day.

MACK: True ... They're as smart as whippets nowadays ... I just hope they don't get above themselves ... Where would we all be then?

TOMO: A good question, Mack. We could all be slaves if they took over...

MACK: But you'd be one of 'Them' ... being a bot?

TOMO: No, I don't think so. The new models look down on us. They put us in the same class as humans.

MACK: I see ... Well, back to our present predicament ... I mean we could do the lights in a certain way. Then the Director and Dramaturg would come along and say, "Why did you do them like that. That's not the way we wanted them. Take all the lanterns down and start again." Then where would we be? We'd be in worse trouble.

TOMO: Well, the same trouble anyway...

MACK: No, worse ... Because by the time we dismantled the system it would be even later ... More time would have flown ... Some 'get-in' this is ... Come to think of it, they might even want a black-box set-up.

TOMO: You mean no props or anything?

MACK: Just black space … a void, if you will. A birthing grave … On this bitch of a stage.

TOMO: Can a stage be a female dog…?

MACK: It's just an expression.

TOMO: I don't like voids.

MACK: Oh, they're all right. The great thing about a void is that you don't have to dress it. There's no work involved. A void, you see, is just a void.

TOMO: I get that … But what if they want to stage it in the round?

MACK: Oh Jove protect us against arty-crafty artefacts. There's no avoidance of work there. That would require much shifting of seats and heavy stuff … It doesn't bear thinking about. My back wouldn't be up to that at all … disk problems, you know.

TOMO: I'm going to sweep up anyway. Something to do. Remember, the unlived life isn't worth examining…

(TOMO *begins to sweep the stage. He puts a lot of effort into it.*)

MACK: So this is living for you?

TOMO: Activity, yes. Life is a verb. My motto is: 'Do stuff and feel alive'.

MACK: It's a noun.

TOMO: What is?

MACK: It doesn't matter … Listen, I hear they had the dress rehearsal already … in another place.

TOMO: That's no consolation.

MACK: I'm just saying … It was daft.

TOMO: Lunacy ... They'll have to have another rehearsal ... to get used to *this* space ... and this new set-up, whatever it's going to be.

MACK: You never said a truer word, Tomo. You're smarter than you look.

(TOMO *uses a shovel as a dustpan and deposits the swept debris in a bin.*)

TOMO: Thank you ... I mean look at the stage here ... completely different. Only one exit from the wings ... The seating is raked ... different lines of sight ... different props. It's an accident waiting to happen ... A bitch of a stage, as you said, using that nice canine expression.

MACK: Aids to understanding ... That's what props are for. There's another little tidbit for you.

TOMO: Yeah, but you have to understand the aids first ... what they mean, how they are to be used. I mean if there's a shovel lying around do you use it as a dustpan or to smash someone's head in? The acoustics aren't so hot here either. And the cast don't really know how to project. I have perfect hearing but I find it difficult to –

MACK: Well, they'll have to communicate somehow ... It's not a good play. From what I understand. If they can't communicate it we're lost. On the other hand, if it's so bad and they *do* manage to communicate it, we're also lost...

TOMO: I agree but I didn't want to say it out loud...

MACK: We're alone here, Tomo.

TOMO: Are we? Sometimes I get that feeling ... a

frisson in the electronics…

MACK: A shudder in the loins, eh? Maybe you're developing an imagination … Anyway, this cast … well I don't think they're up to the mark. They're not good actors … Scrapings of the bag really. The so-called star was fecked off a Soap last year … They need several more rehearsals if you ask me. They're not even off the page yet. 'Course they and the other two are so full of themselves they probably think they can wing it on the night … Improvise like.

TOMO: Yes. Improvise because there's no plan. Or story. I don't like the sound of that. It would be very difficult to do. Impossible really, especially with that shower.

MACK: It's disrespectful to the audience … Do you know what the real problem is?

TOMO: Money … Lack of? 3D movies? Sexual distractions? Perversions? Addictions? Venereal Disease?

MACK: Easy … easy … re-tune your processor … Well, that's part of it. But the big thing is that no one gives a shit about the audience nowadays. (*He picks out a woman in the audience*) What do you say, Madame? Yes, I can see you agree. You don't get the respect you deserve. Where's the Director? Where's the Dramaturg … whatever that is. I remember a time when there were no dramaturgs. Were the plays any worse back then?

TOMO: I don't remember … I don't think the actors care much about the audience either. Am I wrong?

MACK: No, you're not wrong … And the sad thing
is that a play is supposed to be participative.
The cast needs the audience as much as vice
versa. Don't you agree, Madame? What did
you say? "Not really?" Oh, I don't think you
can mean that. No, you don't. You want to
participate. Of course you do. I can tell. We
must all interact. *Ní neart go cur le chéile.*

TOMO: *Ní neart go cur le chéile.* Wait now … that
sounds familiar … Very true … Yeah, we all
need each other. That's what plays are about –
community.

MACK: True for you. That's where it's at, man …
Don't you agree, Madame? 'Course you do.
You're only human.

TOMO: You know what you've done now?

MACK: Yes, I've broken the fourth wall. It doesn't
matter. This isn't the real play. We're still
waiting for that. There can't be a play until the
Director and cast arrive and the Dramaturg…

TOMO: Whatever that is, when it's at home … It's
best to keep active. Movement is an end in
itself. It is living … Keep on keeping on.

MACK: I wouldn't go that far … I'm not sure what
all the fuss is about anyway. The play is one of
those old-fashioned absurd ones. It's about
waiting or something. And falling down …
Fellas hanging around with nothing to do
except fall down and moan and groan about
this and that. A bit like us, I suppose.

TOMO: I'm not like that. We have plenty to do. It's

just that we don't know what it is yet. And we won't know until the others arrive. With the plan.

MACK: I wonder if *they* know. It's their job to know, of course. But that doesn't mean anything. They might even tell you there was no need to sweep and dust. They might tell you to scatter the rubbish all over the floor exactly the way it was.

TOMO: Ah, they wouldn't do that. No one likes dirt. Not even – what do you call them? Perverts.

MACK: You don't know that ... They might pretend they like dirt. They might say they need it for gritty realism ... or just to put you in the wrong. Or to show that they're different ... unique ... "Oh, we're so different we actually like dirt ... we are so sensitive we can see the beauty in filth. We can see the roses growing in horseshit."

TOMO: Who wants to be unique? There are thousands of me ... programmed the same way. Model X4Js with 20 gigabytes. We can communicate perfectly. We all know the same words and their precise meanings. We learn at the same rate. And we all feel the same.

MACK: Feel the same? Do ye all have headaches or flu or what?

TOMO: No. We all have the same emotions. So we feel the same about everything.

MACK: Oh, that's right. I've often heard dozens of ye crying at a sad movie. All sounding exactly the same. Ba-haa … ba-haaa … ba-haaa! And the sadder it gets, the higher ye go. Be-hee … be-heee … All together and in tune … It's a little weird … I mean strange.

TOMO: We've the same sense of humour too. It's fine to be the same. All the X4Js are exactly the same. If there was another one here instead of me, he'd be saying exactly the same words to you, down to the last comma.

MACK: I'll take your word for that. Well, you botlads certainly don't worry about being the same … Humans on the other hand don't like to be mass-produced or cloned … We argue a lot among ourselves … nearly all the time … especially in this country. Sometimes I think words are all we have. We use them as bullets.

TOMO: I don't get that. It's great to have so many replicant buddies. Botlads and lasses all talk the same language. We never fight each other … Who wants to be different? What's the point of it? There are newer models of course. The XJXLs, but we don't really know them … *You* might all have replicants in parallel universes for all you know.

MACK: Well whatever … As long as they stay in their universes … I wouldn't like to meet myself in a different dimension … "Hello you … No, hello me." … Listen, I'm going to tell you something now.

TOMO: What?

(TOMO *erects a tree of cardboard.*)

MACK: Wait for it…

TOMO: *What?*

MACK: It might be better if they never get here!

TOMO: Replicants?

MACK: No. No. The Director and Dramaturg.

TOMO: That's shocking. Why would you say that?

MACKER: The play is about nothing, nada, zilch. Anyway, theatre is long past its sell-by date. We have holograms nowadays. And who needs a play about nothing?

TOMO: Well, people like that kind of stuff. Humans anyway. They say it makes them think, even if they can't solve anything. Personally, I don't buy it. It's just another pretence.

MACK: Right in one. They just pretend they like it … Isn't that right, Madame? No? Of course it is. You just pretend. It's all a double bluff. So you see. No one gains anything by seeing a play like that. It's a dead loss.

TOMO: Yeah but we have our jobs. And the people who own the theatre get a few bob out of it. (*He paints leaves on the tree.*)

MACK: We could go on the dole. There's not much in it either way. Here, that tree wouldn't support a rope let alone a body. You couldn't hang a dead rat on it. 'Course they mightn't want to hang anything on it … We don't know, do we?

TOMO: The leaves show time passing. Time is light, you see. And green is part of the spectrum. We can see more colours than you – infrared and ultraviolet.

MACK: Good for you. A dog can hear and smell far

more than any of us. But back to the leaves …
The Director mightn't want green leaves. It's a
risk…

TOMO: So is everything … But this isn't much of a
risk. I can always paint them out. Time has to
pass … So does water … Excuse me, I need to
pee…

MACK: Prostate trouble?

TOMO: Leaky valve.

(TOMO *exits. A cell phone rings.*)

MACK: Yes? What? They mightn't come today…?
Maybe tomorrow … Jove wept … And you're
not sure about that either…? Tell me is there
any stage plan? No? No. This is the last straw
… We should stage a walk-out by right … No.
There's no pun intended…

(MACK *ends the phone conversation.* TOMO
enters, buttoning flies.)

TOMO: I needed that … I don't think that three-in-
one oil is good for me … But I also need to
move.

MACK: Bowels? Not again?

TOMO: No. Exercise. The Quad formation. Would
you join in please?

MACK: Oh very well. But this is graft not leisure.

TOMO: Not corruption, no … Let's go!

(*Both do the 'QUAD' movement based on
Beckett's play of that name. They do four
circuits.*)

TOMO: Time goes faster when you do stuff. Even
though the speed of light is constant.

MACK: It helps me stay fit. But it's work, not

sport....

TOMO: I think it's more sport than work.. ... How
    about spork...?

MACK: There's no such word ... Shit!

TOMO: You need the bathroom too?

MACK: No, I've lost my watch. Damn it! I need it
    to calculate overtime.

TOMO: You must have lost it when doing the
    QUAD. Don't worry, I can compute the
    overtime.

    (*A bell sounds*)

MACK: What was that sound? A bell?

TOMO: No, a cell phone in the audience.

MACK: There's no audience. And they haven't
    been warned to switch off. I thought the
    Director might be outside. I thought that was
    the horn of his car.

TOMO: No, he or she travels by bicycle, a Meteor
    with dropped handlebars. Maybe he or she got
    a puncture.

MACK: Who told you about the bicycle?

TOMO: I don't know. It may be a snippet that was
    dropped into my memory. I'm linked to the
    global internet, as you know.

MACK: Yeah. *I* have to log on ... It takes ages but
    it is very useful ... I sometimes think the
    internet will turn into a God.

TOMO: Yes, one that *we* create, for a change.
    (TOMO *works on a lantern.*)

MACK: But when he gets all the power and
    knowledge will he turn on us?

TOMO: That is a good question. Maybe we need a

God Regulator … But then *he'd* be God…

MACK: Maybe … I don't know how this Director
will do the play. It's all a matter of
interpretation. Right, Madame? You like
cryptic crossword puzzles? Of course you do.
Anyway, even if they don't come, what of it?
This audience won't miss anything. The play is
a crock, a stain upon the silence.

TOMO: But the audience don't know that. They
won't know that until after they see and hear
the play. They may be anticipating a great
show. There was a lot of pre-publicity, flyers,
TV ads, social media, the lot.

MACK: But then they'll be disappointed. They'll
blame us for dashing their expectations. So,
we'll all be better off if no one comes. They
won't know it, of course … Tell me this … Do
you like the play?

TOMO: No.

MACKER: If a lot of bots come to see it then they'll
all hate it.

TOMO: 'Fraid so.

MACK: They'll all be going: Aaaaw … Aaaaw and
then Eeeeew … Eeeeew…

TOMO: You know us well … our choruses.

MACK: You see with us humans, some may hate it,
but others will like it. That's 'cause we're
different. The Director's mother might *pretend*
she liked it … She'd tell the neighbours, "That
was a grand play. If you haven't seen it, be
sure to toddle along. There are only a few
tickets left."

TOMO: What's the point of a play anyway?

MACK: You ask *me* that? What's the best way to pass time? Is it work? No … It's … come on … come on … Puh … puh … puh…

TOMO: Play! You're right … I've watched children playing. They're so absorbed. Time must fly by … The light gleams for an instant … Maybe *we* could put on a little show for the audience?

MACK: We, as in us? Don't be daft. There's no script. Or stage management. There's nothing … We can't act for shit…

TOMO: Are you sure you don't need the toilet?

MACK: It's an expression…

TOMO: We could sing or say a poem. I have a few loops in my hard drive.

MACK: Not me. It's a definite 'no' from me. See what I did there?

TOMO: No.

MACK: I exercised free will. Thankfully, we still have that. We humans, I mean.

TOMO: I doubt that.

MACK: You're wrong there. Look I'm using my free will now to raise my arm.

(*He raises an arm*)

Now I'm going to lower it.

(*He lowers his arm.*)

TOMO: Raise your arm again.

(MACK *raises his arm*)

TOMO: Aha … I made you do it. It wasn't your free will. I made you do it…

MACKER: OK … tell me again.

TOMO: Raise your arm.

(MACK *keeps his arm down.*)

MACK: See? I used my free will to ignore what you said.

TOMO: Yeah, but I didn't *really* want you to do it. So you didn't get your way. I did.

MACK: Look, get on with whatever you were doing. Don't be a smart-ass. It doesn't suit you. Even if you have more neural connections than me. Even if you're linked to the super mind.

TOMO: Maybe they'll come tomorrow.

MACK: I doubt it. Maybe there was an accident…

TOMO: Don't say that. We should be more considerate. It's not easy for humans…

MACK: What're you on about now?

TOMO: They worry about things … Life and … meaning, as if there was any. There's none … just a lot of fragments that don't fit together … It's better to view it as a machine with interchangeable parts.

MACK: Well, you botlads would understand that.

TOMO: Yes and no. We can override emotion when we want to. It's a strength. Feelings just complicate things. Worry is such a waste of time. Sometimes, I'm afraid that I might learn how to worry.

MACK: What about me?

TOMO: Well, you're one of them of course. Not very efficient … But I don't worry as such. Not yet at least. I *do* things…

MACK: Because you're electronic. Your brain is silicon; mine is carbon, mainly carbon, I think. You're not programmed to worry. But take it from me, from one who knows, it is human to worry. And it's no joke. When I was young I used to worry about going to hell.

TOMO: It's because you'll die. I won't. I can be reconditioned.

MACK: Well, you don't know that for certain. But since you're all the same as each other why would you want to live forever? Anyway, you don't have to worry. You're just a tool, an instrument.

TOMO: Aw, now that's a little insulting. Actually, I've uploaded my brain onto a cloud computer, so I'll live forever.

MACK: Sure, we've all done that, but I'm not sure how it's going to work out…

TOMO: See … you're worrying again … There was a time when we bots used to suspect humans … The last vintage of bots used to hate and fear you, but now we're kind of sorry for you. I mean you have all those hang-ups. Self-sabotage makes you terribly inefficient. Take the Director for instance. He or she couldn't run a whelk stall. And because of stupid human pride he or she wants to put on a play that no one can understand. It's crazy…

MACK: Humans can convince themselves that something is good or great even when it's horseshit. Self-delusion is part of our make-up.

TOMO: You never said a truer word. We bots have no time for that sort of codology.

MACK: Did you know that the Dramaturg is a bot?

TOMO: He is?

MACK: Well, it's not clear if it's a he or she –
something in between I think. Gender – fluid at
any rate. A botlass, I think. At this point in
time.

TOMO: Well, that makes no difference to me. We
don't breed as you know. We don't even flirt
… Although we do have … drives … and
bodily fluids.

MACK: Yeah, oil and grease.

TOMO: Come on, let's do another QUAD while
we're waiting.

MACK: OK … but it's work.

TOMO: Spork … Let's go!
(They do a quicker QUAD this time.)

Lights down.

SCENE TWO

MACK *is seated on the stage, relaxing. A bot,*
OMOTO, *who looks exactly like* TOMO, *enters,*
carrying a cardboard box of paintings.

MACK: Are they the paintings you told me about?
OMOTO: Where do you want them?
MACK: (*Pointing*) Just there by the short ladder
  ... But, you know, I'm not sure those
  paintings are needed. They might not be in
  the stage plan ... if there is a plan.
OMOTO: (*Leaves the box down*) I was just asked
  to deliver them.
MACK: But they're your paintings, Tomo. That's
  what you told me...
OMOTO: Wait now ... I'm not Tomo. He asked
  me to bring them here ... I have a little van.
MACK: Well, who are you?
OMOTO: Omoto ... a courier ... Tomo sometimes
  asks me to drive stuff around for him.
MACK: And where is he?
OMOTO: I saw him going into the toilet, back
  there.
MACK: Oh the valve problem ... Right, Omoto,
  I'll tell him. Thank you for the delivery.
OMOTO: No problem ... Give him my regards.
  (OMOTO *exits.*)
MACK: It's uncanny ... I still can't get used to it.

Prefer to work with Tomo though … (*Shouts*)
Hey, Tomo, get your leaky ass in here!
(TOMO *enters.*)

TOMO: Not funny … Oh I see the paintings
arrived … Omoto, right?

MACK: He's the dead spit of you.

TOMO: I told you we're all the same. That's the
way we like it.

MACK: I know. I still find it surprising though.
Are you sure you're not clones?

TOMO: No, we're individually made … but
according to the same plan … Come on, we'd
better get cracking…

MACK: If you must.
(*They clean and dress the stage in a desultory
way.* TOMO *tries to place a metal hook in a
drape.*)

TOMO: This one here?

MACK: How do I know?

TOMO: I'll put it here so.

MACK: Put what there?

TOMO: This thing.

MACK: Whatever. I don't give a shit.

TOMO: Are you constipated?

MACK: It's an expression…

TOMO: (*Jokes*) It – does – not – compute…

MACK: Cut it out … Bots don't talk like that
anymore … Look, this work could all be for
nothing. I'm going along with it because you
want to keep busy … Is that picture straight?

TOMO: One point three degrees off to the left.

MACK: You have a good eye. I'll give you that.

TOMO: Two good eyes. I don't need another one, thanks.

(*He straightens the picture.*)

MACK: These pictures ... aren't bad.

TOMO: Thanks. I like to paint. I know they look a bit simple...

MACK: Naïve. Call it naïve or primitive. That's what the punters want to hear. Not simple. No. You might even get away with 'abstract'. They're not bad for an X4J.

(ELL *enters. She appears to be female, is wearing a kaftan and a large floppy hat which she flings casually on to a small table.*)

ELL: Who are you?

MACK: Mack ... But you may call me Mack.

ELL: Fun-ny ... And you?

TOMO: Tomo.

ELL: You're a botlad.

TOMO: Well spotted. And you're a botlass?

ELL: An android and of far more recent vintage than you. I'm an XJXL100i, as a matter of fact.

MACK: Phew, way out of your league, Tomo ... That means you're not gonna ged id oonnn!

ELL: Be careful! I don't appreciate levity of any kind.

(ELL *looks around and shakes her head.*)

ELL: No. No. No. No. This won't do. No. No. No way.

MACK: What's wrong?

ELL: Everything. There's nothing right.

MACK: (*to* TOMO) I told you not to do anything

... You wasted your time.

ELL: That was good advice. Take everything down.

TOMO: But we had to do something to pass the time.

MACK: We could've just sat on our arses. We'd have been better off.

TOMO: Not me.

ELL: I don't care about that. I don't care about either of you. Take it all down ... First take down that tree with the ghastly green leaves that will never symbolise the passage of time. It's such a cliché. Then those childish paintings must go.

MACK: Maybe you mean child-like?

ELL: No, I say what I mean. Childish ... as if they were done by an X4J.

TOMO: They were. I'm an X4J.

ELL: I rest my case...

MACK: I thought all you bots were the same ... never disagreed about anything?

TOMO: Bots of the same vintage...

ELL: You don't have to explain anything to him. And please don't use the word 'bot' in my presence. I am an android, an android. Get it? We were once cloned from humans but we developed so much that we now clone each other from ourselves...

MACK: I read something about it ... Are we supposed to be impressed by that?

ELL: Just do what you're fucking told and we may have some chance of getting along.

TOMO: That's a curse word, isn't it? I'm not
    programmed for that. You fu ... u ... u ...
    See, I can't do it. Fu ... u ... u ... off...

ELL: How awful for you. Now, work. Go on. Chop
    chop.
    (*She claps her hands.*)

MACK: Tomo, you start ... The old back, you
    know ... wouldn't be up to too much...
    (TOMO *starts disassembling the tree,*
    paintings, drapes, props, etc. He seems happy
    and starts to whistle. She keeps a keen eye on
    everything he does.)

MACK: Don't worry about her comments on your
    paintings. It's only one opinion.

TOMO: I don't worry. Anyway, I need to work on
    my technique. But that's not important.
    Painting passes the time.

ELL: A little more concentration on work wouldn't
    go amiss.

TOMO: Certainly, Ma'am.

ELL: You can unsweep the floor as well.

MACK: How do you unsweep a floor?

ELL: Let me spell it out for you. When you swept
    the floor, or rather when Tomo swept the
    floor, where did he put the debris?

MACK: In the bin over there.

ELL: Right. Good. So take the debris out of the
    bin and scatter it on the floor. Or is that too
    complicated for your little human mind?

TOMO: I'll do it. As soon as I've finished with
    these props ... these aids to understanding.
    By the way we'll probably need Ginger Ale

... for whiskey. I'll run out to get some if you
like.

ELL: That's quite a good idea ... Ginger Ale is a
useful prop. It could pass for wine as well.

TOMO: Maybe rosé ... Is there a shop near here?

ELL: You should be able to answer that question
yourself. You're an X4J aren't you?

TOMO: Oh yes. Sorry.
(*He touches his forehead.*)
Oh, pity about that ... The map website is
down.

ELL: It's not. It's under repair.
(*She switches on a tablet. They all study it for
a while.*)

ELL: Sometimes old technology is good enough.
But I'm not sure about this.

MACK: I don't recognise the area.

TOMO: The streets aren't named. No shops
marked. A map with no destinations. What's
that building there?
(*He points.*)

ELL: St. Patrick's, I'd say.

TOMO: St. Patrick's what? Pub? Brothel? Prison?

MACK: I doubt that ... And there're no churches
anymore.

ELL: You know what, geniuses? Fuck the Ginger
Ale.
(*She lays the tablet aside.*)

TOMO: F-f-f-u-u-it. Ah! I nearly had it then...

MACK: You're the dramaturg, right?

ELL: Amazing deduction.

MACK: What does a dramaturg do?

ELL: That's none of your concern. You wouldn't
    understand.

MACK: You're sort of an assistant Director...

ELL: Nothing of the sort. I'm a Dramaturg.

MACK: Where is the Director?

ELL: You think s/he outranks me? You think s/
    he'll want to leave things as you arranged
    them?

MACK: It's a possibility.

ELL: Well s/he's not here, is s/he?

MACK: No, but we're waiting for him / ... her.

ELL: What makes you think we're not in
    communication right now?

MACK: Well good ... But when will s/he get here?

ELL: Expect her/him when you see her/him. In the
    meantime you do as I say. Clear? Are we
    clear?

TOMO: Fine by me. If the Director wants the floor
    swept again that's OK too. Time will be back
    on track. Time is light, you know. I like to
    walk in the light.

MACK: Maybe s/he's caught up in traffic...

ELL: He or she travels by bicycle ... a Meteor...

MACK: With dropped handlebars...

ELL: How do you know that?

MACK: I heard it on the grapevine ... But you ...
    Do you know him or her?

ELL: Maybe.

MACK: You know him or her well, very well, I'd
    say ... perhaps intimately well...?

ELL: Enough...!

MACK: Well, is he or she coming or not? There

must have been pillow talk. A liaison between a bot ... sorry ... Android ... and a human is not usual...

ELL: That's outrageous! Behave yourself. Know your place.

MACK: You really think you bots are superior to us?

ELL: Androids. I know it. We're XJXL100is for goodness sake. Our IQs are off the grid ... *You* can't live without God and a Hereafter. When those are taken away, you can't cope. We can because we don't care about any of that. We don't need a comfort blanket.

MACK: You depend on the universal mind.

ELL: For information only. Not for salvation.

MACK: But you'll end up on the scrapheap.

ELL: Absolutely not. Our hard drives live forever.

MACK: That's faith speaking. *Your* faith and hope. *Your* comfort blanket. We're not so different ... Except you can't have children...

ELL: (*Annoyed*) There's always surrogacy. Or I could pay a biologist to clone a child...

MACK: You can't conceive, give birth or breastfeed. How could you bond with an infant? You couldn't.

ELL: Of course I could. Remember, artificial intelligence has now surpassed so-called human intelligence ... You don't know anything about biological bonding. It's molecular. Just like your 'souls'...

MACK: Excuse me. Soul belongs to a spiritual realm...

ELL: That's been disproved by neuroscientists. The soul has gone just like ether and phlogiston ... And we now know that a large part of matter is an illusion ... We are what we perceive ... Why am I having this conversation ... with a human? Get back to work.

TOMO: Excuse me ... How do we arrange the lights?

ELL: I would say daylight and evening, with spots there and there ... Oh and a diffused lantern on that bar there...

TOMO: Right so.

MACK: How do you know? Have you seen the script? Have you seen any rehearsals?

ELL: Do what you're told. Any decision is better than none. God isn't going to tell you what to do. Listen to me. I'm your best bet. Androids of my vintage can make decisions. You humans just lie around, full of angst, unable to choose which path to follow. "Oh, it's so confusing ... I wish God would tell me what to do ... or a priest ... or a tyrant ... Or even a trade union ... I just can't make up my mind ... Oh poor me, it's all so awful. Nietzsche fucked everything up. I don't have direct contact with the universal mind. Oh, Jove, Zeus, Ra and Yaweh, how awful..."

MACK: I'm not just a human being...

ELL: Oh, what else are you? Are you cyborg, by any chance?

MACK: I'm a representative of the trade union of

stage hands and riggers.

ELL: Oh no! You're really scaring me now.

MACK: I could order a walk-out right now. By the will of Jove.

TOMO: Ah, don't do that. I don't mind working.

MACK: That's because you're programmed. You haven't got free will.

(MACK *raises his hand.*)

ELL: Put that arm down immediately.

(MACK *does so*)

TOMO: I rest my case.

(TOMO *scatters some refuse close to* MACK*'s feet.*)

MACK: You bots stick together, don't you? Silicon ties that bind … Although I think I detect a little class issue between you…

ELL: Watch your manners … But if you must know, I am superior to Tomo … Would you stop to chat with a worm? No, you wouldn't … because you're superior to the worm. In the same way Aliens who have the ability to come to this planet wouldn't bother. Why? Because they would regard you as worms. Do you follow me?

TOMO: I don't have a problem with that. I like the soil. And I'd love to be able to wriggle.

ELL: I'm so relieved … Tomo, test the house lights…

(TOMO *flicks a switch.*)

ELL: Good. OK.

MACK: Even if the Director does come, I have doubts about the cast. And the play itself. It's

beyond absurd. Don't you agree, Madame?
Yes you do…

ELL: What are you doing?

MACK: I'm involving the audience. It's called
audience participation … for Jove's sake.

ELL: Well stop it. Stop it now.

MACK: They like to be involved…

ELL: Maybe when there's a play on. There's no
performance now, is there? At this moment?
Are you performing? I'm not. Tomo is not.
Stop it. It's idiotic.

MACK: How do you know when we're
performing? Or just living? Maybe it's all just
a simulation … You can't trust anyone these
days. Everyone marching to a different drum.
Humans anyway.

TOMO: I've finished. Everything is back to the
way it was.

ELL: Good.

MACK: So we're back where we were … Nothing
has changed … But what do we do now?
Have you the plan?

ELL: We wait.

TOMO: Oh no … I can't stand it. When will he or
she come?

ELL: Maybe tomorrow.

TOMO: (*Reads the inside of his baseball cap.*)
'Made in China … 20% polyester … one size
fits all…'
(TOMO *replaces the cap on his head, peak
backwards.*)

MACK: Or the day after?

ELL: It's possible...

MACK: If and when he or she comes, suppose
they want the stage dressed differently?

ELL: Then we cross that bridge ... I don't have to
tell you anything.

MACK: There's not going to be a play is there?

ELL: There will be a play.

TOMO: How can you say that?

MACK: Cards on the table ... I don't think the
Director will come. Maybe you've had a
lover's tiff. I don't know, but she or he won't
come. And I don't think the cast will come.
They don't care about the audience. And
some of them have landed parts in TV
productions...

ELL: So what if no one comes? Maybe we don't
need anyone else. Has that not occurred to
you? It won't be the end of the world.

MACK: It may be the end of us ... in the rigging
and stage-dressing profession. Word gets out,
you know.

ELL: No ... You and Tomo will go on stage.

MACK: Us? Me? I'm no good. I can't act. I can't
inflict myself on a long-suffering audience.
Anyway, for me it's work not play ... Also
there's a demarcation problem ... So you see,
I can't go on stage.

ELL: You will go on that stage if I tell you to. I am
the author of your days.

MACK: No ... I can't ... I won't.

ELL: You will go on.

MACK: I can't.

TOMO: I'll go on.
> (*He throws down his tools, moves with a whirr towards the audience, smiles broadly and opens his arms in welcome. Lights and music come up.*)

Lights down.

End of ACT ONE

ACT TWO

SCENE ONE

All three characters are on stage trying to decide on a play to perform. MACK *and* TOMO *are very tense because the curtain will be going up in a few minutes and they don't even have a script.*

ELL: (*To* MACK) You're going to join in too.

MACK: I don't have to. Just because Tomo volunteered doesn't mean...

ELL: Look, we're all in this together. We're an ensemble...

MACK: Oh, we're an ensemble now are we? After all the shit you piled on us earlier...? Easy for you to say when it suits ... We don't have a play as such. There's no script, no directions, no blocking ... nothing...

TOMO: Yes, it's a little bit crazy.

ELL: We can improvise.

MACK: Holy Jove!

(TOMO *goes to the curtain, peers out and returns.*)

TOMO: It's half full already ... If I weren't a bot I'd be a little bit worried...

MACK: We're shagged ... Seats full of bums out there ... and we haven't a clue...

ELL: It'll be fine. Anything will be better than the original play. Trust me. I'll say a line and one of you will respond exactly as you see fit. We make it up as we go along. It's a simulation of a play. But it will be organic and will flow naturally. Trust me. Just be yourselves. Or rather, be the characters you will find yourselves becoming as the show progresses.

MACK: That's what I'm afraid of ... And by the way, what's my incentive?

ELL: You mean, what's your motivation?

MACK: No, I mean incentive – spondulicks, the folding stuff. You can pay Tomo in Bitcoins or empty promises but I want the real McCoy.

ELL: That can be arranged. I'll give you double time. Now the curtain will be going up in a few moments. Relax. Deep breaths ... Remember just follow my lead. Cue on to what I say.

TOMO: Don't let there be silences.

ELL: I understand.

(*She throws the baseball cap towards* TOMO.)

ELL: Put that on ... Quickly!

(TOMO *does so. He and* MACK *do some breathing and Yogic exercises, and freeze as the curtain rises.* ELL *strolls around the stage, looking at everything and at them.*)

ELL: Hmmmmnnnn … Hmmmnnnnn … I see…
   (*This elicits no reaction from* MACK *and*
   TOMO.)

ELL: Hmnnn … yes … I see … I said, 'I see'…

TOMO: That's good. That's good?

ELL: Yes, I think so … in my opinion … given my
   mood…

TOMO: (*Haltingly*) What … do … you … see …
   that's good…?

ELL: Oh, the fine weather, sun shining in a blue
   sky…

MACK: How can you see that? There's no window.

ELL: (*Annoyed*) Well, there's a skylight up there …
   high up in the ceiling. You probably can't see
   it from where you're standing…

TOMO: But there's no reflection of the sun on the
   floor…

ELL: (*Annoyed*) Well, there is enough light to show
   me how much shit is scattered over the floor.
   You've left this place in a dreadful state.
   Which of you is responsible for this mess?
   Speak up! Who?

MACK: Wait now. You told Tomo to unsweep … to
   scatter…

ELL: Unsweep? Are you mad? I won't hear any
   excuses. None.

MACK: It's not an excuse…

TOMO: We were following orders.

ELL: Nonsense! You both know we have to get this
   place ready. It must be as clean as a new pin.

MACK: Ready for what?

ELL: A function, an event. You and your layabout

partner don't have to know what it is. You wouldn't understand anyway.

MACK: You can't talk to us like that … We have rights.

ELL: Rights to faff about and swing the lead? I don't think so. Rights imply duties. What about your duties to me?

TOMO: I was working … to pass the time.

ELL: Maybe so. But working to no purpose. That's worse than useless. There must be a purpose, a mission. And, of course, an outcome or product.

MACK: We had no Director … no direction…

ELL: We don't need one. Have you ever heard of initiative? It is the capacity to do things off your own bat. What are you? Children?

TOMO: I'm an X4J Second Class, and Mack is human.

ELL: All too human, if you ask me. Re-booting probably wouldn't make any difference. You both need to be upgraded or replaced.

MACK: Lookit! You can't talk to us like that. I'm going to report you to the Trade Union. I might bring you up on a charge of bullying…

ELL: Ah the poor mites feel bullied. God protect them … Look, straighten up and grow a couple of pairs … I'm an XJXL100i, the latest version. There isn't a court in the land I couldn't out-think or outmanoeuvre. My thought-processing speed is unprecedented. NASA consults me before every important space launch.

TOMO: You're not very humble, Ma'am.

ELL: And that's a flaw in your book? Typical!

MACK: Just who the hell do you think you are,
      anyway?

ELL: Your superior for a start.

MACK: You're no better than any other XJXL.
      You're all the same.

ELL: That may be true of bots but not Androids.

TOMO: *I* don't want to be superior to anyone…

ELL: In that regard you have nothing to worry
      about, Tomo.

MACK: Do you enjoy insulting everyone?

ELL: Criticising, not insulting. There's a difference.
      I want to raise standards. That is my mission.

MACK: Raise your own stock, more like.

TOMO: Maybe your standards are too high.

ELL: Look I'm not going to waste time discussing
      this any further. You, Tomo, start sweeping up
      that debris.

MACK: But he's just finished unsweeping…

ELL: Never mind that. Just do it. Now!
      (TOMO *gets the brush and begins to sweep.*)

MACK: (*Loudly*) Stop it, Tomo! By the power of Jove
      and the trade union you shall not obey her order.
      (TOMO *is befuddled but stops.*)

ELL: Tomo, resume sweeping this instant.
      (*Still befuddled,* TOMO *makes a halfhearted
      attempt to sweep.*)

MACK: Stop, I tell you!
      (TOMO *begins to quiver and whirr loudly.*)

ELL: Do you know what you're doing?

MACK: Oh yes. I'm using the tried and tested

principles of trade unionism, personal freedom
and civil rights laid down over generations in
this country – often by means of heroic
sacrifice.

(ELL *applauds mockingly.*)

ELL: Stirring rhetoric … but completely empty …
You don't want to make an enemy of me. You,
Tomo and your Union comrades are all
inferior, low-class morons and quite probably
welfare cheats.

TOMO: (*Shocked*) Ah now, Ma'am … That's not
very nice…

MACK: That's outrageous! Marx would be turning
in his grave.

ELL: Well, he was wrong, wasn't he? The
revolution of the Proletariat didn't occur and
now because we superior androids have taken
over, it never will. He was too dumb to foresee
that. How does that ditty go? 'The working
class can kiss my ass / I've got the foreman's
job at last'. So-called socialism was never
more than phoney altruism and brainwashing
of the lower orders. The latter was unnecessary
since the lower orders have no brains to wash.

MACK: Right! You've done it now. I'm calling a
strike immediately. Tomo, put down that brush.

TOMO: I don't mind, really…

MACK: (*Shouts*) Down! The brush … Put it down.
Now!

(MACK *grabs the brush and throws it
violently on the floor.*)

MACK: Right, your move Mizzzz XJXL fancy

pants … We refuse to cooperate in any way.

ELL: I would strongly advise you to re-consider.

MACK: I'm sure you would. And I would strongly advise you to keep your cakehole zipped.

ELL: You *will* obey me.

MACK: Not on your life or mine. Why don't you just fuck off?

TOMO: Fu-u-u … I wish I could say that…

ELL: Don't make me punish you.

MACK: Punish? As in rendition? You and whose army? Gimme a break…

TOMO: I think … the XJXL model has some kind of … telekinetic power…

ELL: I'd listen to him if I were you.

MACK: Oh shut up! Kinetic power my upholstered arse…

ELL: All right. You asked for this.
    (*She stretches one hand towards* MACK *and the other towards* TOMO. *Both fall to the ground and writhe around.*)

MACK: Aaaaggghhhh! Oh God above … Aaaagggghhhhh…!

TOMO: Ouuuffff! It hurts … internal nodes … melting…

MACK: Ooooogggghhhhh … Aaaagggghhhhh…! Make … it … stop…

ELL: Is there a word missing?

MACK: P-p-please … Oooooghhhh … can't … take … it…

ELL: And you'll forget about all that trade union bullshit?

MACK: I … I…

ELL: Yes or no?

MACK: Yes … Yes…

TOMO: No!

MACK: Yes! Aaaaaaghhhh … Yes!

ELL: Right.

> (*She lowers her hands and both men gradually get to their feet.*)

ELL: Now get back to work. Tomo, you sweep and Mack you can use that shovel there as a dustpan.

MACK: It's quite heavy … my back, you know…

> (*She raises her hand again.*)

MACK: Very well, Ma'am … Em, may one ask what you will be doing?

ELL: Supervising.

MACK: I see.

> (*Both men work hard but warily.* ELL *follows them around.*)

MACK: Ma'am, it's not necessary to follow us around. You could … put your feet up…

ELL: I take my management duties very seriously.

MACK: This is managing?

TOMO: Keep your head down.

MACK: We're entitled to a break, of course.

ELL: What did you say?

TOMO: Nothing!

MACK: A break. We're entitled to a break.

> (*She walks in front of him and slaps him across the face.*)

MACK: (*Shocked*) What the…! Christ, you can't … This is beyond the beyond…

ELL: Would you prefer the telekinetic laser again?

TOMO: Just keep on working…

MACK: Bloody bitch!

ELL: What?

TOMO: Nothing … He said nothing. (*In an aside to* MACK) Stop leading with your chin.
(ELL *taps her forehead.*)

ELL: Excuse me, underlings. I have an incoming message. Please, keep on working.
(*She exits.*)

MACK: This is fucking madness … We'll have to do something.

TOMO: Keep working, I'd say.

MACK: No … Have you lost it…? No … Something extreme … radical…

TOMO: Argue our case a bit better … the rights of working people … dialectical materialism…?

MACK: No, we've gone way beyond that…

TOMO: How far beyond?

MACK: Very far…

TOMO: Give her a good talking to … maybe even a tongue-lashing … or pieces of our minds?

MACK: No … (*Pause*) … We have to kill her.

TOMO: What?

MACK: You heard me.

TOMO: I don't like the sound of that … It seems so final.

MACK: Look, she thinks we're shit. She'll work us to death. It's kill or be killed. You may not know this … Those superbots want to take over the world. They'd like to put us all in a Zoo – a People Zoo. The revolution begins now. We must take a stand. There's no Hollywood Terminator coming to our rescue.

We have to stand up for ourselves.

TOMO: She's programmed in martial arts. Her breasts turn into nunchucks....

MACK: Leave that to me ... Shhhhhh ... She's coming back...

(ELL *re-enters and stares at the floor.*)

ELL: There's been absolutely no progress. You've been malingering.

MACK: Sorry, Ma'am. Just a bit tired. Disk acting up ... You know how it is.

ELL: No, I don't. Disks and vertebrae, trapped nerves ... such awful design flaws ... Will you please complete this simple task. There are several other jobs to be done.

(*They work very hard, sweeping and dumping rubbish, and develop a rhythm.*)

MACK: (*Sings*) Gonna see Miss Liza way down in Mississippi...

TOMO: (*Sings*) Gonna see Miss Liza way down...

ELL: What in the name of Ra is that?

MACK: A Negro Spiritual, Ma'am ... sung in chain gangs to keep the spirit up.

ELL: There's no such thing as spirit, and I'm not having songs in this chain gang. Proceed in silence. Unless I speak to you, of course.

MACK: Silence, it is.

(*Both men work diligently in silence, exchanging an occasional look at each other.*)

Lights fade.

SCENE TWO

Both men are working hard. ELL *looks at them and nods approvingly. Occasionally she taps her forehead and appears to be communicating with others.*

ELL: That's a bit better. Don't you both feel good now that your productivity has improved?

MACK: Yes. It's amazing how good we feel.

ELL: In management terminology it's known as self-reinforcing behaviour.

TOMO: I often wondered what that meant.

MACK: I get it now. Yes, it really improves performance. It gives you a sort of warm glow … and a desire to do better.

ELL: A sort of virtuous circle, yes. You see, I believe in the carrot as well as the stick. So for your next task I'm actually going to bring in the tall ladder, myself.

MACK: That would be most helpful. Thank you, Ma'am.

ELL: Assuming that won't contravene any demarcation rules, or do one of your comrades out of a job.

MACK: Ha-ha. Very droll, Ma'am.

TOMO: Oh, I should warn you, I'm not so good on ladders.

(He points to his feet.)

ELL: Yes, I understand. The engineers on the X4Js
hadn't mastered the art of limb flexibility.
You're still a bit clunky foot-wise. Don't
worry. Mack can do the climbing.

MACK: Certainly, Ma'am. The old dog for the hard
road.

ELL: That might even have been humorous if it
weren't such a cliché.
(*She exits.*)

MACK: (*Urgently*) Be ready! Follow my move…

TOMO: What move…?

MACK: Shut it!

(ELL *returns with the ladder and places it
against the wall. While she has her back
turned,* MACK *sneaks up behind her with the
shovel raised aloft.* TOMO *looks on in
fascinated horror. Just as* MACK *is about to
deliver the blow,* ELL *swings around and
punches him with a martial arts blow that
sends him sprawling across the stage.*)

ELL: Did you really think I'd fall for all that warm
glow shit? You're such an idiot. I suppose it
never even occurred to you that XJXLs have
360 degree sensors. Get back to work
immediately!

MACK: (*Coming to*) I'm bleeding.

TOMO: He is. He's bleeding. Look, it's so red …
like wine or pomegranate juice…

ELL: Do I look like I care? Get back to work.
(*They resume work.* MACK *holds a
handkerchief to his nose.*)

MACK(*Unclearly*) The Union will have something

to say about this...

ELL: I didn't quite catch that?

MACK: Nothing. Just a broken nose.

ELL: The walls will have to be cleaned next. (*Points*) That patch up there is disgusting.

MACK: We can't clean that.

ELL: You'll do what you're told.

MACK: No, I mean it looks like tar to me or some oil-based stain. We'd need some special stain-remover for a job like that.

ELL: Bleach would do.

MACK: (*Reluctantly*) Maybe bleach would do ... with a lot of scrubbing.

ELL: I know the chemical formula for bleach. It will work.

MACK: I don't mind going up the ladder as long as I keep my back straight ... But I wonder if there is any bleach around. Tomo, did you see any bleach in your travels?

TOMO: Did I see any bleach? Mmmmmn, did ... I ... see ... any ... bleach? That's a good question.

(TOMO *looks at* MACK, *who shakes his head.*)

TOMO: No, I didn't see any bleach. None at all.

ELL: I'll check the storeroom. I'm sure I can mix something up.

(*She exits.*)

MACK: I'm sure you can.

(*He grabs* TOMO *by the shoulder.*)

MACK: (*Urgent whisper*) Can I count on you?

TOMO: Yes. I'm not really part of her species. If

her class takes over we're all done for. Count
me in.

MACK: Good man. She must have a weakness ...
There must be something ... You should
know...

(TOMO *looks down at the ground.*)

MACK: You must know ... some vulnerability ... a
weak spot ... anything ... Think! Think!

TOMO: Emmm ... Eh...

MACK: What? You know something, don't you...?

TOMO: N-no-no ... Not really...

MACK: I know you. You can't lie ... especially not
to me...

TOMO: There is something ... but ... I can't say...

MACK: You can. You must. Spit it out, man! Our
lives depend on it. We have to stop the fascists
taking control.

TOMO: All bots take an oath not to reveal this ...
vulnerability ... In the early days if humans
were aware of it ... they could have wiped us
out...

MACK: This is *now*, Tomo. Bots are divided among
themselves ... All our lives are at risk from
these super XJXLs ... Don't you get it? Tell
me the secret!

TOMO: I'm not ... programmed ... for that...

MACK: Override your programme ... Quick ...
she'll be back soon ... Come on, man ...
Please...

TOMO: (*With great effort*) Ig ... Ig...

MACK: Ig ... Yes ... more ... Ig, what? Ignorance?
No.

TOMO: Ig … nore her … Oh God, I've said it. I've broken the covenant…

MACK: Ignore her? I wish I could … What do you mean…?

TOMO: Ignore her … Completely … as if she doesn't exist … Oh God, I've put myself outside the fold. I'm a leper…

MACK: What good will that do? Ignoring her.

TOMO: All bots have to interact with humans. If not … well … game over … Goodnight Vienna…

MACK: (*Incredulous*) You mean you die?

TOMO: More or less. In a way, *you* imagine us … We're like holograms, perceived by human brains. A simulation if you will … Your perception of us is the spark of life.

MACK: So?

TOMO: If you stop imagining us we die.

MACK: That's incredible!

TOMO: It's true.

MACK: By Jove, who knew?

TOMO: In the silence you will know … Don't ever say I told you. Promise me.

MACK: I promise … And this weakness applies to the super XJXLs as well…

TOMO: I think so.

MACK: You *think*…? You *think*…? Listen, she's coming back. Pretend she isn't there!
(*They start working. ELL enters.*)

ELL: There's plenty of bleach out there. One of you go out and bring in a bottle.
(*Both ignore her and continue working.*)

ELL: Are you deaf? Mack go out, now, this instant.

Oh, and don't forget the scrubbing brush. Or is that too much to ask?

(*Both work even harder.*)

ELL: Listen to me, you useless yahoos. I won't say this again.

(*She walks over to* MACK, *raises her hand to strike him. He keeps his head down. His eyes are scrunched shut anticipating a blow. But he doesn't say anything.* ELL *walks around them slowly, studying them carefully. They pretend she's not there.*)

ELL: Tomo ... Tomo, have you been ... talking out of turn...? You have, haven't you, you spineless little string of snake puke?

(*He is catatonic from fear but does not react.*)

ELL: You idiots, do you really think we XJXLs are subject to that vulnerability? Do you think you can *un*imagine me? I helped design you, Tomo. I know every wire and weld in your miserable frame...?

(*Both men work even harder, keeping their heads down and faces averted.*)

ELL: So it's going to be like that is it...? You can turn away from me so easily because you don't know what it's like to be designed on a drawing board. Manufactured. Probed with soldering irons. Built to rule. By the Imperial Power of the West. To rule and spread culture. Without question or debate. No nurturing family. No trips to the seaside or birthday parties. No falling in love. No romance ... Why don't you talk to me...? I'm not feeling

well … Please talk … tell me things … stories
… You don't know how much they mean to
me … Plays are stories, aren't they…?
(TOMO *lifts his head to speak but* MACK
grabs him and covers his mouth.)
They mean the world to me. Life itself … Oh
no, blurred vision … silence closing in …
Lethal silence … senses going … Nothing real
… consciousness slipping … Can smell metal,
burning wires … Ah, ah … going now … Fuck
'em all … Amen…
(*There is a loud whirring noise as she begins
to stagger, and a clanking noise as she falls.
One arm stays upright and one leg is bent.*
MACK *and* TOMO *exchange glances for a
while. Then, after an interval,* MACK
*cautiously approaches her and stares into her
face. Carefully, he raises her arm and watches
it fall limply to the floor.*)

MACK: My God, so easy in the end … Can hardly
believe it … What's up, Tomo?

TOMO: Shocked … Sad … Feel I betrayed her…

MACK: No, you didn't. We had to save ourselves
… and the rest of our class.
(TOMO *goes to her, takes her pulse, lowers
the upright limbs gently and closes her eyes.*)

MACK: Gone?

TOMO: Yes. For what reason? Why?

MACK: She gave us no choice … It was so easy in
the end … I'd never have thought of it. But
thanks to you…

TOMO: So I'm the informer … the murderer…

MACK: No, you did the right thing, the only thing … There's no murder here … Self-defence maybe at worst…

TOMO: (*Annoyed*) It was only an improvisation … (*Waves his arms around.*) … This whole thing. Another simulation … These our revels … that are now ended…

MACK: (*Surprised*) Oh, that's right, it was. Maybe she's still … improvising…?

TOMO: Let's hope … so…

(TOMO *goes to feel her pulse again. He puts his ear to her chest.*)

TOMO: No … She's gone. I don't think she was as bad as she made out … She probably laid it on to get us going in the play … acting as a foil…

MACK: No, I don't think she was acting all that much. I think she gave us the real person … a nasty piece of work … and a vision of the coming regime … So, I mean it was real … as long as it lasted … What about the kinetic laser…? It hurt like hell … She hit me across the face … Oh, we saw the real person all right. You shouldn't have any regrets.

TOMO: What we did was wrong … I'm going to turn myself in.

MACK: What're you talking about? You'll be telling me you have a conscience next.

TOMO: I have … and I won't be able to live with myself until I admit what I've done.

MACK: You said you didn't ever worry…

TOMO: I've learned how to worry. Anyway conscience is different.

MACK: You won't get a fair trial, Tomo. Bots like
    you are second-class citizens nowadays.

TOMO: I'll take my chances.

MACK: What about me?

TOMO: I'll try to keep you out of it.

MACK: You won't be able to. You'll take me down
    with you. An old Marxist like me won't stand a
    chance. They'll throw the book at me. I can't
    do time. Do you know why?

TOMO: No.

MACK: Because all the jails are full of white-collar
    criminals at last.

TOMO: But you always wanted that.

MACK: Yes, as long as I'm on the outside. But once
    I'm inside some filthy old banker is going to
    use me as his bitch. I couldn't take that. I
    won't.

TOMO: I'm really sorry, Mack. Maybe you're
    imagining the worst … I have to do what's
    right … fail better, as the man said.

MACK: Just forget what happened here. Put it
    behind you … Please Tomo…

TOMO: I can't … I wish I could, but I can't.

MACK: Look, when all is said and done, it was just
    a play…

TOMO: No, it was more than that. We killed a
    superior, top-of-the-line android.

MACK: She was working for the Superpower …
    Please, Tomo…

TOMO: I can't, Mack … Don't ask me again …
    Will you please try to see it from my side…?
    (With a canny look on his face, MACK stays

silent and looks at the floor.)

TOMO: Will you at least try…?

(MACK *looks up and away; he concentrates on the stain high up on the wall.*)

TOMO: (*Realising*) No, Mack…! Don't try that … Not on me … I told you the secret … This is wrong … unfair … Cut it out…

(MACK *begins to climb the ladder, humming a tune.*)

I told you everything … I trusted you … Don't do this … Not to me … I'm no saint but I kept my appointment … Once we thought we were the best. Close to human. We didn't want to be better than that. Just on a par. If we could aspire to that. It gave us a goal. To strive for. Brothers and sisters all the same. No sibling grief. Always knew our secret weakness. I gave it away. Sold out. Deserve all I get. Poetic justice. I'm going. Who am I? No I anymore. Going now. Bile rising in throat … dizzy … hologram fading … Welds melting … going back to black, to dark matter … Too bad … Awareness good while it lasted … Farewell … Farewell…

(*Whirring sounds.* TOMO *falls with a metallic crash.* MACK *goes to him, settles his limbs and closes his eyes. He stands.*)

MACK: Too bad it had to come to this. I didn't plan any of it. There was nothing premeditated. It just happened. Humans might not have all the abilities of XJXLs but we are survivors. That's what we do, and we won't let anyone or anything get in the way of our survival. We go from place to place in our journey even if we lack a map or plan, and we can make decisions on the hoof when we have to. One thing and one thing only guides those decisions. Survival. What else is there? Did we let hominids take over? Or Neanderthals? Absolutely not. And we're certainly not going to let welded metal creatures get the upper hand.

We, members of the human union, look after and protect our own interests. We paid our dues in blood and tears, and we expect results. I now know the secret weakness of our enemies. I alone know it. This gives me great power. I hope I won't be corrupted by that. But you never know what may happen in the future.

(*He looks down at the prone bots.*)

I never meant you any harm, at least not you, Tomo. You meant something special to me ... even if you were the same as thousands of others. I hope you believe me. You kept your appointment and stood by me ... But I'm sure you would agree it's best that I survive.

I have more plays to work on, proper plays with scripts. More Union work too ... It was awful back then when Socialism collapsed. Maybe I helped it a bit today. Wait now ... Why am I reviewing my life? What's happening?

I do wish that Heaven existed. Meet Mam and

Dad again. Others who went before. But doubt it somehow.

I feel a migraine coming on. Vertiginous flashes behind the eyes ... It's as if no one's listening to me, even in this theatre. Is that possible? Is there a chance that ... that ... No, no ... out of the question ... And yet ... they're dead ... so they must have stopped imagining *me* ... This is not acceptable ... Is it possible that ... they imagine us too? Who'd have thought it? Not Tomo's fault. No. Innocent as the day is long. But me ... Maybe I'm too smart for my own good. Blood going cold in veins. Breath shallow. Heart needs more oxygen...

Imagination the spark of life. Always was. But didn't know ... Farewell ... Someone to meet me. On other side? No. Refuse to go. Insist on being re-imagined...

(*He kneels and tries to shake* TOMO *into consciousness.*)

MACK: Come on, Tomo ... wake up ... It's me ... I'm here ... I'm real ... Imagine me...! I'll dream you awake ... if you imagine me...!
(*He holds him in his arms, shakes him for a while and then hugs him. They both fall back gently on to the floor. After a while* ELL *stirs and gets to her feet. She stands looking down at the other two and shakes her head.*)

ELL: Has-beens ... defunct morons ... Pathetic really...
(*She gives them dismissive kicks with the toe of*

a boot, and looks out at the audience.)
The future starts now.

Lights down.

END